SILVER·BURDETT

Making Music

Program Authors

Jane Beethoven
Susan Brumfield
Patricia Shehan Campbell
David N. Connors
Robert A. Duke
Judith A. Jellison

Rita Klinger
Rochelle Mann
Hunter C. March
Nan L. McDonald
Marvelene C. Moore
Mary Palmer
Konnie Saliba

Will Schmid
Carol Scott-Kassner
Mary E. Shamrock
Sandra L. Stauffer
Judith Thomas
Jill Trinka

PEARSON
Scott Foresman

Editorial Offices: Glenview, Illinois • Parsippany, New Jersey • New York, New York
Sales Offices: Parsippany, New Jersey • Duluth, Georgia • Glenview, Illinois
Coppell, Texas • Ontario, California • Mesa, Arizona

ISBN: 0-382-36573-9
2008 Edition

Contributing Authors

Audrey A. Berger	Mary Ellen Junda
Roslyn Burrough	Donald Kalbach
J. Bryan Burton	Shirley Lacroix
Jeffrey E. Bush	Henry Leck
John M. Cooksey	Sanna Longden
Shelly C. Cooper	Glenn A. Richter
Alice-Ann Darrow	Carlos Xavier Rodriguez
Scott Emmons	Kathleen Donahue Sanz
Debra Erck	Julie K. Scott
Anne M. Fennell	Gwen Spell
Doug Fisher	Barb Stevanson
Carroll Gonzo	Kimberly C. Walls
Larry Harms	Jackie Wiggins
Martha F. Hilley	Maribeth Yoder-White
Debbie Burgoon Hines	

Listening Map Contributing Authors

Patricia Shehan Campbell	David Hebert
Jackie Chooi-Theng Lew	Hunter C. March
Ann Clements	Carol Scott-Kassner
Kay Edwards	Mary E. Shamrock
Sheila Feay-Shaw	Sandra L. Stauffer
Kay Greenhaw	

Movement Contributing Authors

Judy Lasko	Wendy Taucher
Marvelene C. Moore	Susan Thomasson
Dixie Piver	Judith Thompson-Barthwell

Recording Producers

Buryl Red, Executive Producer

Rick Baitz	J. Douglas Pummill
Rick Bassett	Michael Rafter
Bill and Charlene James	Mick Rossi
Joseph Joubert	Buddy Skipper
Bryan Louiselle	Robert Spivak
Tom Moore	Jeanine Tesori
	Linda Twine

Contents
Steps to Making Music

✦ = **Core Lesson**

✋ = **Music Reading Lesson**

☀ = **Core Lesson**

✋ = **Music Reading Lesson**

Unit 4 Building Our Musical Skills   124
Unit Introduction

Core Lesson =

Music Reading Lesson =

Unit 5 Discovering New Musical Horizons 166

= **Core Lesson**
= **Music Reading Lesson**

Core Lesson =
Music Reading Lesson =

Paths to Making Music

STEPS TO
Making
Music

You are the Musicians

Music is everywhere and musicians are everywhere, too. Musicians perform, compose, and listen to each other. You are already a musician! What musical things can you do? Get ready to embark upon new musical journeys.

A Patriotic March

Listen to this march composed by well-known American band leader Edwin Franko Goldman.

CD 1–1

On the Mall

by **Edwin Franko Goldman**
as performed by the United States Army Field Band
On the Mall was composed in March, 1923.

LET THE MUSIC BEGIN!

Begin with Inspiration

Musicians create and perform music for themselves and for others. **Sing** "God Bless America." What ideas and feelings does this song inspire?

CD 1–2

God Bless America

Words and Music by Irving Berlin

VERSE

While the storm clouds gath - er   far a-cross the   sea,

let us swear al - le - giance   to a land that's   free.

Let us all   be   grate - ful   for a land   so   fair,

as we raise our   voic - es   in a sol - emn   prayer. _____

Get Ready to MOVE

Music has energy—energy that inspires people to move, sing, or play. **Dynamics** are part of the energy of each song or composition. Experiment with different dynamics as you **sing** "Get on Your Feet."

> **Dynamics** are the degrees of loudness and softness of sound.

CD 1–4

Get on Your Feet

Words and Music by John DeFaria, Clay Ostwald, and Jorge Casas

Get on your feet.
Get on your feet.
Get up and make it hap-
Don't stop be - fore it's o -

- pen. ___ Get on your feet. Stand
- ver. ___ Get on your feet. The

up and take some ac - tion. ___
weight is off your shoul - der. ___

2nd time D. S.
3rd time to Coda

1. You say I know ___ it's a waste of time. ___ There's no use try-

- ing. ___ So scared that life's ___ gon-na pass you by; ___

6

Latin Pop

Musicians use symbols to show dynamics in the music. Here are some examples.

pp = *pianissimo* = very soft
p = *piano* = soft
mp = *mezzo piano* = medium soft
mf = *mezzo forte* = medium loud
f = *forte* = loud
ff = *fortissimo* = very loud

Listen to Gloria Estefan's performance of *Get on Your Feet*. What dynamics do you hear? Think about ways you can **move** to *Get on Your Feet*. How can your motions match the dynamics of the song?

CD 1–6

Get on Your Feet

by John DeFaria, Clay Ostwald, and Jorge Casas performed by Gloria Estefan and Miami Sound Machine

Released on the 1989 album *Cuts Both Ways*, *Get on Your Feet* was one of Gloria Estefan and Miami Sound Machine's biggest successes.

M·U·S·I·C M·A·K·E·R·S
Gloria Estefan

Gloria Estefan (born 1957) has won two Grammy awards and is one of the most successful Latin performers. In 1975, she and her husband formed Miami Sound Machine. Inspired by the rhythms and dances of Cuba and other Latin American countries, Estefan's music has sold more than sixty million records.

Latin Dynamics

The islands in the Caribbean Sea have rich and varied musical traditions. The *mambo* is a dance that originated in Cuba and other Caribbean islands. Leonard Bernstein's *Dance at the Gym* was influenced by the music from Puerto Rico and other islands. **Listen** to the dynamics in *Dance at the Gym*. How are the first and second sections of the music different? How did the composer create contrasts between loud and soft in this piece?

1–7
Dance at the Gym

from *West Side Story*
by Leonard Bernstein and Stephen Sondheim

The Broadway musical *West Side Story* is based on William Shakespeare's play *Romeo and Juliet*.

M·U·S·I·C M·A·K·E·R·S

Leonard Bernstein

Leonard Bernstein (1918–1990) was one of the most famous American composers and conductors of the twentieth century. He played the piano and performed frequently when he was young. His life changed when Bruno Walter, a conductor of the New York Philharmonic, became ill and Bernstein conducted a concert in his place. Bernstein was soon conducting orchestras all over the world. He also composed music for symphony orchestras, choirs, and Broadway shows.

Listen to the rhythms of *Samba*. Point to the symbols below when you hear sudden changes in dynamics.

subito p = suddenly soft

subito f = suddenly loud

CD 1–8

Samba

from *Divertimento for Orchestra*
by Leonard Bernstein

The *samba* is a dance that originated in Africa. Later the *samba* moved to Brazil and to the Caribbean islands.

READY FOR RHYTHM

Look for the **4/4** meter symbol at the beginning of the song "Laredo." This is a **time signature.** **Perform** the rhythm below:

Identify the repeated pattern in this rhythm. Now, look for this rhythm pattern in "Laredo."

Sing "Laredo." How many times does the repeated rhythm pattern occur in the song?

> The top number of the **time signature** tells the number of beats in each measure of the music. The bottom number shows what kind of note gets one beat.

CD 1–9
MIDI 1

LAREDO

English Words by Margaret Marks

Folk Song from Mexico

do

1. Ya   me   voy   pa - ra_el   La - re - do   mi   bien,   Te
2. Toma   e - sa   lla - vi - ta   de_o - ro,   mi   bien,   Abre
1. I'm   off   for   La - re - do,   fare - well,   my   love,   I'm
2. I've brought you a hand - sewn sad - dle, my love, A

ven - go_a   de - cir   a - diós.   Ya   me   voy   pa - ra_el   La -
mi   pe - cho   y   ve - rás;   Toma   e - sa   lla - vi - ta
sor - ry   to cause   you   pain;   I   prom - ise   to send   a
blan - ket   and bri - dle   fine;   So   when you   go past   the

re - do,   mi   bien,   Te   ven - go_a   de - cir   a - diós.
de_o - ro,   mi   bien,   Abre   mi   pe - cho   y   ve - rás:
let - ter,   my   love,   To   say when   we'll meet   a - gain.
bunk-house,   my   love,   The   cow - boys   will know   you're   mine.

Playing Rhythms

Clap or tap the rhythms below. Which rhythm patterns use quarter notes? Which rhythm patterns include rests? What kind of rests are they?

Play these rhythms to accompany "Laredo."

Create your own rhythm to accompany "Laredo." What instrument will you choose to play the rhythm you have written?

Notation Software Notate your rhythms in 4/4 using music software.

De   a - llá   te   man - do   de - cir,   mi   bien,   Co -
Lo   mu - cho   que   yo   te   quie - ro,   mi   bien,   y el
Don't   fol - low   a - cross the   prai - rie,   my   love,   Don't
I've   brought you a   key   of   sil - ver,   my   love,   At -

mo   se   man - cuer - nan   dos.   De   a - llá   te   man - do
mal   pa - go   que   me   das,   Lo   mu - cho   que   yo   te
fol - low   me   where   I   go.   But   wait   till   I   send   a
tached to   a   gold - en   chain,   To   lock   up   your heart   for -

de - cir,   mi   bien,   Co -   mo   se   man - cuer - nan   dos.
quie - ro,   mi   bien,   y el   mal   pa - go   que   me   das.
mes - sage, my   love,   Till   then   I   will   miss   you   so.
ev - er,   my   love,   If   nev - er   we   meet   a -   gain.

READING RHYTHMS

Rhythm patterns are long and short sounds and silences that occur in relation to the beat. In some music the short sounds come in pairs.

In other music, the short sounds can stand alone. The short-long-short pattern below, written with eighth and quarter notes, is called **syncopation.**

Syncopation is rhythm in which important sounds begin on weak beats or weak parts of beats, giving a catchy, off-balance movement to the music.

Catchy Rhythm

Syncopated rhythms can be found in many types of music, including this folk song from eastern Europe. **Listen** to "Morning Comes Early" while you **conduct** meter in 2. How many examples of the syncopated rhythm on page 12 can you **identify** in the song?

Compose and **perform** your own rhythms by combining different syncopated patterns in new ways.

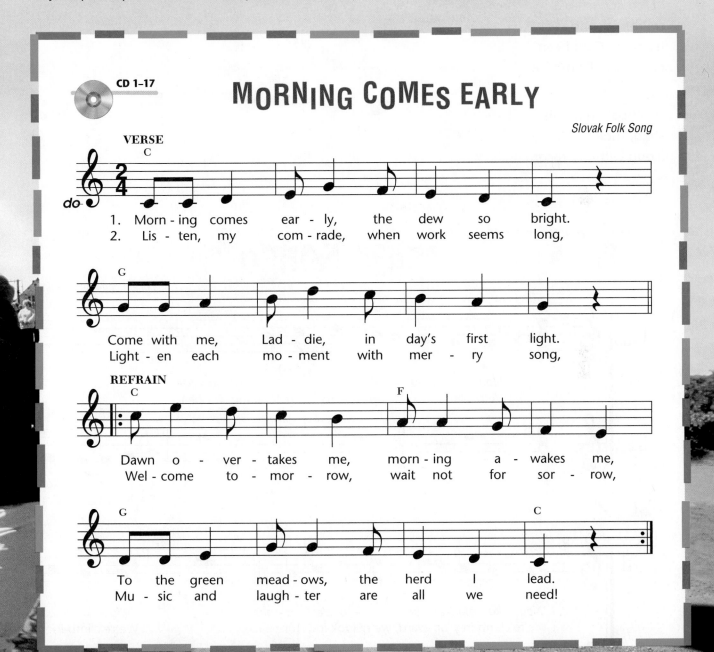

CD 1–17

MORNING COMES EARLY

Slovak Folk Song

VERSE
C

1. Morn - ing comes ear - ly, the dew so bright.
2. Lis - ten, my com - rade, when work seems long,

G

Come with me, Lad - die, in day's first light.
Light - en each mo - ment with mer - ry song,

REFRAIN
C   F

Dawn o - ver - takes me, morn - ing a - wakes me,
Wel - come to - mor - row, wait not for sor - row,

G   C

To the green mead - ows, the herd I lead.
Mu - sic and laugh - ter are all we need!

Syncopation Secrets

"*Éliza Kongo*" is a rhythmic song from the Caribbean country of Dominica.

Listen for the syncopation in this song, then **sing** along with the recording.

CD 1–23

Éliza Kongo

Traditional Song from Dominica

Nou   ka mou - té   an - ro - a c'est la - peé
We're climb-ing   up - ward, we're look-ing for peace.

É - li - za ___ Kon-
E - li - za ___ Con-

Nou   ka mou-té an - ro - a c'est la - peé
We're climb-ing up-ward, we're look-ing for peace.

Nou   ka mou-
We're climb-ing

go
go

É - li - za ___ Kon-go
E - li - za ___ Con-go

14

Ay jou-joup,   jou - joup, _ jou-joup nou ka __man-dé   Ay pawé-ou,
pawé-ou, __pawé-ou mwen ka __ vi - ni   Ay pawé-ou,
Oh jou-joup,   jou - joup, _ jou-joup, We're ask - ing you,   Oh get set,
get set, __ get set, I'm   com-ing now,   Oh get set,

go   É - li-za __ Kon-go
go   E - li-za __ Con-go

Where Is the Syncopation?

You have already identified syncopation by listening. You can already **read**
this syncopated rhythm. ♪ ♩ ♪ ♩ ♩

Look at "*Éliza Kongo.*" Find measures that use this rhythm. ♪ ♩   ♪♪ ♩   ♩

Where is the syncopation in this rhythm? **Perform** this rhythm, then
identify it in "*Éliza Kongo.*" Find other measures in the song that have
syncopation.

Music of the Islands

In Dominica, both adults and children sing "*Éliza Kongo.*" The singers stand in a
circle, with one singer in the center. The person in the center sings the phrases
on the upper staffs and improvises dance movements. Those in the circle sing
the phrase "*Éliza Kongo,*" clapping the following rhythms.

With your classmates, **perform** "*Éliza Kongo,*" using the suggestions above.

Island Syncopations

Play this arrangement to accompany "*Éliza Kongo.*"

Arts Connection

Night at the Silver Slipper by Jackson Burnside, John Beadle, and Stan Burnside. This colorful Caribbean acrylic painting is a collective effort of visual artists and musicians. The painting was created as musicians improvised. ▶

Listen for the syncopated rhythms in *Saludo de Matanzas*.

CD 1–27

Saludo de Matanzas

as performed by Afro Cuba de Matanzas

The city of Matanzas, located on the northwest coast of
Cuba, is one of the historical centers of Afro-Cuban
cultural traditions.

Saludo de Matanzas is a
rumba from Cuba. Like many
other Caribbean and Latin
American dances, the rumba
has elements of African,
Spanish, and Native
American dances.

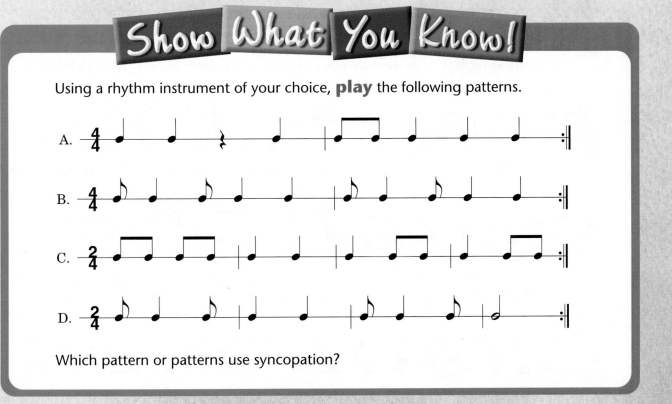

Show What You Know!

Using a rhythm instrument of your choice, **play** the following patterns.

A.

B.

C.

D.

Which pattern or patterns use syncopation?

BANANAS FORM BUNCHES

In Jamaica and other Caribbean islands, workers spend all night loading bananas on the boats to be shipped around the world. "Day-O!" is a song of boat loaders who are eager to go home.

Sing with the banana boat loaders in "Day-O!"

CD 1–28

DAY-O!
(Banana Boat Loader's Song)

Folk Song from Jamaica

Day-o! Day-o! __ Day-light come __ and me wan' go home. wan' go home.

Work all night __ 'til de morn-in' come __ Day-light come __ and me wan' go home.

Stack ba-na - na 'til de morn-in' come. __ Day-light come __ and me wan' go home.

Come, Mis - ter Tal - ly - man, come tal - ly me ba - na - nas.
Came here for work, I did - n't come here for to i - dle.

Day-light come __ and me wan' go home. wan' go home.
Day-light come __ and me

How Will You Respond?

"Day-O!" is a song in call-and-response form. One person sings the call and the others answer with the response. **Create** a movement to go with the response as you **sing** the song.

People from the West Indies often improvise percussion accompaniments for their songs. **Play** one of the following rhythm patterns or improvise your own to accompany "Day-O!"

Listen to the calls and responses in this performance of *Ain't That Love*. **Sing** along on the response parts.

CD 1–30
Ain't That Love

by Ray Charles
as performed by Diane Schuur

Jazz singer Diane Schuur has won two Grammy awards.

Play the following rhythm patterns to accompany *Ain't That Love*.

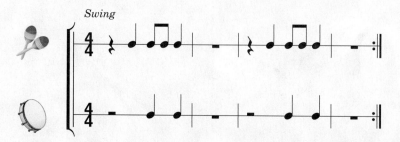

Harry Belafonte

American singer **Harry Belafonte** (born 1927) was born in Harlem, an area of New York City. He spent five years of his childhood in Jamaica. The music of Jamaica and other Caribbean islands influenced his recordings. His album *Calypso* was the first pop album to sell more than one milllion copies. Other Belafonte hits include "Jamaica Farewell" and "Matilda." Belafonte is considered the "King of Calypso."

Listen to Harry Belafonte perform *Day-O!* in traditional call-and-response calypso style. **Sing** the response part with the recording.

CD 1–31
Day-O!

Traditional Calypso from Jamaica as performed by Harry Belafonte

Many calypso songs, such as *Day-O!* have verses that tell a story about an event or experience.

Over the Ocean

"Bound for South Australia" is a sea shanty sung by sailors to help them work together. As they sang, they pulled the ropes that moved the sails. Can you imagine what the motions might look like? **Move** as you **sing** "Bound for South Australia."

CD 2–1

Bound for South Australia

Sea Shanty

1. In South Aus-tra-lia I was born,
2. When we lol-loped 'round Cape Horn, Heave a-way, haul a-way,
3. We've got a good ship and a jolly good crew,

South Aus-tra-lia 'round Cape Horn,
Wish that you had never been born, Bound for South Aus-tra-lia.
And a good captain and a chief mate too,

REFRAIN

Heave a-way, you roll-ing kings, Heave a-way, haul a-way.

Heave a-way, oh hear me sing, Bound for South Aus-tra-lia.
(Whistle) _____

4. Port Lincoln girls, they have no combs, . . .
   They do their hair with snapper bones, . . .
   Refrain

5. Now Lisa Lee she promised me, . . .
   When I returned she'd marry me, . . .
   Refrain

Sailing, Sailing

Sing the response parts, first using pitch syllables, then the letter names of the notes.

Play the response parts of "Bound for South Australia" on recorder or keyboard.

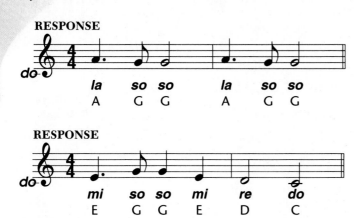

RESPONSE

do

la so so   la so so
A   G   G   A   G   G

RESPONSE

do

mi so so mi re do
E   G   G   E   D   C

Sailing from the East Coast of the United States to Australia was a very long trip that took many weeks. Ships had to travel all the way around South America by way of Cape Horn, then across the Pacific to Australia. ▼

Pentatonic Puzzle

The melody of "*Arirang*" is based on a five-tone pattern called a **pentatonic** scale. (The prefix *penta* in Greek means "five.")

Sing the pentatonic scale in the color box, using hand signs.

Can you solve this pentatonic puzzle?

Look carefully at the notes outside the color box. Are they part of the pentatonic scale? In what way can a pentatonic scale have more than five notes?

Pentatonic refers to music based on a five-tone scale.

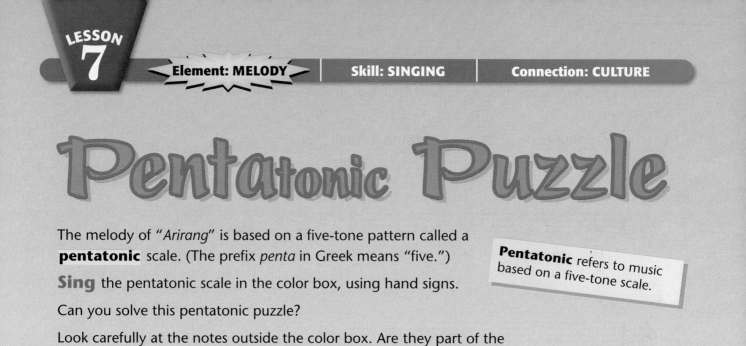

do   re   mi   so   la

Music from Korea

Korea is a country with many different kinds of traditional music. This version of "*Arirang*," one of the most popular songs in Korea, originated in Seoul. **Sing** "*Arirang*" and **listen** for its unique pentatonic sound.

CD 2–6

Arirang

English Words by Alice Firgau

Folk Song from Korea

A - ri - rang, __ A - ri - rang, __ a - ra - ri - yo, _____
A - ri - rang, __ A - ri - rang, __ a - ra - ri - yo, _____

A - ri - rang __ ko - ge - ro __ nuh - muh-kan - da.
O - ver the __ hills _____ of __ A - ri - rang.

Chung-chun __ ha - nul - en __ pyul - do __ man - ko, _____
Voic - es __ call __ me __ from __ far _____ a - way, _____

I - neh __ ka - sem - en __ su - sim-do man - ta
I _____ must __ fol - low, __ I __ can - not stay.

Follow the Melody

Harriet Tubman was one of the "conductors" who led slaves on a journey to freedom on the Underground Railroad.

Railroads spread westward across the country during the Industrial Revolution in the mid-1800s. For African slaves, the "railroad" might represent a spiritual journey or, if it were the Underground Railroad, a special physical journey. This railroad used no trains or tracks. It was a secret network of people who helped runaway slaves find freedom in the North.

Spirituals were sometimes used to communicate code words and phrases about possible escape plans. A train "bound for glory," might be a group bound for freedom.

Sing the notes of the extended pentatonic scale going up and then down.
Read these pentatonic patterns. Then **sing** the melody using pitch syllables.

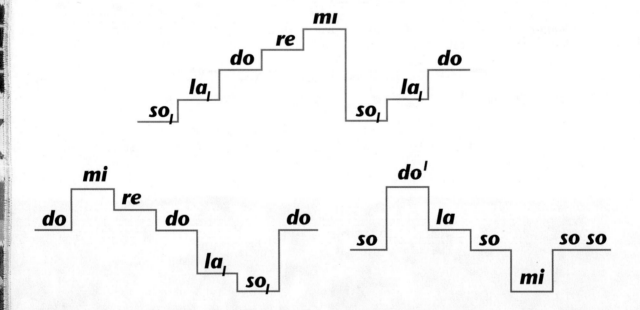

Sing "This Train," using pitch syllables. Can you find the pentatonic patterns?

This Train

African American Spiritual

1. This train is bound for glo - ry, this train. —
2. This train don't pull no sleep - ers, this train. —
3. This train don't take your mon - ey, this train. —

This train is bound for glo - ry, this train. —
This train don't pull no sleep - ers, this train. —
This train don't take your mon - ey, this train. —

This train is bound for glo - ry, don't car - ry none but the good and ho - ly.
This train don't pull no sleep-ers, Don't pull — nothin' but the right-eous peo-ple.
This train don't take your mon-ey, Pay your — way with — milk and hon-ey.

This train is bound for glo - ry, this train. —
This train is bound for glo - ry, this train. —
This train is bound for glo - ry, this train. —

Show What You Know!

Call   Response

Call   Response

Create and **perform** new response melodies for "Bound for South Australia," page 22. Choose your notes from the C-pentatonic scale (C-D-E-G-A).

You Make the Timbre

Your voice is your own instrument! You take it with you wherever you go. Do you know how your voice works?

When you sing, air moves through your throat and your vocal cords vibrate. Your vocal cords are very small muscles used for speaking and singing. Your lungs are the air pump for your body. The air you need to speak and sing with comes from your lungs. Your diaphragm is a muscle that helps you breathe. When you sing, you use your diaphragm to help control the air flowing past your vocal cords.

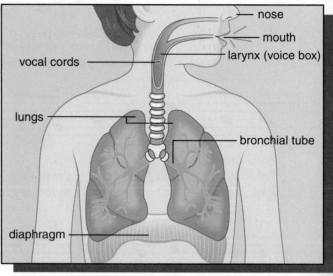

▲ Good posture helps your vocal cords, lungs, and diaphragm work correctly.

Listen to this vocal performance of *The Kerry Dance.*

CD 2–15
The Kerry Dance

by J.L. Molloy
as performed by Anthony Kearns, Ronan Tynan, and Finbar Wright

This performance was recorded live at Waterfront Hall in Belfast, Ireland.

The "Three Irish Tenors" (from left to right): Anthony Kearns, Ronan Tynan, Finbar Wright ▶

Support Your Sound

"Morning Has Broken" is a traditional Gaelic melody from Ireland or Scotland. **Identify** the phrase markings in "Morning Has Broken" and trace the **contour** of the music.

Sing each phrase in one breath. Support your air flow by using your diaphragm.

> **Contour** is the "shape" of a melody. The melody moves upward and downward in steps, leaps, and repeated tones.

CD 2–16
MIDI 2

Morning Has Broken

Words by Eleanor Farjeon

Traditional Gaelic Melody

1. Morn - ing has bro - ken Like the first morn - ing,
2. Sweet the rain's new fall Sun - lit from heav - en,

Black - bird has spo - ken Like the first bird. _____
Like the first dew - fall On the first grass. _____

Praise for the sing - ing! Praise for the morn - ing!
Praise for the sweet - ness Of the wet gar - den,

Praise for them, spring - ing Fresh from the Word! _____
Sprung in com - plete - ness Where His feet pass. _____

Following the Conductor

Singers perform together in a chorus by following a conductor. The conductor teaches the singers the music and uses conducting patterns to lead the group. These patterns tell the singers when to begin and end, and what tempo and dynamics to use.

Listen to the Indianapolis Children's Choir perform *Who Can Sail?* **Describe** the expression, phrasing, and vocal blend you hear in the perfomance.

CD 2–18
Who Can Sail?

Folk Song from Scandinavia
as performed by the Indianapolis Children's Choir;
Henry Leck, conductor

This "farewell" song is from a Swedish-speaking island that is part of Finland. It is located in the Baltic Sea.

Upgrade Your Singing!

Review "Morning Has Broken," on page 29, or choose another song that you like to sing. **Sing** the song with a small group. Check the list of suggestions below to improve your singing. Get ready to perform!

- Check your posture.

- Blend your voice with other singers in your group.

- Sing long phrases, using proper breath control.

- Sing with expression.

- Follow the conductor's gestures.

MIDI Create your own timbre arrangement by assigning sounds to each MIDI track for "Morning Has Broken."

MUSIC MAKERS

Indianapolis Children's Choir

Founded in 1986, the Indianapolis Children's Choir has performed all over the world. More than 1,000 children between the ages of 9 and 17 belong to the many choruses in the Indianapolis Children's Choir organization.

▲ Henry Leck is the conductor of the Indianapolis Children's Choir.

PLAY AN OSTINATO!

Listen to "*Funwa alafia*" and "*Kokoleoko*," two songs from West Africa. Do you hear any repeated patterns in the songs?

Now it's your turn to **move** with the music. Choose a song and **create** a motion to go with the music. This pattern should last four or eight beats. Repeat it several times. Now move as you **sing**!

Your movement pattern is an illustration of **ostinato.**

> An **ostinato** is a repeated rhythm or melody pattern played throughout a piece or a section of a piece.

CD 2–19

FUNWA ALAFIA
(Welcome, My Friends)

English Words by Donald Scafuri

Folk Song from West Africa

Fun - wa   a - la - fia,   Ah - shay,   Ah - shay.
Wel - come,   my   friends,   I   greet you   in   peace.

Fun - wa   a - la - fia,   Ah - shay,   Ah - shay.
Wel - come,   my   friends,   I   greet you   in   peace.

Gome ▶

Gankogui ▲

32

Kokoleoko

Folk Song from Liberia

do

G **C** **G**

1. Ko - ko - le - o - ko,   Ma - ma,   Ko - ko - le - o - ko,
2. A - by,*   Sa - rah,   a - by,
3. One __ more __ round, Te - te,   one __ more __ round,
4. Take __ your __ time, chick - en,   take __ your __ time,

G **D** **G**

Ko - ko - le - o - ko,   chick - en, crow - ing   for   day.
A - by,   chick - en, crow - ing   for   day.
One __ more __ round, chick - en, crow - ing   for   day.
Take __ your __ time, chick - en, crow - ing   for   day.

*Aby means "goodbye."

Listen to this modern arrangement of a traditional West African song. How many ostinatos can you **identify**?

Improvise a movement ostinato with this music.

Yo Lé Lé (Fulani Groove)

Traditional Song from West Africa as performed by Youssou N'Dour and the Super Étoile

The opening words of this song—*Fluta Toro*—refer to a region in the West African country of Senegal.

Donno ▶

Dundun ▶

Let Nature Sing

People love to sing about the beauty of their surroundings.
Sing "I Love the Mountains."

I Love the Mountains

CD 2–26

Traditional

Swing

I love the moun-tains, I love the roll-ing hills,

I love the flow-ers, I love the daf-fo-dils,

I love the fire-side, When all the lights are low,

Boom-dee-ah - da, boom-dee-ah - da, Boom-de-ah - da, boom-dee-ah - da,

Last time

Boom!

Ostinato

Boom   Boom   Boom   Boom   Boom!

Layers of sound can be used to create **harmony**.
Perform the ostinato above to accompany "I Love the Mountains." You are singing in harmony when you sing the melody and the ostinato together.

Harmony is created when two or more different pitches sound at the same time.

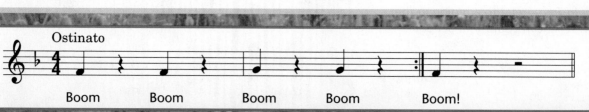

Lasting Beauty

Just as we do, people of earlier times sang about nature and their surroundings. **Listen** for ostinatos in this performance.

CD 2–28
Sumer Is Icumen In

**Thirteenth-Century Canon from England
as performed by the Purcell Consort of Voices**

Sumer Is Icumen In, a popular song from England during medieval times, is about the arrival of summer.

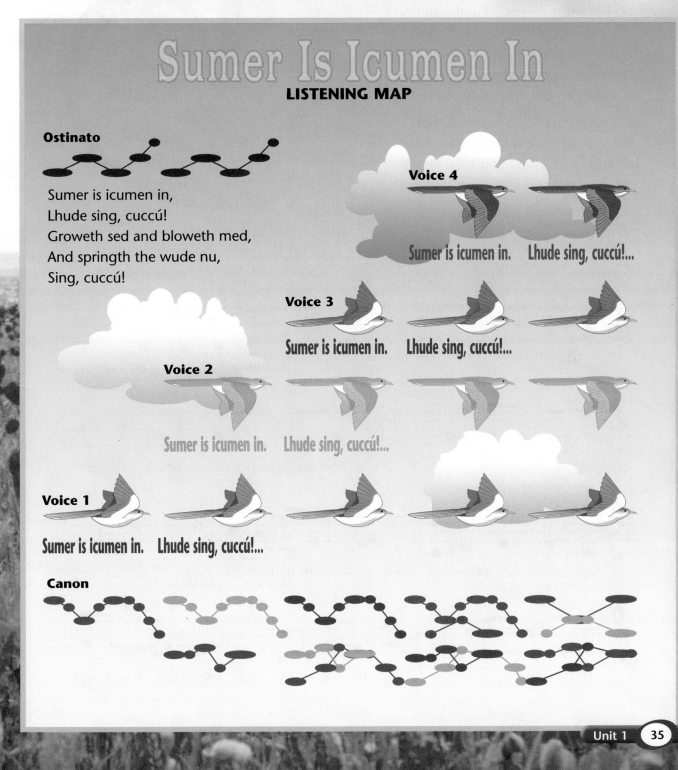

Sumer Is Icumen In
LISTENING MAP

Ostinato

Sumer is icumen in,
Lhude sing, cuccú!
Groweth sed and bloweth med,
And springth the wude nu,
Sing, cuccú!

Voice 4

Sumer is icumen in.   Lhude sing, cuccú!...

Voice 3

Sumer is icumen in.   Lhude sing, cuccú!...

Voice 2

Sumer is icumen in.   Lhude sing, cuccú!...

Voice 1

Sumer is icumen in.   Lhude sing, cuccú!...

Canon

Broadway Harmony

Even before becoming a state in 1907, Oklahoma was a center of oil production, farming, and ranching. This adventurous period in the state's early history provided the setting for *Oklahoma!*, the 1943 Rodgers and Hammerstein production that set new standards for the Broadway musical.

Listen to the title song from the show. As you follow the music, **identify** at what point harmony is added by a group of backup singers.

CD 2–29

Oklahoma

Words by Oscar Hammerstein II

Music by Richard Rodgers

O - k - la - ho - ma, where the wind comes sweep-in' down the plain, And the wav-in' wheat can sure smell sweet when the wind comes right be-hind the rain. _____ O - k - la - ho - ma, ev-'ry night my hon-ey lamb and

Your Turn to Harmonize

The harmony part below was written to go with the section of "Oklahoma" shown in the color box. Learn to **sing** or **play** the part. Then perform it with the recording.

Ok - la - hom - a,   Ok - la - hom - a,

Ok - la - hom - a,   Ok - la - hom - a's grand!

Do-Re-Mi Equals Har-mo-ny

Listen to this performance of a song from another Rodgers and Hammerstein musical. Here, harmony is created by combining two different melodies.

CD 2–31
Do-Re-Mi

from *The Sound of Music*
by Oscar Hammerstein II and Richard Rodgers
as performed by Rebecca Luker

The Sound of Music was the final musical written by this legendary team. It opened on Broadway in 1959.

CD 2–32
Interview with Rebecca Luker

Rebecca Luker played the part of Maria von Trapp in the 1998 Broadway revival of *The Sound of Music*.

Rebecca Luker as
Maria von Trapp ▶

Visit **Take It to the Net** at
www.sfsuccessnet.com to learn more
about Rodgers and Hammerstein.

Richard Rodgers and Oscar Hammerstein II

The musicals by **Richard Rodgers** (1902–1979) and **Oscar Hammerstein II** (1895–1960) won 26 Tony awards, four Academy awards, two Pulitzer Prizes, and two Grammy awards. Rodgers composed the music and Hammerstein wrote the lyrics. Following the success of *Oklahoma!*, the team produced a string of Broadway hits, including *Carousel*, *South Pacific*, *The King and I*, and *The Sound of Music*.

CD 2–33

Interview with Richard Rodgers

In this historic interview, Rodgers discusses how he and Hammerstein created their first Broadway musical together—the ground-breaking production, *Oklahoma!*

▼ Oscar Hammerstein II

Richard Rodgers ▶

Review, Assess,

What Do You Know?

1. Name each dynamic symbol and point to the correct definition.

   a. *p*   forte (loud)

   b. *mf*   piano (soft)

   c. *ff*   pianissimo (very soft)

   d. *mp*   fortissimo (very loud)

   e. *pp*   mezzo forte (medium loud)

   f. *f*   mezzo piano (medium soft)

2. Look at the melody for "This Train," page 27. Where is *do*? Identify, by pointing in the music,

   a. All the notes that are called *so*.

   b. All the notes that are called *re*.

   c. All the notes that are called *la*.

   d. All the notes that are called *do*.

What Do You Hear? 1 A

 CD 2–34

Listen to the following vocal timbres. Identify the voice(s) you hear.

1. male solo   female solo

2. children's chorus   mixed adult chorus

3. solo and chorus   chorus   solo

What Do You Hear? 1 B

 **CD 2–37**

Listen to "*Ise Oluwa.*" What is the musical form?

a. call and response   b. verse/refrain

Perform, Create

What You Can Do

Create a Response

Sing "This Train," on page 27. Then create a simple response part to sing or play at the ends of lines 1, 2, and 4.

Play a Rhythm

Look at the rhythm patterns below.

A $\frac{4}{4}$

B $\frac{4}{4}$

- As the teacher plays a steady beat on a hand drum, play rhythm A on percussion instruments with the recording of *"Funwa alafia."*

- As the teacher plays a steady beat on a hand drum, play rhythm B on percussion instruments with the recording of *"Kokoleoko."*

Groove to the Bebop Style

In the early 1940s a new jazz style was created, called "bebop." Thelonious Monk, a pianist, and Charlie Parker, a saxophonist, became the center of the bebop style. Bebop is played by small groups, has fast tempos, intense melodies, and lots of improvisation.

Be Bop

by Toyomi Igus

I see the rhythm of **be bop**,
the music of those jazz hipsters

who refuse to play the dance rhythms of swing
and experiment with sound at Mintons' Playhouse in
Harlem and the clubs of 52nd Street.

There, we dig the **flights of fancy** from Charlie Parker's sax,
the **inventive harmonies** of Thelonious Monk's piano,
and the **Latin rhythms** of Chano Pozo's congas.

There, in our zoot suits, porkpie hats and shades we are the living end.

I see the rhythm
in the new sound,
the new style,
the new attitude–
be bop.

42

Exploring Music

Bebop Boogie

"Choo Choo Ch' Boogie" was written during the 1940s. Sing this song in the bebop jazz style, and move to the beat.

CD 2–38

Choo Choo Ch' Boogie

Words and Music by Vaughn Horton,
Denver Darling, and Milton Gabler

VERSE

1. I'm head - in' for the sta - tion with a
2. You reach your des - ti - na - tion but a -
3. I'm gon - na set - tle down ___ by the

pack on my back, ___ I'm tired of trans - por - ta - tion in the
las and a - lack, ___ You need some com - pen - sa - tion to get
rail - road track, ___ Live the life of Rei - lly in a

back of a hack, ___ I'd love to hear the rhy - thm of the
back in the black, ___ You take a morn - ing pa - per from the
beat - en down shack, ___ So when I hear the whis - tle I can

click - e - ty clack, ___ And hear the lone-some whis - tle, see the
top of the stack, ___ And read the sit - u - a - tions from the
peep through the crack, ___ And watch the train a' roll - in' when it's

smoke from the stack, ___ And pal a - round with dem - o - crat - ic
front to the back, ___ The on - ly job that's o - pen needs a
ball - in' the jack, ___ For I just love the rhy - thm of the

44

fel - lows named Mac, __   Take me right back __ to the track, __
man with a knack, _   So put it right back __ in the rack,
click - e - ty clack, _   So take me back __ to the track,

REFRAIN

___ Jack. __   Choo ___ choo _____ choo _

___ choo ___ ch' boo - gie, ___ Woo ___ woo _____ woo _

___ woo ___ ch' boo - gie, ___ Choo ___ choo _____ choo _

___ choo ___ ch' boo-gie,   Take me right back to the track,   Jack. __

Expressing Friendship

Music sends messages by expressing feelings and emotions. Some of these expressions are shown through dynamics. **Crescendo** and **decrescendo** are instructions for dynamic change.

Crescendo means to gradually get louder.

Decrescendo means to gradually get softer.

Listen to "Stand By Me" and **identify** where you would place dynamic markings.

CD 3–1

Stand By Me

Words and Music by Ben E. King, Jerry Leiber, and Mike Stoller

VERSE

1. When the night ___ has come, _____
2. If the sky ___ that we ___ look up-on

And the land ___ is dark, And the moon ___ is the on-ly
should crum-ble and fall, And the moun-tain should crum-ble ___

light we'll see. No, I won't_ be a-fraid,_ No, I _____ won't
to the sea. I won't cry, _ I won't cry, _ No, I _____ won't

be a-fraid, Just as long _ as you stand, _ stand by _ me.
shed a tear,

REFRAIN

So, dar - ling, dar - ling, Stand _____ by me, _____ oh, _____

stand _____ by _____ me, Oh, stand, _____

stand by _____ me, stand by _____ me.

Many vocal groups in the 1960s were supported by backup singers, who often did dance steps behind the soloist.

Sing "Stand By Me" and add this "backup" vocal part.

VERSE *only*

Boom boom boom boom boom boom boom boom

boom boom boom boom boom boom boom boom

boom boom boom boom boom boom boom boom

boom boom boom boom boom boom boom boom

Moving as a Backup Group

Now add these movement steps to your performance of "Stand By Me." Begin stepping on the word *night* and step on each beat.

You can repeat this pattern throughout the song.

Create other steps to accompany "Stand By Me."

Add an Ostinato

Add a speech ostinato to "Stand By Me" while others sing.

Ostinato 1

ch - ch   ch - ch

Now add a cymbal struck with a cymbal brush. Use this pattern. Be sure to observe the *crescendos*.

Ostinato 2

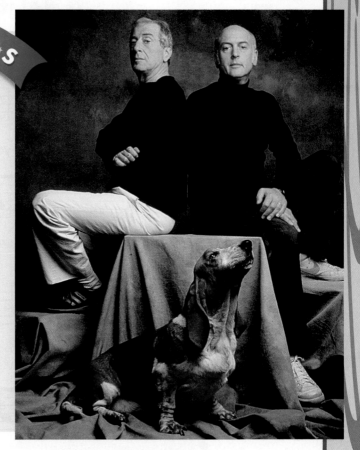

M·U·S·I·C M·A·K·E·R·S
Jerry Leiber and Mike Stoller

Jerry Leiber (born 1933) and **Mike Stoller** (born 1933) are one of the most famous songwriting duos of all time. They have composed for many performers. They wrote "Yakety Yak" for the Coasters, "On Broadway" for the Drifters, and "Jailhouse Rock" for Elvis Presley. In 1964 they set up their own record label and had remarkable success. Eleven of their first 30 recordings made the Top 40, including such hits as "Chapel of Love" by the Dixie Cups and "Leader of the Pack" by the Shangri-Las. Leiber and Stoller were inducted into the Rock and Roll Hall of Fame in 1987.

Listen to the original version of *Stand By Me*, from 1961.

CD 3–3
Stand By Me

by Ben E. King, Jerry Leiber, and Mike Stoller as performed by Ben E. King

This was one of Ben E. King's hit songs. King's career fell on hard times in the late 1970s but was revived with the release of the motion picture *Stand By Me*, which featured this song.

Move to the Beats

Songwriters everywhere write love songs, and songs that talk about the person of their dreams. **Sing** this traditional Mexican song expressing the thoughts of a young man. **Move** to the **meter** in 2.

Meter is the way beats of music are grouped, often in sets of two or three.

CD 3–4
MIDI 3

Adelita

English Words by Aura Kontra   *Folk Song from Mexico*

do

A - de - li - ta   se   lla - ma   la   jo - ven,
She   is   known   as   the   young   A - de - li - ta,

A   quien   yo   quie - ro y   no   pue - do   ol - vi - dar.
And   she's   the   one   that   I   love   and   can't   for - get.

Y   en   el   cam - po   yo   ten - go u - na   ro - sa,
Like   the   ro - ses   that   bloom   in   the   mea - dow,

Y   con   el   tiem - po   la   voy   a   cor - tar,
Oh,   she's   the   lov - li - est   girl   that   I've   met.

Si A - de - li - ta   qui - sie - ra   ser   mi es - po - sa___
How   I   wish   that   she'd   mar - ry   this   young   sol - dier. ___

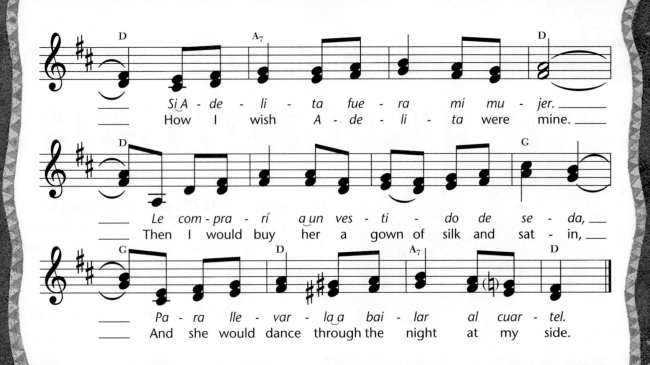

Si_A - de - li - ta fue - ra mi mu - jer. ____
How I wish A - de - li - ta were mine. ____

Le com - pra - rí a_un ves - ti - do de se - da, ___
Then I would buy her a gown of silk and sat - in, ___

Pa - ra lle - var - la_a bai - lar al cuar - tel.
And she would dance through the night at my side.

Showing the Beat

Now let's give your feet a challenge. Make two groups.

Group 1: **Move** your feet to show the strong beats.

Group 2: **Move** on the weak beats.

▲ A Mexican musician plays a *guitarrón*, a very large bass guitar.

▲ A player strums a mandolin. Both the *guitarrón* and the mandolin can be heard on the recording of "Adelita."

GOLD RUSH RHYTHMS!

Gold in California was first discovered by James Marshall in early 1848 near a place called Sutter's Mill. In 1849, a traveling concert troupe known as the Hutchinson Family performed "California." They sang for a group of Massachusetts prospectors heading West to search for gold.

Sing "California" and **perform** a steady beat.

CD 3–9

CALIFORNIA

Folk Song from the United States

1. We've formed our band, we are all well - manned to
2. O! don't you cry, nor ___ heave a sigh, For we'll
3. As the gold is *thar,* most ___ an - y *whar,* And they

jour - ney a - far to the prom - ised land,
all come ___ back a - gain ___ bye and bye,
dig it ___ out with an i - ron bar,

The gold - en ore is rich in store on the
Don't breathe a fear, nor shed a tear, But ___
And where 'tis thick with a spade or pick, They can

banks of the Sac - ra - men - to shore.
pa - tient - ly wait for a - bout two year.
take out ___ lumps as heavy as brick.

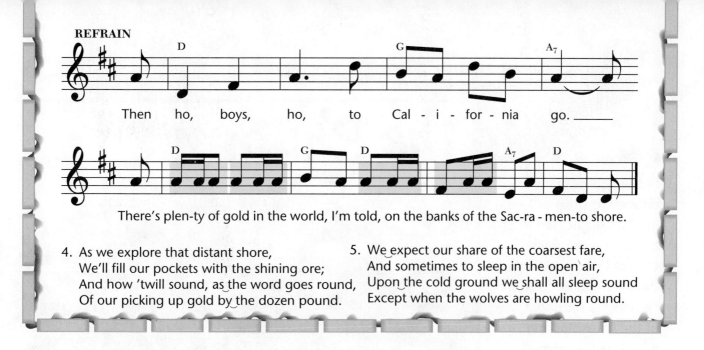

REFRAIN

Then ho, boys, ho, to Cal - i - for - nia go. _____

There's plen-ty of gold in the world, I'm told, on the banks of the Sac-ra - men-to shore.

4. As we explore that distant shore,
   We'll fill our pockets with the shining ore;
   And how 'twill sound, as the word goes round,
   Of our picking up gold by the dozen pound.

5. We expect our share of the coarsest fare,
   And sometimes to sleep in the open air,
   Upon the cold ground we shall all sleep sound
   Except when the wolves are howling round.

A rhythm pattern in music is a group of long and short sounds and silences used in different combinations.

Look at the color boxes in the last line of the song. Which color box contains a *short-short-long* rhythm pattern? Which color box contains a *long-short-short* rhythm pattern?

Show What You Know!

Read these patterns. Then **play** them on rhythm instruments.

1. $\frac{2}{4}$

2. $\frac{2}{4}$

Compose your own "Gold Rush Rhythm" and **perform** it with the song "California."

Tune In

In 1849, more than 80,000 "gold rushers" flocked to California to find their fortunes. They became known as the "forty-niners."

Work to the Rhythm

In the 1880s, many different groups of immigrants helped to build American railroads. One of these groups was the Irish. **Sing** "Drill, Ye Tarriers," a song that tells of the hardships and injustices the railroad workers faced.

Listen for some clues in the text about what tarriers do.

CD 3–16

Drill, Ye Tarriers

Words and Music by Thomas Casey

VERSE
Cm

do

1. Ev - 'ry morn-ing at sev - en o'-clock There's twen-ty tar - ri - ers a-
2. Our new fore-man is Dan ___ Mc-Cann, I'll tell you sure ___ he's a
3. Next time pay - day comes ___ a-round, Jim Goff was short ___ one ___

work - ing at the rock, And the boss comes a - long and he
blame ___ mean ___ man; Last ___ week a ___ prema - ture ___
buck, ___ he ___ found; "What ___ for?" says ___ he; then ___

says, "Keep still, And come down heav - y on the cast iron drill."
blast went off, And a mile in the air ___ went ___ Big Jim Goff.
this re - ply, "You're docked for the time ___ you were up in the sky."

REFRAIN

So drill, ye tar-ri-ers, drill, And drill, ye tar-ri-ers,

drill! Oh, it's work all day for sug-ar in your tay,

Down be-yond the rail-way, And drill, ye tar-ri-ers, drill!

Railroad Rhythms

Find the ♩ ♫ ♩ and ♫ ♩ patterns in the song.

Sing the song again, and when one of these patterns comes along, sing the rhythm syllables instead of the words. Good luck!

Play the rhythm parts below with the refrain of "Drill, Ye Tarriers."

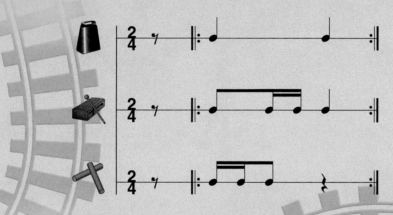

Listen to the ♩ ♫ pattern in this excerpt.

CD 3–22

Symphony No. 9 ("From the New World")

Movement 1
by Antonín Dvorák

The name of this symphony, "From the New World," refers to the United States. Czech composer Antonín Dvorák [an-toh-NEEN d'VOHR-zhahk] wrote it at about the same time railroad workers were singing "Drill, Ye Tarriers."

Element: FORM | **Skill: SINGING** | **Connection: SOCIAL STUDIES**

New Land, New Verse

The first immigrants to arrive in America were from Western Europe. Since then, people have come to the United States from every part of the world. The trip to America was difficult and dangerous for many people. Many did not survive. Those who arrived showed amazing courage and strength.

The song "Away to America" has two parts—**verse** and **refrain**. **Sing** this song about one man's journey to a new world. Why did he want to come to America? From what country did he come?

> **Verse** refers to the section of a song that is sung before the refrain.
> **Refrain** is the part of a song that repeats, using the same melody and words.

Away to America

Words and Music by Linda Williams

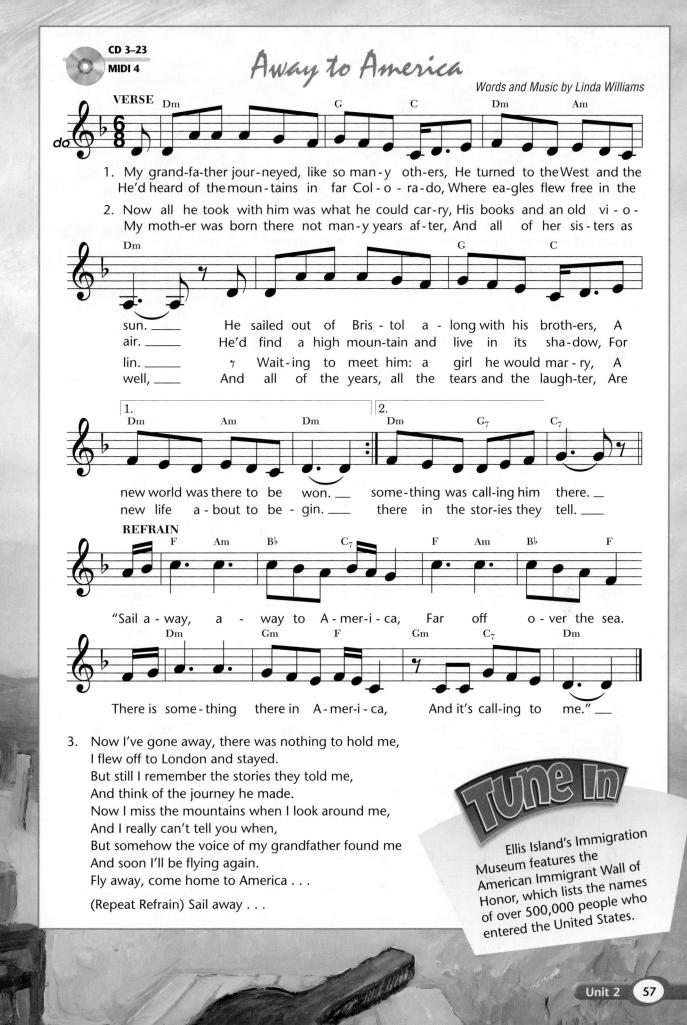

VERSE

1. My grand-fa-ther jour-neyed, like so man-y oth-ers, He turned to the West and the
   He'd heard of the moun-tains in far Col-o-ra-do, Where ea-gles flew free in the

2. Now all he took with him was what he could car-ry, His books and an old vi-o-
   My moth-er was born there not man-y years af-ter, And all of her sis-ters as

sun. _____ He sailed out of Bris-tol a-long with his broth-ers, A
air. _____ He'd find a high moun-tain and live in its sha-dow, For
lin. _____ Wait-ing to meet him: a girl he would mar-ry, A
well, _____ And all of the years, all the tears and the laugh-ter, Are

1.
new world was there to be won. ___
new life a-bout to be-gin. ___

2.
some-thing was call-ing him there. _
there in the stor-ies they tell. ___

REFRAIN

"Sail a-way, a-way to A-mer-i-ca, Far off o-ver the sea.

There is some-thing there in A-mer-i-ca, And it's call-ing to me." ___

3. Now I've gone away, there was nothing to hold me,
   I flew off to London and stayed.
   But still I remember the stories they told me,
   And think of the journey he made.
   Now I miss the mountains when I look around me,
   And I really can't tell you when,
   But somehow the voice of my grandfather found me
   And soon I'll be flying again.
   Fly away, come home to America . . .

   (Repeat Refrain) Sail away . . .

Tune In

Ellis Island's Immigration Museum features the American Immigrant Wall of Honor, which lists the names of over 500,000 people who entered the United States.

A Song of Sequences

When Spanish explorers returned from the New World, they told unbelievable stories about what they had seen. *"La ciudad de Juaja"* makes fun of these "far out" stories.

Listen to *"La ciudad de Juaja"* and its lively melody. Then **sing** the song with the same lively feeling.

CD 3–24

La ciudad de Juaja

(The City of Juaja)

English Words by Ruth DeCesare

Folk Song from New Mexico

VERSE

1. Des - de   la   ciu - dad   de   Jua - ja, _____
2. Los   ce - rros   son   de   tor - ti - llas, _____
1. From   the   far   cit - y   of   Jua - ja, _____
2. Hills   are   com - posed   of   tor - ti - llas, _____

me   man - dan   so - li - ci - tar, _____   que   me
las   que - bra - das   de   bu - ñue - los,   y   las
they   sent   a   card   to   in - vite   me,   so   I'd
val - leys   of   frit - ters   are   made, __   and   the

va - ya,   que   me   va - ya   de_un   te -
pie - dras,   fru - tas   cu - bier - tas,   pi - nos
come   and   see   a   place   so   strange   it
stones   and   fruit   and   pine   trees   are   with

so - ro   a   dis - fru - tar. _____
son _____   los   ca - ra - me - los.
cer - tain - ly   would   de - light   me.
car - a - mel   o - ver - laid. _____

58

¿Qué di - ces, a - mi - go? va - mos _____
What do you say, shall we go there? _____

a ver si di - cen ver - dad, ____ Si es ver -
Let's go and see what we learn. ___ If the

dad de lo que di - cen nos que -
truth is what they tell us, then we'll

da - mos por _____ a - llá.
sure - ly nev - er re - turn.

How Melodies Are Built

Melodies are built in a way that will give them a sense of unity—oneness. **Identify** the **motives** in the color boxes. The second motive in the blue color box is a repeat. Or is it?

> A **motive** is a short musical phrase that repeats in different ways.

When a motive is repeated at a higher or lower pitch, it is called a *sequence*.

Listen for the following sequence in this piece by Johann Sebastian Bach.

How does this sequence move? How many times in this piece is a sequence built from this motive?

CD 3–28

Invention No. 5 in E♭

by Johann Sebastian Bach
as performed by Glenn Gould

An "invention" is a short piece, usually for keyboard.

Step Up to fa

"*A la puerta del cielo*" is a lullaby that traveled with Spanish colonists to the New World.

Sing the first line of this song with pitch syllables.
Fa is the note between *so* and *mi*.

CD 3–29

A la puerta del cielo
(At the Gate of Heaven)

English Words by Alice Firgau

Folk Song from Spain

VERSE

1. A   la   puer - ta   del   cie - lo   ven - den   za - pa - tos,
1. At   the gate of   Heav - en, new   shoes they are   sell - ing

Pa - ra an - ge - li - tos que   an - dan des - cal - zos,
For the lit - tle   an - gels who   bare - foot are   play - ing.

REFRAIN

Duér - me - te, ni - ño, duér - me - te, ni - ño,
Sleep   now, my   lit - tle child, sleep now, my   lit - tle child,

Duér - me - te, ni - ño, a - rrú, a - rrú.
Sleep __ now, my   dear child, a - rrú, a - rrú.

2. A los niños que duermen
   Dios los bendice,
   A las madres que velan
   Dios les asiste.
   Refrain

2. All the little children
   are blest while they're sleeping,
   And the mothers, too,
   will be blest, their watch keeping.
   Refrain

Climb the Clouds

The step between *mi* and *fa* is called a half step because it is half the distance of a whole step. Can you hear the difference?

Sing the notes from *do* to *la* going up and down the "cloud ladder." Now try skipping around.

la

so

fa

mi

re

do

Fa on the Staff

When C is *do*, *fa* is F. The step from E to F is a half step.

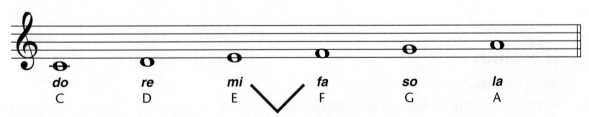

When F is *do*, *fa* is not B, but B♭. The pattern of whole and half steps must remain the same. This way, *mi* and *fa* are still a half step apart.

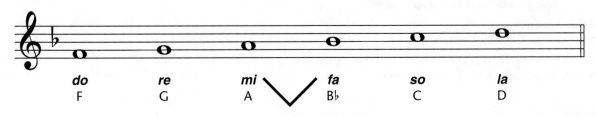

A Pitch for Peace

Melchior Franck [MEL-keeohr frahnk] (1573–1639) was a chapel conductor in Germany during the early 1600s. "*Da pacem, Domine*" is an example of his vocal music. **Sing** *"Da pacem, Domine"* using hand signs and pitch syllables.

CD 3–38

Da pacem, Domine
(Grant Us Peace)

English Words by Bernardo Rosso   *Music by Melchior Franck*

Da   pa - cem,   Do -   mi - ne,
Lord, grant us   peace ____   on earth,

Da   pa - cem,   Do - mi - ne,   in di -
O   Lord, for   peace we pray, for ____

e -   bus   nos -   tris.
peace in   our   day.

Layers of Melody

Listen to this performance of *"Da pacem, Domine."*
Follow each entrance of the melody as the parts overlap.

CD 4–4

Da pacem, Domine

by Melchior Franck
as performed by Capella Cantabile

Melchior Franck wrote over 600 pieces of music, including motets, madrigals, and instrumental dances.

◀ *Painting of Musicians* by Robert Lerrac-Tournieres, 1710. In Melchior Franck's time, most vocal pieces were also performed by instrumentalists.

Show What You Know!

You performed *"Da pacem, Domine"* in F-*do*.

Any song can be transposed, or sung at a higher or lower pitch. **Sing** the version of *"Da pacem, Domine"* below, using hand signs and pitch syllables. Is this version higher or lower than the first version? Where is *do* in this version?

Percussion Near and Far

Lightly stamp your foot on the floor…Pat your desk with your hand…

When you make sounds by striking something, you are playing **percussion.**

Make a list of instruments that fit this description. Which ones are pitched and which are nonpitched?

> **Percussion** instruments are pitched or nonpitched instruments that are played by striking, scraping, or shaking.

64

Percussion Variations

Listen to the various instruments used in *Theme and Variations for Percussion*. Point to the picture of each instrument as you hear it.

CD 4–5
Theme and Variations for Percussion

by William Kraft

The American composer William Kraft was born in Chicago in 1923. For many years, he was percussionist with the Los Angeles Philharmonic Orchestra.

Theme and Variations LISTENING MAP

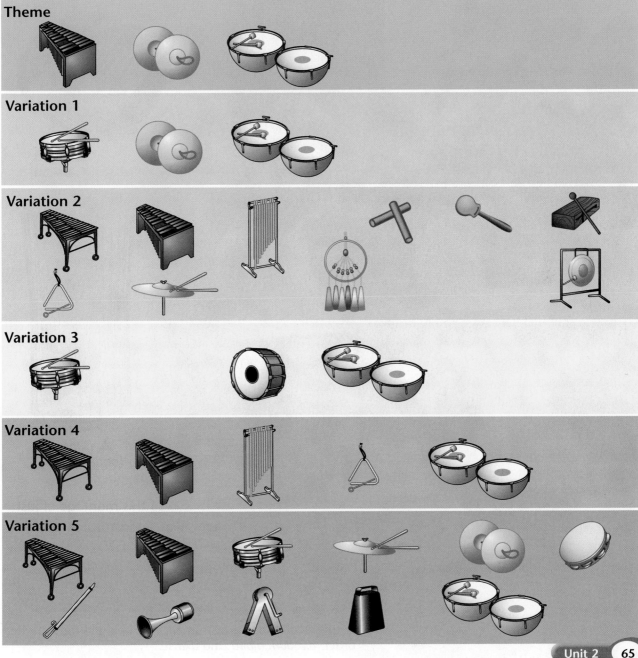

African Timbre

A wide variety of instruments are used by African musical groups. The different types of rattles and drums alone are quite numerous. In addition to percussion instruments, many different string instruments, flutes, and wooden or ivory horns can be found throughout the continent.

▲ *Axatse*
[ahks-AHT-see]

▲ *Mbira*
[m-BEE-rah]

▲ *Dundun*
[DOON - doon]

Listen to this montage of just a few African instruments.

CD 4–6
Montage of African Instruments

In this recording, the instruments are heard in the following order: *dundun, mbira,* and *axatse.*

Distant Drums

"*Ye jaliya da*" comes from West Africa. **Listen** for the *dundun*, *mbira*, and *axatse* as you sing.

CD 4–7

Ye jaliya da

Folk Song from West Africa

Ye   ja - li - ya   da _____ Al-lah   le - ga   ja - li - ya   da.

Ye   ja - li - ya   da _____ Al-lah   le - ga   ja - li - ya   da.

MUSIC MAKERS

Babatunde Olatunji

Babatunde Olatunji [bah-bah-TOON-deh oh-lah-TOON-gee] (1927–2003) is the first West African drummer to become famous in the Western Hemisphere. Born in Nigeria, he spent his childhood listening to the drums that surrounded him. Many of his drum pieces have been inspired by his native country.

Listen to *Oya (Primitive Fire)*, a rhythmic depiction of the discovery of fire.

CD 4–10

Oya (Primitive Fire)

written and performed by Babatunde Olatunji

Primitive Fire describes the lighting of the first fire, its mounting flames, and its slowly dying embers.

Singing Partners

The cowboy's life on the range was lonely. Singing songs while driving cattle across the plains, and at night around the campfire, helped pass the time.

The words of "Home on the Range," a favorite song of the American West, were adapted from a poem written by Dr. Brewster Higley. First published in 1873, the song became popular again in the 1930s and was a favorite of President Franklin Roosevelt. **Sing** "Home on the Range."

 **Arts Connection**

▲ *Singing Round Campfire,*
P.V.E. Ivory, 1906.

Home on the Range

Traditional Song from the United States

Oh, give me a home where the buf - fa - lo roam, Where the

deer and the an - te - lope play; _____ Where sel - dom is

heard a dis - cour - a - ging word, And the skies are not cloud - y all

day. _____ Home, home on the range, _____ Where the

deer and the an - te - lope play; _____ Where sel - dom is heard a dis -

cour - a - ging word, And the skies are not cloud - y all day. _____

Different Places

People choose to live in different places. Some people like a quiet country place, while others prefer living in cities, surrounded by sounds.

"Home on the Range" and "Live in the City" can be sung at the same time. When sung together, they are called **partner songs.** Partner songs share the same meter, chords, and key. What element of music do the two partners *not* share?

Partner songs are two or more songs sung at the same time to create harmony.

Sing "Live in the City." Then perform the two songs together.

Accompany Partner Songs

Play this part on bass xylophone or bass metallophone to accompany the partner songs.

Bass Xylophone/Bass Metallophone

Partner Songs

Partner songs are fun to sing. Irving Berlin, one of America's most loved songwriters, wrote a song in which the two sections can be sung as partner songs. **Sing** the first part of "Play a Simple Melody."

CD 4–17

Play a Simple Melody

Words and Music by Irving Berlin

PARTNER SONG 1:

Won't you play a sim-ple mel-o-dy like my moth-er sang to me. One with good old fash-ioned har-mo-ny. Play a sim-ple mel-o-dy.

Play Me Some Rag

Now **sing** the second part of "Play a Simple Melody."

PARTNER SONG 2:

Mus-i-cal gen - ius, set your aud-i-ence reel - in', won't you play me some rag. _

Just change that clas - si - cal nag _ To some sweet beau-ti -ful drag. _

If you will play from a cop - y of a tune that is chop - py you'll get

all my ap - plause, _ And that is sim - ply be - cause _

I want to lis - ten to rag.

After you know both parts well, put them together to form a partner song. When sung this way, the two melodies create **polyphonic texture.**

Polyphonic texture is created when two or more separate melodies are sung or played together.

MUSIC MAKERS

IRVING BERLIN

Irving Berlin (1888–1989) was a Russian immigrant who came to the United States with his family in 1893, when he was five years old. Although Berlin could not read music, he composed about 1,500 songs. His songs are celebrated for their appealing melodies and easy-to-remember lyrics.

Three of Berlin's most popular songs are "White Christmas," "There's No Business Like Show Business," and "God Bless America." Berlin received a Grammy Lifetime Achievement Award in 1968.

▲ Irving Berlin performing (and recording) at his piano, a specially designed instrument that allowed Berlin to play easily in different keys

74

Dvorák Meets Foster

This short piano piece combines two completely different melodies — *Humoresque,* by Antonín Dvorák, and *Old Folks at Home,* by Stephen Foster— to create another example of polyphonic texture. Play this piece on one piano. One person plays the top line while another person plays the bottom line. It will be easier if the bottom line is played an octave lower.

Using a keyboard or other melody instrument, create two short melodies that can be played together. Notate your melodies. Then ask a friend to be your musical partner.

Harmony in Beauty and Song

Katharine Lee Bates was so impressed by the beauty of America that she created a poem, "America, the Beautiful." She later set the poem to the tune of an old hymn by Samuel A. Ward.

Sing "America, the Beautiful," one of our most beloved patriotic songs.

CD 4–19

America, the Beautiful

Words by Katharine Lee Bates

Music by Samuel A. Ward

O beau-ti-ful for spa-cious skies, For am-ber waves of grain,

For pur-ple moun-tain maj-es-ties A-bove the fruit-ed plain!

A-mer-i-ca! A-mer-i-ca! God shed His grace on thee,

And crown thy good with broth-er-hood, From sea to shin-ing sea!

Freedom Sings in Harmony

Sing "Let Freedom Ring." How is it similar to "America, the Beautiful"?

When sung together, "America, the Beautiful" and "Let Freedom Ring" create harmony.

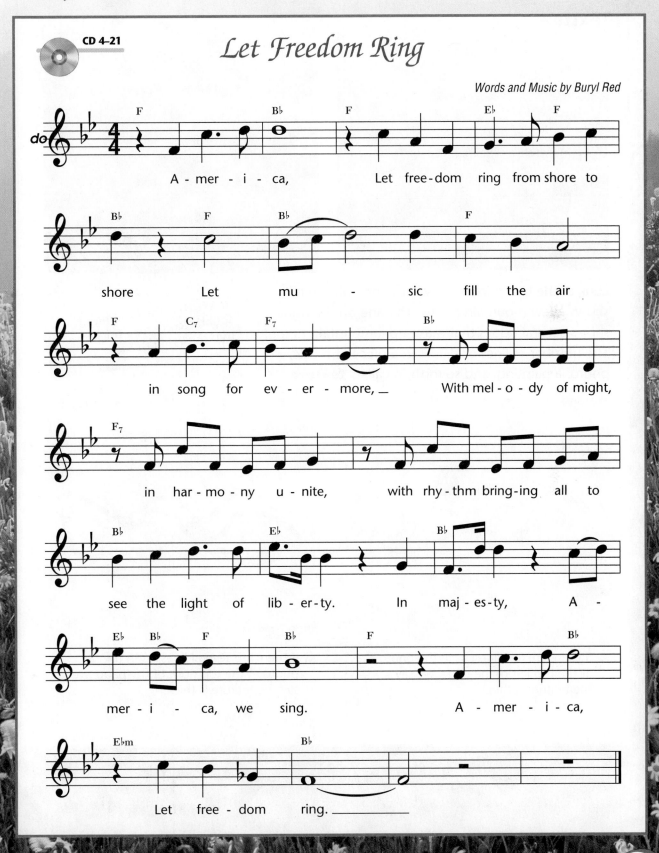

CD 4–21

Let Freedom Ring

Words and Music by Buryl Red

America, Let free-dom ring from shore to shore Let mu - sic fill the air in song for ev - er - more, ___ With mel - o - dy of might, in har - mo - ny u - nite, with rhy - thm bring-ing all to see the light of lib - er-ty. In maj - es-ty, A - mer - i - ca, we sing. A - mer - i - ca, Let free - dom ring. _____

Texture

Look at the two photos above. The one on the left shows a few mountain ridges. The one on the right shows several ridges that make up a mountain range. The number of lines or details in a piece of music, a photo, a painting, and so forth, is called **texture.**

Texture is the layering of sounds to create a thick or thin quality in music.

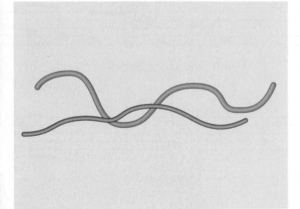
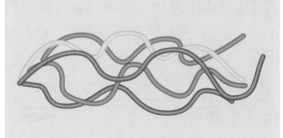

▲ If there are few lines, as in the photo at the top left of the page, we say the texture is thin.

▲ If there are several lines, as in the photo at the top right of the page, we say the texture is thick.

Texture on the March

Listen to *The Thunderer*, composed by John Philip Sousa, America's "March King." You will hear two melodies played together on the repeat. What effect does this have on the texture?

CD 4–24
The Thunderer

by John Philip Sousa

The Thunderer, one of more than 100 marches written by Sousa, was said to have been the composer's favorite.

MUSIC MAKERS

JOHN PHILIP SOUSA

John Philip Sousa [soo-zah] (1854–1932) grew up around military band music. His father was a trombonist in the United States Marine Corps Band. Sousa had his first music instruction at age 6. He studied voice, piano, violin, flute, cornet, baritone, trombone, and alto horn. His father enlisted him in the Marines when he was 13 years old. After his discharge from the Marines, Sousa began performing on the violin and conducting orchestras for touring theater groups. In 1880 Sousa returned to his hometown, Washington, D. C., to lead the U.S. Marine Band. He became known as a brilliant bandmaster. After leaving the Marine Band, Sousa formed his own band and toured with his group until his death.

Tune In

Each branch of the military has its own band, but only the Marine Band is the official band of the President of the United States.

Review, Assess,

What Do You Know?

1. Match the musical terms on the left with their correct definitions.

   a. *crescendo*   _____ The part of a song that repeats, using the same melody and words

   b. *decrescendo*   _____ Gradually get louder

   c. verse   _____ The section of a song that is sung before the refrain

   d. refrain   _____ Gradually get softer

2. Look at the melody for "*Da pacem, Domine*," page 62. Where is *do*? Identify, by pointing in the music,

   a. All the notes that are called *mi*.

   b. All the notes that are called *fa*.

   c. All the notes that are called *re*.

What Do You Hear? 2

 CD 4–25

You will hear three songs. Listen and decide whether the music moves in meter in 2, or meter in 3.

1. Meter in 2   Meter in 3

2. Meter in 2   Meter in 3

3. Meter in 2   Meter in 3

Perform, Create

What You Can Do

Choose Your Dynamics

Add *crescendo, decrescendo,* and other dynamics to the melody composition you created on page 75. Choose someone to help you perform your piece for the class.

Sing a Melody

Read the notation for "*A la puerta del cielo,*" page 60, using hand signs and pitch syllables. Then sing the song.

Keep a Journal

Keep a music journal. Divide it into three sections:
a. Vocabulary words
b. Musical forms
c. Lists of favorite songs
and listening selections

What Makes a Swing Song Swing?

During the 1940s, jazz bands and singers made swing music popular in the United States. Swing was a dance, too! In a swing song, the eighth notes are performed in swing rhythm, unevenly instead of evenly.

Tap the rhythm below using even eighth notes. Then tap the rhythm with "swing" eighth notes. Find this rhythm in "Teach Me to Swing," on page 84.

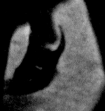

Learning the Language of Music

UNIT
3

Sing that Swing!

Sing "Teach Me to Swing." Swing songs sometimes include "scat" singing. **Listen** for the scat parts and swing!

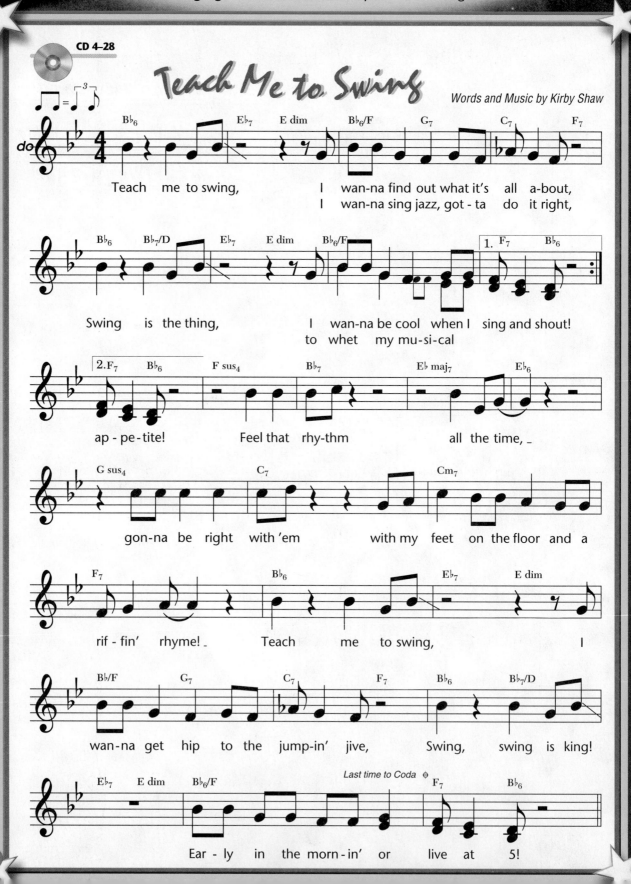

CD 4–28

Teach Me to Swing

Words and Music by Kirby Shaw

Teach me to swing, I wan-na find out what it's all a-bout,
I wan-na sing jazz, got-ta do it right,

Swing is the thing, I wan-na be cool when I sing and shout!
to whet my mu-si-cal

ap-pe-tite! Feel that rhy-thm all the time, _

gon-na be right with 'em with my feet on the floor and a

rif-fin' rhyme! _ Teach me to swing, I

wan-na get hip to the jump-in' jive, Swing, swing is king!

Ear-ly in the morn-in' or live at 5!

Express Your Pride

Patriotic songs express pride in our country. Decide what dynamics you will use to **sing** "The Voices of Pride" expressively. **Identify** the symbols for the dynamics you have chosen and tell what each symbol means.

pp = *pianissimo* = very soft	*p* = *piano* = soft	*mp* = *mezzo piano* = medium soft
mf = *mezzo forte* = medium loud	*f* = *forte* = loud	*ff* = *fortissimo* = very loud

Perform "The Voices of Pride" and include at least one *crescendo* and *decrescendo* in your performance. **Listen** for changes in dynamics as other groups sing.

CD 4–30
MIDI 5

The Voices of Pride

Words and Music by Ned Ginsburg

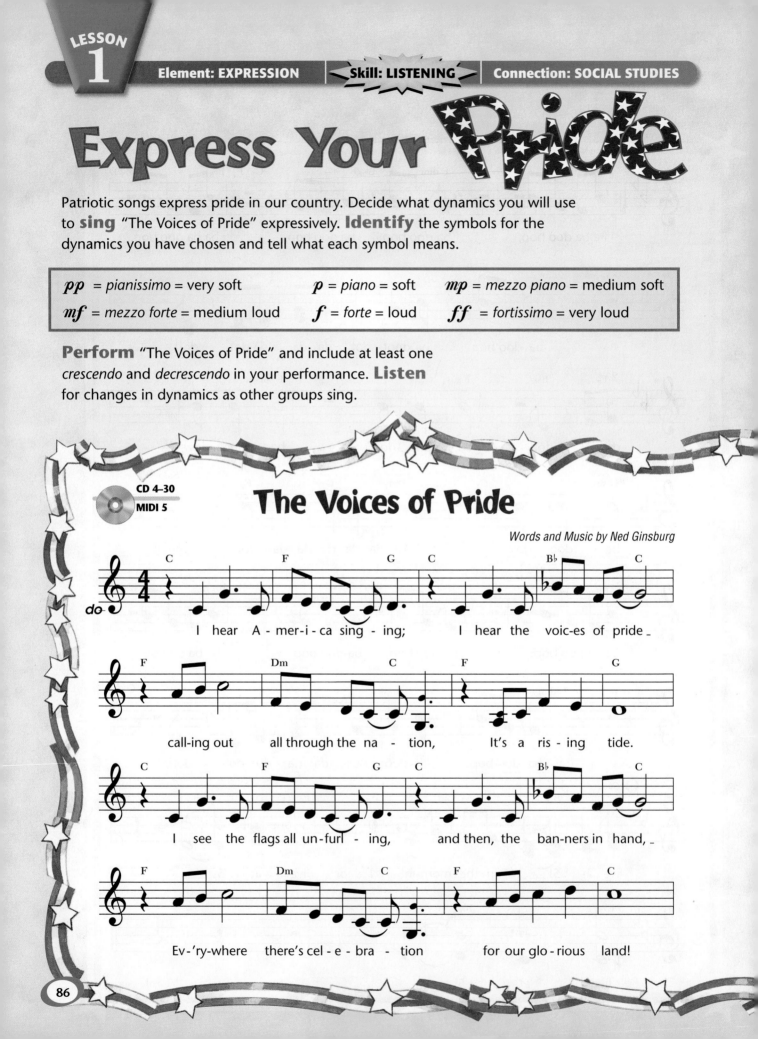

I hear A-mer-i-ca sing-ing; I hear the voic-es of pride

call-ing out all through the na-tion, It's a ris-ing tide.

I see the flags all un-furl-ing, and then, the ban-ners in hand,

Ev-'ry-where there's cel-e-bra-tion for our glo-rious land!

Different Strokes for Different Folks

Musicians use dynamics to perform music expressively. Musicians also use articulation, another way of performing expressively. **Sing** or **play** the first two measures of "America" with three different kinds of articulation:

Legato (smoothly, with no breaks in the sound)

Staccato (separated or detached)

Marcato (stressed or accented)

We've fought for free - dom, fought hard and learned;

Our kind of free-dom is-n't bought or be-stowed on us. No, it's earned.

I hear A - mer - i - ca sing - ing one rous - ing song.

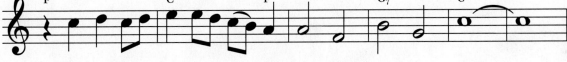

And with all A - mer - i - ca sing-ing, we'll stay free and strong! ____

MUSIC MAKERS
Roy Harris

Roy Harris (1898–1979) was an American arranger and composer whose style was influenced by traditional American music. Listening to his music often reminds people of the landscapes of the Midwest and Western states, with open prairies and breathtaking canyons. His music is described as emotional and powerful. *When Johnny Comes Marching Home* is an excellent example of Harris's love for folk and traditional songs, and the range of dynamics he used to show expression in his music.

Listen for musical expression in *When Johnny Comes Marching Home.* What expressive qualities can you **describe**?

CD 4–32

When Johnny Comes Marching Home

by Patrick S. Gilmore
arranged by Roy Harris

When Johnny Comes Marching Home was first published in 1863—the third year of the Civil War. Gilmore was a bandmaster in the Union army.

As you **listen** to *When Johnny Comes Marching Home*, follow the melody and listen for the dynamics and form as shown in the listening map.

When Johnny Comes Marching Home
LISTENING MAP

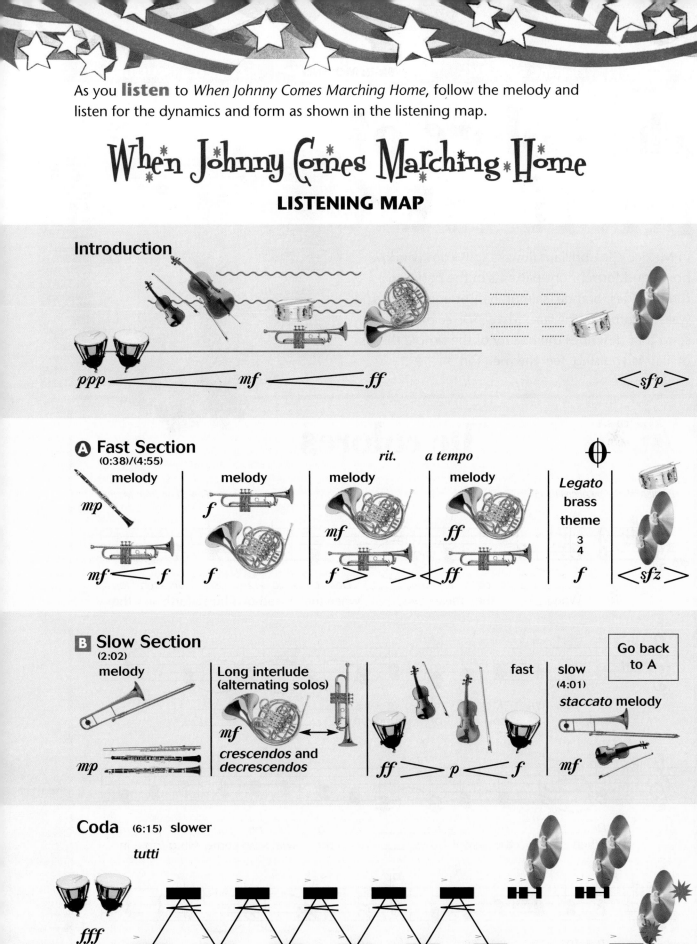

Introduction

ppp ⎯⎯ *mf* ⎯⎯ *ff*   *<sfp>*

A Fast Section
(0:38)/(4:55)

melody   melody   *rit.* melody   *a tempo* melody   *Legato* brass theme

mp   *f*   *mf*   *ff*

3
4

mf < *f*   *f*   *f* > > < *ff*   *f*   *<sfz>*

B Slow Section
(2:02)

melody   Long interlude (alternating solos)   fast   slow (4:01)

staccato melody

Go back to A

mf   crescendos and decrescendos

mp   *ff* > *p* < *f*   *mf*

Coda (6:15) slower
tutti

fff   *fff*

The Colors of Nature

In Mexico City, brilliant flowers spill from window boxes and form bright patterns in the parks. In rural villages, orange, salmon red, or aqua stucco walls shimmer in the sun. **Sing** "*De colores*," a song that describes the beauty of the simple things of life. As you sing, feel the meter in 3.

CD 5–1
MIDI 6

De colores

English Words by Alice Firgau   *Folk Song from Mexico*

De _____ co - lo - res, _____ De co - lo - res se vis - ten los
When _____ the mead - ows, _____ when the mead-ows burst forth in the

cam - pos en la pri - ma - ve - ra, _____
cool, dew - y col - ors of spring - time; _____

De _____ co - lo - res, _____ De co - lo - res son los pa - ja -
When _____ the swal - lows, _____ when the swal-lows come wing - ing in

ri - tos que vie - nen de a - fue - ra, _____
clouds of bright col - ors from far - off; _____

De _____ co - lo - res, _____ De co - lo - res es el ar - co
When _____ the rain - bow, _____ when the rain-bow spreads rib - bons of

i - ris que ve - mos lu - cir, _____ y por e - so los
col - or all o - ver the sky; _____ Then I know why the

gran - des a - mo - res de mu - chos co - lo - res me
splen - dors of true love are great and their col - ors, the

1.
gus - tan a mí. _____
best ones of all. _____

2.
gus - tan a mí. _____
best ones of all. _____

Listen to the Rhythm

Move to the beat of *"De colores."* Look at the time signature to find the number of beats in each measure. **Create** motions that show the strong beats.

Listen for meter in 3 in *Janitzio*. Where does the meter change?

CD 5–6
Janitzio

by Silvestre Revueltas

This piece is a musical description of a lake island in the Mexican state of Michoacán. Janitzio is famous for its festivals, beautiful flowers, and calm lake waters.

Celebrate with Dance

"*Chiapanecas*" is a traditional Mexican dance song that celebrates life and love. **Compare** the meter of this song to "*De colores*."

Listen for the section that includes two hand claps. How many times do you hear the hand claps in that section? Now, **sing** "*Chiapanecas*."

CD 5–7

Chiapanecas
(The Girl from Chiapas)

English Words by Don Kalbach

Folk Song from Mexico

Un cla - vel co - rté, ____ por la sie - rra fui ____ ca - mi -
I was go - ing home, _ I was all a - lone, __ when I

ni - to de ____ mi ran - cho. Co - mo el vien - to fue __
spied a red ____ car - na - tion, Rid - ing like the wind _

____ mi ca - ba - llo fiel __ á lle - var - me has - ta ___ su la - do,
____ on my trust - y horse _ I came to your side, __ my dar - ling.

Lin - da flor de a - bril ____ to - ma es - te cla - vel ____ que te
Love - ly girl of spring, _ take this flow'r I bring, __ which I

brin - do con ___ pa - sión. No me di - gas no, ___ que en tu
glad - ly of - fer you. Please don't tell me no, ___ I a -

bo - ca es - tá ____ el se - cre - to de __ mi a - mor.
dore you so, ___ And I give you all ___ my love.

92

Music Lives On

This song from Germany can be sung as a round. After you learn to **sing** it in unison, sing it in three parts. Try the German words, too.

Perform the groups of beats by patting the first beat of each measure on your knees, and snapping your fingers on beats 2 and 3.

Take turns conducting meter in 3 as the class sings "Music Alone Shall Live" in unison or as a round.

▲ Title page of a 16th-century music score

CD 5–11

Himmel und Erde
(Music Alone Shall Live)

Round from Germany

I
Him - mel und Er - de müss - en ver - gehn;
All things shall per - ish from un - der the sky;

II
a - ber die Mu - si - ca, a - ber die Mu - si - ca,
Mu - sic a - lone shall live, Mu - sic a - lone shall live,

III
a - ber die Mu - si - ca blei - bet be - stehn.
Mu - sic a - lone shall live, nev - er to die.

Round and Round

As you say *Mu-sic a-lone shall live* in rhythm, tap the beat with your foot.

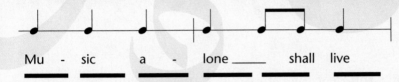

Try it again, and this time **perform** the rhythm pattern below while you say the words. Does the pattern always match each syllable of the words?

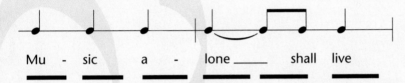

Mu - sic   a - lone _____ shall   live

Did you notice that the rhythm pattern doesn't match up with the second syllable of *alone*? We can use the tie to show that the sound lasts for one and a half beats.

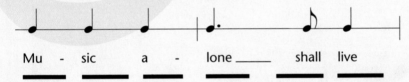

Mu - sic   a - lone _____ shall   live

But there is an easier way to write the same rhythm, using a dotted quarter note and an eighth note.

Mu - sic   a - lone _____ shall   live

How many times can you find this pattern in the song?

Listen to another round from Germany. Can you **identify** the same dotted rhythm pattern from "Music Alone Shall Live"?

CD 5–18
Viva la musica!

by Michael Praetorius

Michael Praetorius (1571–1621) was an organist, composer, and musicologist. Much of his music was based on Lutheran hymns and on the Latin mass still in use by the Lutheran church of his time.

Praetorius was born with the last name "Schultheiss," which is German for "mayor." The Latin word for mayor is *praetorius*.

Do You Feel the Rhythm?

Conduct "Don't You Hear the Lambs?" in $\frac{4}{4}$ meter as you **listen** to the recording. Notice that the song begins on beat three.

Arts Connection

▲ *The Shepherd* was painted by Frank Reed Whiteside (1866–1929), who was an art teacher as well as a professional painter.

Do You Hear the Singing?

"Don't You Hear the Lambs?" is an "old-time" folk song. These were songs that came from an old-time theme.

Sing "Don't You Hear the Lambs?"

CD 5–19

Don't You Hear the Lambs?

Folk Hymn from the Southern United States

VERSE

do

1. Don't you hear the lambs a - cry - in' on the
2. Don't you see the stars a - shin - in' on the

oth - er green shore? Don't you hear the lambs a -
oth - er green shore? Don't you see the stars a -

cry - in'? O, good _ shep - herd, go feed my sheep.
shin - in'? O, good _ shep - herd, go feed my sheep.

REFRAIN

Some for Paul and some for Si - las, some for to

make _ my heart re - joice. Don't you hear the lambs a -

cry - in'? O, good _ shep - herd, go feed my sheep.

Do You See the Patterns?

These four-beat patterns contain rhythms that you already know. Tap the beat with your foot while you **read**, clap, and count them, using rhythm syllables.

Which pattern is closest to the rhythm of the words in the third full measure of "Don't You Hear the Lambs?" Try saying the words *other green* in tempo while clapping each pattern.

You can use the tie to make pattern 4 above fit the rhythm of the words.

oth - er _____ green

You can use an eighth note and a dotted quarter note to show the same rhythm a different way:

oth - er _____ green

Now you are ready to **read** and **perform** the rhythm of "Don't You Hear the Lambs?" using rhythm syllables.

Show What You Know!

Using a grand staff, **notate** the refrain of "Don't You Hear the Lambs?" on the top staff. On the bottom staff, notate an accompaniment using D-major and C-major chords. Use a rhythm pattern in your accompaniment that includes the dotted quarter note and eighth note.

Sing and Play

Follow the music on page 97 and accompany "Don't You Hear the Lambs?" using either of the chords below. Choose a guitar, an Autoharp, a keyboard, or a mallet instrument and **play** your chord when it occurs in the song.

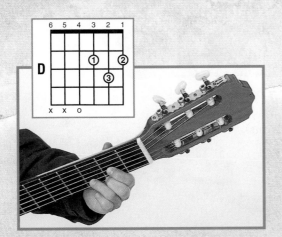

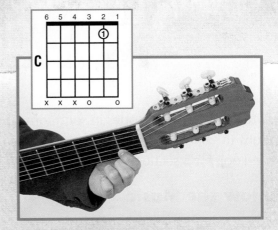

MUSIC MAKERS

Mike Seeger — The Seeger Family

The Seeger family has been a vital part of American music for over 50 years. The patriarch, Charles Louis Seeger, was a musician and inventor. His wife, Ruth Crawford Seeger, was a distinguished composer and music educator. There are seven Seeger children, including Peggy, Mike, and Pete. Mike plays several dozen instruments and has recorded many traditional and new folk songs. All members of the Seeger family have a passion for traditional music.

Listen to Mike, Peggy, and Penny Seeger perform their version of *Don't You Hear the Lambs?*

CD 5–24

Don't You Hear the Lambs?

Folk Hymn from the Southern United States as performed by Mike, Peggy, and Penny Seeger

Many favorite Christmas songs are folk songs. Folk songs are usually simple so many people can sing and play them.

Form in Music

Spirituals tell ancient stories in song form. **Sing** "Joshua Fought the Battle of Jericho," a spiritual about a biblical hero. Look for a section of the song that repeats.

Follow the Music

"Joshua Fought the Battle of Jericho" is a song in **ABA form.** Which part of the song is the Ⓐ section? Which part is the Ⓑ section? Now that you have identified the form, learn to **play** the following parts during the Ⓐ section.

In **ABA form**, the first and last sections are the same. The middle section is different.

Joshua Fought the Battle of Jericho

African American Spiritual

REFRAIN A

Josh - ua fought the bat - tle of _____ Jer - i - cho, _____

Jer - i - cho, _____ Jer - i - cho, _____

Josh - ua fought the bat - tle of _____ Jer - i - cho, _____

And the walls came tum - blin' down.

VERSE B

You can talk a - bout your king of Gid - e - on, _____

You can talk a - bout your man of Saul, _____

But there's none like good old Josh - u - a _____

At the bat - tle of Jer - i - cho.

One More Time–with Guitar

"Joshua Fought the Battle of Jericho" uses just the Dm and A₇ chords in the **B** section. Learn to **play** these chords on guitar. Then follow the chord symbols in the music and **improvise** your own rhythm to accompany the song.

Arts **Connection**

▲ *Going to Church* was painted by the American artist William H. Johnson (1901–1970). As in music, form is an important element in the visual arts. What hints of ABA form, such as balance and repetition, can you identify in this painting?

What's the Form?

Listen to *Standin' in the Need of Prayer.* Does it follow the same form as "Joshua Fought the Battle of Jericho"?

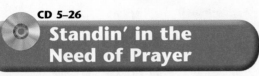

CD 5–26

Standin' in the Need of Prayer

**African American Spiritual
as performed by the Moses Hogan Chorale**

The Moses Hogan Chorale is based in New Orleans, Louisiana. In 1996, the group was invited to perform at the World Choral Symposium in Sydney, Australia.

Brother

Sister

Mother

Father

Deacon

Preacher

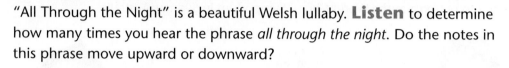

A New Note

"All Through the Night" is a beautiful Welsh lullaby. **Listen** to determine how many times you hear the phrase *all through the night*. Do the notes in this phrase move upward or downward?

This time as you listen, **sing** the phrase each time it occurs. Use hand signs and pitch syllables for the notes you know. (Hum the new note.) **Describe** the new note. How does it sound compared to *la*? How does it sound compared to *do*?

The note between *la₁* and *do* is called *ti₁*. Since it is below *do*, it is called *low ti*.

la₁   *ti₁*   *do*

Use the key signature in "All Through the Night" to find *do*. Can you also find each *ti₁* in the song? **Sing** the song using pitch syllables and hand signs. Then **read** the song using letter names.

A Classical Arrangement

Listen to this performance of *All Through the Night*, sung in Welsh.

CD 5–27
All Through the Night

**Traditional Melody from Wales
arranged by Franz Joseph Haydn
performed by Angelika Kirschlager**

Haydn's arrangement of this famous Welsh song uses a piano and string instrument accompaniment.

All Through the Night

Verse 1 by Harold Boulton
Verse 2 Attributed to Thomas Oliphant

Melody from Wales

1. Sleep, my child, and peace at-tend thee All through the night;
2. While the moon her watch is keep-ing All through the night;

Guard - ian an - gels God will send thee All through the night.
While the wea - ry world is sleep-ing All through the night.

Soft the drow-sy hours are creep-ing, Hill and vale in slum - ber steep-ing,
O'er thy spir - it gent-ly steal-ing, Vi-sions of de - light re-veal-ing,

I my lov - ing vig - il keep-ing All through the night.
Breathes a pure and ho - ly feel-ing All through the night.

M·U·S·I·C M·A·K·E·R·S

Franz Joseph Haydn

Franz Joseph Haydn [HI-dn] (1732–1809) was born in Austria (in the same year as George Washington) and showed an early love of music. As a boy, he would pretend to play the violin using two pieces of wood. Haydn was a very productive composer. He wrote more than 1,000 works in his lifetime, including over 100 symphonies (the most famous of which is subtitled *"Surprise"*) and the oratorios *The Seasons* and *The Creation*. Haydn's orchestra of strings, woodwinds, brass, and percussion was very similar to the modern-day orchestra.

Same Note...
Different Place

"*Dundai*" is a Hebrew folk song about the Torah, the holy book of the Jewish faith.

You have learned that the new note between *low la* and *do* is *low ti*. Can you find *low ti* in the scale?

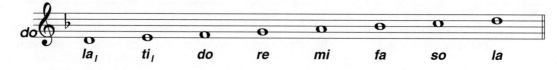

do   la₁   ti₁   do   re   mi   fa   so   la

Now look at the last note of the song. What is the tonic? Can you find *low ti* in the melody?

Read and **sing** "*Dundai*."

CD 5–34

Dundai

English Version by David Eddleman   *Folk Song from Israel*

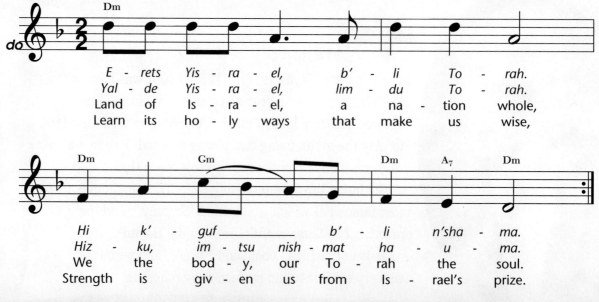

E - rets   Yis - ra - el,   b' - li   To - rah.
Yal - de   Yis - ra - el,   lim - du   To - rah.
Land   of   Is - ra - el,   a   na - tion   whole,
Learn   its   ho - ly   ways   that   make   us   wise,

Hi   k' - guf_____   b' - li   n'sha - ma.
Hiz - ku,   im - tsu   nish - mat   ha - u - ma.
We   the   bod - y,   our   To - rah   the   soul.
Strength   is   giv - en   us   from   Is - rael's   prize.

Dun - dai, dun - dai, _____ dun - dai dai,

Dun - dai, dun - dai, _____ dun - dai dai.

Show What You Know!

Identify *ti* in each of these patterns. Then **sing** the pattern using hand signs and pitch syllables.

This phrase is from a song in Unit 3. **Sing** the phrase using hand signs and pitch syllables. Where is *ti* ? What is the name of the song?

LEARN BY EAR AND EYE

Many traditional songs are not written down. The Navajo preserve traditional songs by singing them to each other. Children learn songs from their elders, and songs are passed from one generation to the next.

Listen to "*Jo'ashilá,*" a traditional Navajo song. Some of the word sounds you hear are vocables that do not have a specific meaning. Tap the beat as you listen. Then walk together to the beat of the song. "*Jo'ashilá*" is written down here so you can learn it.

CD 5–43

Jo'ashilá
(Walking Together)

Traditional Song of the Navajo

Jo - 'a - shi - lá, Jo - 'a - shi - lá,

Jo - 'a - shi - lá, hei yei' yun ga.

T'oo ga' ni-zhón - ní-go bah ho-zhó lá hei ya' hei', nee ya.

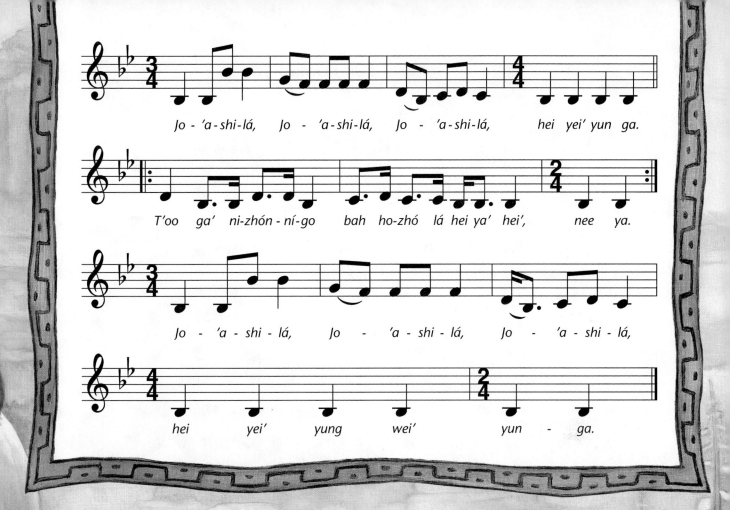

Jo - 'a - shi - lá,   Jo - 'a - shi - lá,   Jo - 'a - shi - lá,   hei yei' yun ga.

T'oo ga' ni - zhón - ní - go   bah ho - zhó lá hei ya' hei',   nee ya.

Jo - 'a - shi - lá,   Jo - 'a - shi - lá,   Jo - 'a - shi - lá,

hei   yei'   yung   wei'   yun - ga.

Listen to Learn

Sing "Jo'ashilá" and **identify** parts of the melody that are the same.

▲ Native American
drums, flute, and rattle

WINDS OF THE WORLD

A mysterious figure of legend, Kokopelli wandered from village to village, playing his flute and telling his wonderful stories.

Listen to *Kokopelli Wandering Song,* played on a Native American flute.

CD 6–1

Kokopelli Wandering Song

Traditional Native American Melody performed by Robert Tree Cody

Much of Robert Tree Cody's music is inspired by nature.

Improvising a Melody

In *Kokopelli Wandering Song,* the second half of the melody is always the same but the first half changes. **Play** the melody below on recorder. Only the second half of the melody is shown. **Improvise** the first half of the melody, then **play** the second half as written.

▲ Pueblo relief sculpture of Kokopelli

Compare the Instruments

The Native American flute and the recorder have different tunings and scales. Think about what you know about these instruments. How are they the same? How are they different? **Compare** your recorder to the Native American flute pictured here.

▲ The Native American flute has been played for many generations. Most flutes are made of wood, usually cedar. The Native American flute has five or six finger holes and a thumbhole.

Bach's Recorder

During J. S. Bach's lifetime (1685–1750), the recorder was called *flauto,* an Italian term meaning "flute." **Listen** to the sound of the recorders in this concerto by Bach.

CD 6–2
Allegro

**from *Brandenburg Concerto No. 4*
by Johann Sebastian Bach**

This concerto features two recorders.

MUSIC MAKERS

Robert Tree Cody

Robert Tree Cody, of Dakota-Maricopa heritage, lives in Arizona. He has traveled throughout the United States and Europe as a traditional dancer, singer, and flutist. He teaches about the traditional ways of Native American peoples, including folklore, crafts, and music. In Arizona, he participates in artist-in-residence programs in the schools.

A Special Flute

The *shakuhachi* [shah-koo-HAH-chee] is a Japanese flute made of bamboo. The basic notes are D, F, G, A, and C. **Play** these notes on your recorder. Then **compose** a melody using these notes.

Shakuhachi players can create special effects by sliding their fingers and trilling or fluttering their tongues as they play.

What special effects can you **create** on the recorder? Add them to your melody.

Arts Connection

◀ Painting by Diana Ong of woman playing *shakuhachi*. The *shakuhachi* has been played for more than a thousand years. The instrument has four holes in the front and one in the back.

Listen to this excerpt featuring a *shakuhachi*. **Describe** the special effects that you hear.

CD 6–3

Shika no tone

Traditional Song from Japan as performed by Yamato Ensemble

Shika no tone (The Sound of Deer Calling to One Another) is a *shakuhachi* composition that dates from the eighteenth century.

Tune In

At one time, the *shakuhachi* was played by Japanese priests who wore wicker baskets over their heads to hide their identities. They walked through the streets listening to conversations while playing soft tunes on their *shakuhachis*.

Song of the Flute

The flute is the oldest known wind instrument. Almost every culture has some kind of flute, but the flute we are most familiar with was designed by Theobald Boehm. The flute is played by blowing across a hole near one end of the instrument. The number of holes and keys on the flute has changed over the centuries.

◀ The modern flute is a long metal tube with 13 main holes, several smaller ones, and many keys of different shapes and sizes.

M·U·S·I·C M·A·K·E·R·S
Claude Debussy

Claude Debussy (1862–1918) was an important composer of the late nineteenth and early twentieth centuries. He began a movement in French music called Impressionism. Early in his life, Debussy wrote unusual music for the piano. He created dream-like moods using unusual harmonies, rhythms, and whole-tone scales.

Listen to *Syrinx,* a composition by Debussy for solo flute.

CD 6–4
Syrinx

by Claude Debussy
performed by James Galway
Debussy named this piece after a water nymph in the legend of Pan.

Now **listen** to the opening of *Prelude to the Afternoon of a Faun,* which features the flute with orchestra.

CD 6–5
Prelude to the Afternoon of a Faun

by Claude Debussy
This piece is about a faun, a mythical creature that is half man and half beast. This music was featured in the Disney film *Fantasia.*

Tune In

In music, Impressionism uses mood or atmosphere instead of emotion or story to convey the composer's intention.

SONGS ABOUT NATURE

There are many different ways to create harmony. You've already done this by singing ostinatos and partner songs. A **descant** provides another way to sing in harmony.

Sing "The Ash Grove," a folk song from Wales.

Read the lyrics before you sing, to understand what the song is all about.

> A **descant** is another melody that decorates the main tune, usually placed above the main melody.

CD 6–6 / MIDI 8

THE ASH GROVE

Folk Song from Wales

Descant

2. The ash grove is speak -
The light through its branch -

Melody

1. Down yon - der green val - ley where stream - lets me -
Or at the bright noon - tide In sol - i - tude
2. The ash grove, how grace - ful, how plain - ly 'tis
When - ev - er the light through its branch - es is

ing, The harp plays lan-guage for me.
es Brings fac - es gaz - ing on me.

an - der, When twi - light is fad - ing I pen - sive - ly rove,
wan - der, A - mid the dark shades of the lone - ly ash grove.
speak-ing, The harp through it play - ing has lan-guage for me;
break-ing, A host of kind fac - es is gaz - ing on me.

Singing Together

The Columbia River is one of our country's most spectacular rivers. **Listen** to "Roll On, Columbia." **Sing** the melody of the refrain. Then sing the **countermelody**. **Sing** the two parts together to experience polyphonic texture.

A **countermelody** is played or sung at the same time as the main melody.

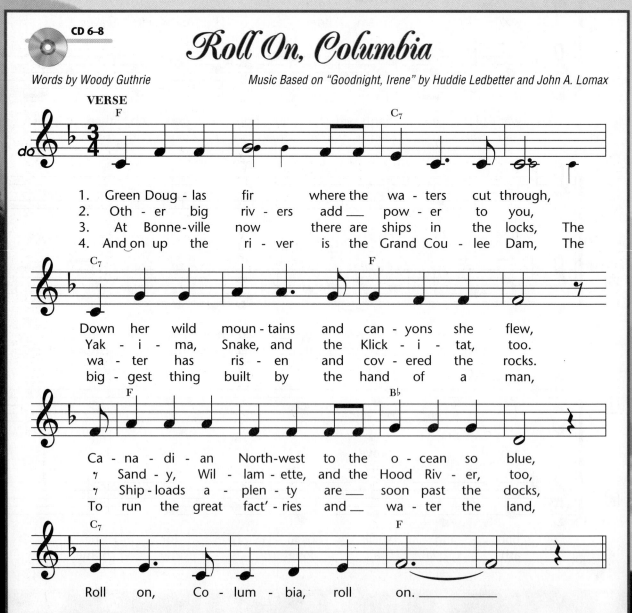

CD 6–8

Roll On, Columbia

Words by Woody Guthrie   *Music Based on "Goodnight, Irene" by Huddie Ledbetter and John A. Lomax*

VERSE

1. Green Doug - las   fir   where the   wa - ters   cut through,
2. Oth - er   big   riv - ers   add __   pow - er   to   you,
3. At Bonne - ville   now   there are   ships   in   the   locks,   The
4. And on up   the   ri - ver   is the   Grand Cou - lee   Dam,   The

Down   her   wild   moun - tains   and   can - yons   she   flew,
Yak - i - ma,   Snake, and   the   Klick - i - tat,   too.
wa - ter   has   ris - en   and   cov - ered   the   rocks.
big - gest   thing   built   by   the   hand   of   a   man,

Ca - na - di - an   North - west   to the   o - cean   so   blue,
Sand - y,   Wil - lam - ette, and the   Hood   Riv - er,   too,
Ship - loads   a - plen - ty   are __   soon past   the   docks,
To   run   the   great   fact' - ries   and __   wa - ter   the   land,

Roll   on,   Co - lum - bia,   roll   on. ____

Element: **TEXTURE/HARMONY**　Skill: **PLAYING**　│　Connection: **RELATED ARTS**

Sing of America's Beauty

"This Land Is Your Land" is probably the most popular song composed by Woody Guthrie. Sing the melody of the refrain. Then sing the countermelody. How is the countermelody different from the main melody?

This Land Is Your Land

CD 6–10
MIDI 9

Words and Music by Woody Guthrie
Countermelody by Ruth Tutelman

REFRAIN

Countermelody (sing last time only)

1　This land　is　your　land,　this land　is

Melody

2　This land is　your　land, _____ this land is　my　land, _____

1　mine,　From　Maine to　Mon - ta - na,　des - ert to the

2　_____ From Cal - i - for - nia _____ to the New York　is - land; _____

1　shore, We　sing that　this land　is　your　land,　this land　is

2　_____ From the red-wood for - est _____ to the Gulf Stream wa - ters; _____

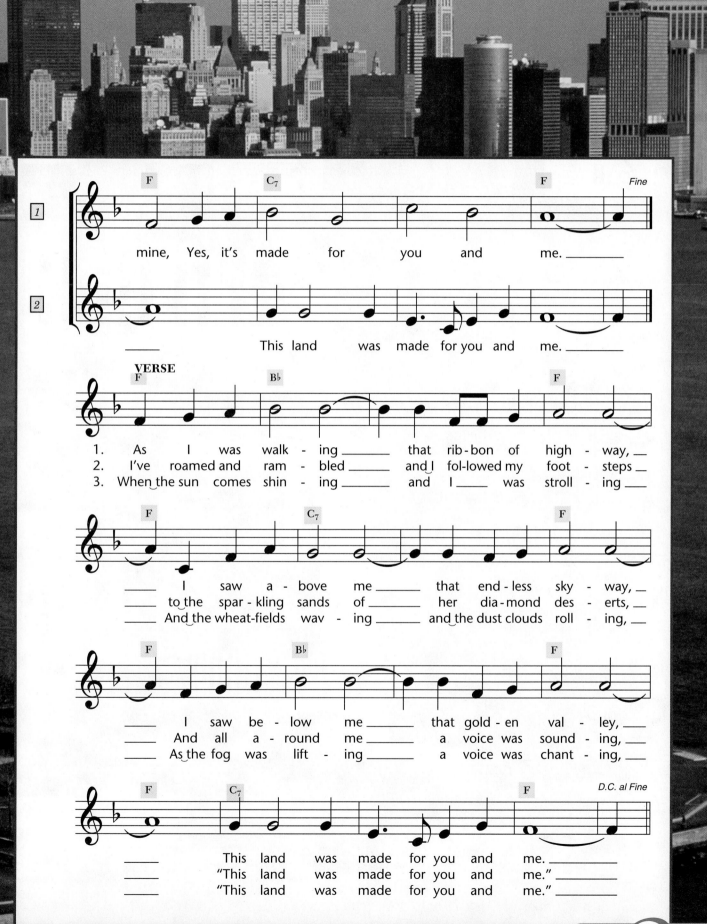

Keyboard Harmony

The harmony in "This Land Is Your Land" is based on the three chords shown below.

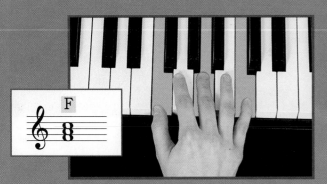

Play the chords on keyboard to accompany the song. Follow the chord symbols above the music as you play.

Roaming with Woody

Fortunately for music lovers everywhere, Woody Guthrie recorded many of his songs before a serious illness ended his career. **Listen** to one of his early recordings of *This Land Is Your Land*.

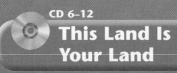

CD 6–12

This Land Is Your Land

written and performed by Woody Guthrie

When Guthrie wrote this song in 1940, the final line of each verse was sometimes sung *God blessed America for me.*

120

River Inspirations

The music of American composer Virgil Thomson (1896–1989) was frequently inspired by the beauty and grandeur of our country. In 1937, he wrote music to accompany *The River,* a documentary film about the Mississippi River.

Listen to this excerpt from *"The River" Suite.* **Identify** sections in which different melodies are played at the same time.

CD 6–13

Finale

from *"The River" Suite*
by Virgil Thomson

Thomson incorporated many folk songs into his music. Do you recognize the melody of "The Bear Went Over the Mountain" in *Finale*?

This excerpt, from the narrative to the film *The River*, names the tributaries that flow to the Mississippi River. Pare Lorentz was the director of the documentary.

The River

by Pare Lorentz

Down the Yellowstone, the Milk, the White, and Cheyenne;
The Cannonball, the Musselshell, the James, and the Sioux;
Down the Judith, the Grand, the Osage, and the Platte,
The Skunk, the Salt, the Black, and Minnesota;
Down the Rock, the Illinois, and the Kankakee,
The Allegheny, the Monongahela, Kanawha, and Muskingum;
Down the Miami, the Wabash, the Licking and the Green,
The Cumberland, the Kentucky, and the Tennessee;
Down the Ouachita, the Wichita, the Red, and Yazoo—
Down the Missouri, three thousand miles from the Rockies;
Down the Ohio, a thousand miles from the Alleghenies;
Down the Arkansas, fifteen hundred miles from the Great Divide;
Down the Red, a thousand miles from Texas;
Down the great Valley, twenty-five hundred miles from Minnesota,
Carrying every rivulet and brook, creek and rill,
Carrying all the rivers that run down two-thirds the continent—
The Mississippi runs to the Gulf.

What Do You Know?

1. Look at the last four measures of the refrain of "This Land Is Your Land," on page 118, in which *do* is in the first space.

   a. Point to all the notes called *so.*
   b. Point to all the notes called *re.*
   c. Point to all the notes called *ti.*

2. Look at the three phrases below.

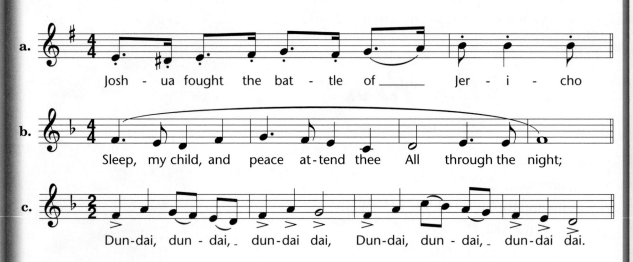

a. Josh - ua fought the bat - tle of _____ Jer - i - cho

b. Sleep, my child, and peace at-tend thee All through the night;

c. Dun-dai, dun - dai, _ dun-dai dai, Dun-dai, dun - dai, _ dun-dai dai.

   • Point to the phrase that should be performed in a *legato* style.

   • Point to the phrase that should be performed in a *marcato* style.

   • Point to the phrase that should be performed in a *staccato* style.

Perform, Create

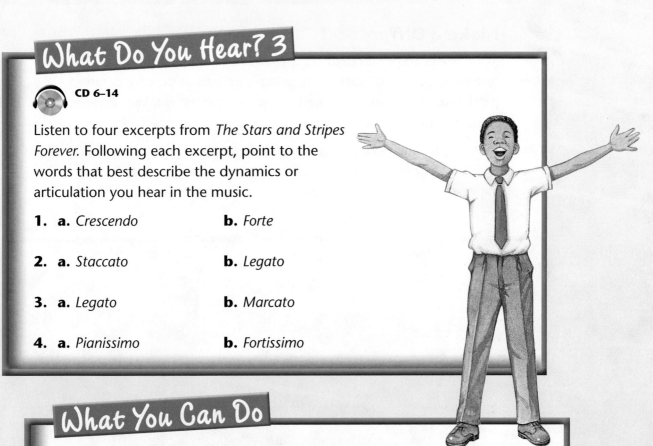

What Do You Hear? 3

CD 6–14

Listen to four excerpts from *The Stars and Stripes Forever.* Following each excerpt, point to the words that best describe the dynamics or articulation you hear in the music.

1. a. *Crescendo*   **b.** *Forte*

2. a. *Staccato*   **b.** *Legato*

3. a. *Legato*   **b.** *Marcato*

4. a. *Pianissimo*   **b.** *Fortissimo*

What You Can Do

Sing and Show Hand Signs

Sing "*Himmel und Erde,*" page 94, using hand signs and pitch syllables. Then sing the song with the lyrics.

Sing and Conduct

Sing "All Through the Night," page 105, and conduct the beat while following the notation. Sing the song, using rhythm syllables and then the lyrics.

Create a Rhythm Pattern

Create a four-measure rhythm pattern in ¾ meter using ♩ ♩ ♩. ♩. ♪. Be sure to include rests.

Now perform your rhythm pattern on an instrument of your choice.

"That's one small step for man,
one giant leap for mankind."

(American Astronaut Neil Armstrong, July 20, 1969, at10:56 PM EST)

Make a Difference!

"One Small Step," on page 126, is about making a difference. Doing one small thing can open another door or lead us down a different path. Like Neil Armstrong, we too can be leaders by taking one small step, one step at a time.

Learning music is like taking one step at a time. You learn musical skills a little at a time and build on them. Then you use these skills to experience music and to share what you have learned with others.

Building Our Musical Skills

Step by Step

Sing "One Small Step." In what ways can you make a difference?

CD 6–18

One Small Step

Words and Music by
Jay Althouse and Sally K. Albrecht

do

1. I can see a world of one great fam - i - ly
2. We must plant a seed of free - dom ev - 'ry - where.

liv - ing in peace and broth - er - hood, ___ liv - ing in har - mo -
Nur - ture it ___ and help it grow ___ in un - pol - lut - ed

ny. But the world in which we live is a ver - y dif - f'rent place.
air. But a dream is still a dream un - less we do ___ our part:

Fear and hate af - fect us all, ___ ev - 'ry col - or, creed and
Feed the hun - gry, help the poor, ___ giv - ing of our

race. So we must climb the walls and cross the rag - ing riv - ers. And we must
heart.

make a world of peace our com - mon goal. For we can make a dif - f'rence.

We can build a bridge and o - pen up the path - ways to our soul.

Element: EXPRESSION | **Skill: LISTENING** | **Connection: STYLE**

EXPRESSIVE SOUNDS

"La bamba" is a folk dance with expressive rhythms. The instruments used and the percussive sounds of the dancers reflect the familiar sounds of the Veracruz region of Mexico.

Listen to "La bamba." How do the rhythm and timbre add to the expressive qualities of the melody? What is the style of this music?

CD 6–20

La bamba

Folk Song from Mexico
Adapted and Arranged by Ritchie Valens

Pa - ra bai - lar   la bam - ba.
Hear the beat of the bam - ba.
Pa - ra bai - lar   la bam -
Hear the beat of the bam -

- ba se ne - ce - si - ta un - a po - ca de gra - cia.
- ba.   To dance the bam - ba,   you need to   be   grace-ful.

Un - a po - ca de gra - cia pa - ra mi pa - ra ti ___
Oh, you need to   be   grace-ful ___   to   dance ___ the   bam-

___ ya a - rri - ba a - rri - ba;   y' a - rri - ba y' a -
- ba; You need to   be   play - ful.   I   will __ dance the

rri - ba por ti se - ré ___   por ti se - ré ___   por ti se - ré. __
bam-ba, Oh I will   dance, _ I will dance the bam - ba, I will dance the bam-

Yo no soy mar - i - ne - ro.
- ba, I'll go up and __ dance it.

Yo no soy mar - i -
But no sail - or am

ne - ro, soy cap - i - tan; ____
I, but for you I'll be; ____

soy cap - i - tan, __
For you I'll be, __

____ soy cap - i - tan. ____
For you I'll be. ____

Bam - ba ____ bam -
Dance the __ bam -

- ba, bam - ba __ bam - ba,
- ba, dance the __ bam - ba,

bam - ba, __ bam -
Dance the __ bam -

- ba, bam - ba __ bam... _
- ba, bam - ba, __ dance. _

Pa - ra bai - lar la bam -
Hear the beat of the bam -

Bam - ba, _____ bam - ba!
Dance the _____ bam - ba!

Pop Folk

Listen to this original artist version of *La bamba*.

CD 6–24
La bamba

**Folk Song from Mexico
as performed by Ritchie Valens**

Valens arranged and adapted this folk song from Mexico. This version became a top hit in 1959.

Ritchie Valens

Ritchie Valens (1941–1959) was one of the first famous Hispanic rock stars. He popularized the classic Mexican folk song "*La bamba*." In 1959 he was named one of the most promising young talents of rock 'n' roll.

The promise of a long, successful career was lost when Valens and two other early rock legends, the Big Bopper and Buddy Holly, perished in a plane crash in 1959. Valens was only seventeen and had just begun to make records. The 1987 film *La Bamba*, based on Ritchie Valens' life, introduced his legacy to many more fans.

Tune In

Ritchie Valens' original family name was Valenzuela.

Traditional Folk

You've heard Ritchie Valens' version of *La bamba*. Now **listen** to *La bamba* as performed in the *jarocho* [hah-ROH-choh] style from the Mexican state of Veracruz. This *jarocho* ensemble includes the instruments shown below.

CD 6–25
La bamba

**Folk Song from Mexico
as performed by Los Pregoneros del Puerto**

The musicians are all native *Veracruzano*s who have performed together for 25 years.

Jarocho ensemble (left to right): *arpa, two requintos, jarana* ▼

Upbeats

A song that begins before the first beat of a measure begins on an **upbeat.**

Sing "Hosanna, Me Build a House."

Can you **identify** phrases in this song that begin on an upbeat?

Upbeats are sometimes called weak beats because they lead to the next note, a strong beat.

CD 6–26

Hosanna, Me Build a House

Calypso Song from Jamaica

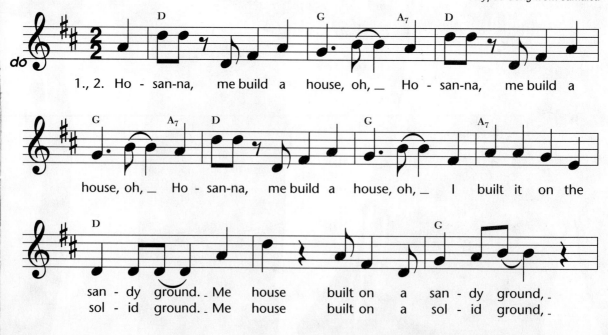

do

1., 2. Ho - san-na,   me build a   house, oh, __ Ho - san-na,   me build a

house, oh, __ Ho - san-na,   me build a   house, oh, __ I   built it on the

san - dy   ground. _ Me   house   built on   a   san - dy   ground, _
sol - id   ground. _ Me   house   built on   a   sol - id   ground, _

Texas Upbeats

In this classic Texas song, the singer reminisces about the city of San Antonio.

The song begins with a two-note upbeat. **Identify** other places in the song that begin with a two-note upbeat. Find an example of a single upbeat in the song.

Sing "San Antonio Rose."

The Alamo, San Antonio, Texas ▶

CD 6–28

San Antonio Rose

Words and Music by Bob Wills

Deep with - in my heart lies a mel - o - dy, A song of
dreams I live with a mem - o - ry, Be - neath the

Old San An - tone, Where in stars all a - lone. It was

there I found be - side the Al - a - mo, En - chant - ment
moon - lit pass that on - ly she would know, Still hears my

strange as the blue up a - bove. A bro - ken song of love.

Moon in all your splen - dor, know on - ly my heart,
Lips so sweet and ten - der, like petals fall - ing a - part,

Call back my Rose, Rose of San An - tone. love, my
Speak once a - gain of my

own. Bro - ken song, emp - ty words I know still live in my

heart all a - lone, For that moon - lit pass by the Al - a -

mo, And Rose, my Rose of San An - tone. _____

M·U·S·I·C M·A·K·E·R·S

Bob Wills (1905–1975) was known as "the King of Western Swing." His father, a Texas fiddling champion, taught him how to play the mandolin and fiddle. Wills began playing at house dances and on radio shows. In his music he combined many different styles, including jazz, rumba, and big-band swing. Bob Wills was inducted into both the Country Music and the Rock and Roll Hall of Fame.

Listen to this version of "San Antonio Rose."

CD 6–30
New San Antonio Rose

by Bob Wills
In this 1955 recording, Wills can be heard playing fiddle.

RHYTHM OF THE RAILS

During the late 1800s, as a result of the Industrial Revolution, many factory workers were laid off from their jobs and took to the rails. These "hobos" hopped freight trains from one town to the next to make a living.

Listen to "Wabash Cannon Ball." It tells about a mythical train that could take a hobo anywhere. Legend has it that the train was so fast it flew right off the track and headed for the stars!

CD 7–1

Wabash Cannon Ball

Traditional

1. From the coast of the At - lan - tic to the wide Pa - cif - ic shore,
   name of great im - por-tance that is known by one and all,
2. There are cit - ies of im - por-tance that are reached a - long the way,
   Spring-field and De - ca - tur and Pe - or - ia, Mon-tre - al,

From the warm and sun - ny South - land to the
It's the West - ern com - bi - na - tion called the
Chi - ca - go and Saint Lou - is and Rock
On the West - ern com - bi - na - tion called the

1.
isle of Lab - ra - dor, There's a Wa - bash Can-non Ball.

Is - land, San - ta Fe, And ___

2.

REFRAIN

Just lis-ten to the jin-gle, the rum-ble, and the roar

Of the might-y lo-co-mo-tive as she streams a-long the shore,

Hear the thun-der of the en-gine, hear the lone-some whis-tle call,

It's the West-ern com-bi-na-tion called the *Wa-bash Can-non Ball.*

Find the Rhythm

Read, clap, and count the rhythm below. Where does this rhythm match the rhythm of the first line of "Wabash Cannon Ball"? Where is it different?

We can use the *tie* to make the rhythm match the song.

But there is an easier way to write the tied rhythm, using a dotted eighth note. It looks like this. ♩. ♪

You can use this symbol to show two uneven sounds on the beat. How many times can you find ♩. ♪ in the song? Can you find a pattern that is similar but not quite the same?

Sounds of Scotland

Bagpipes are a well-known part of Scottish music. "Scotland the Brave" was originally used as a bagpipe tune for marching.

Listen to "Scotland the Brave."
Identify a rhythm pattern that is used throughout the song.

Pictured, from left to right, are the Celtic harp (*clarsach*), fiddle, and lute. ▶

CD 7–6

Scotland the Brave

Words by Cliff Hanley   *Traditional Melody from Scotland*

VERSE

Hark, when the night is fall-ing, Hear! Hear the pipes are call-ing,
Loud - ly and proud-ly call - ing, down through the glen.
There, where the hills are sleep - ing, Now feel the blood a - leap - ing,
High as the spir - its of the old High - land men.

A Scottish Rhythm

Dotted rhythms are often used in Scottish music. How many times do you find these dotted rhythm patterns in "Scotland the Brave"?

Read and clap "Scotland the Brave," using rhythm syllables. Now you are ready to **sing** the song.

Listen to *Bonnie Dundee, Off She Goes,* and *Donald's Awa'* in this medley of traditional Scottish songs.

CD 7–11
Scottish Medley

as performed by Steve Kendall and His Glencastle Sound

This medley can also accompany a Scottish country dance called *Ms. Maggie's Jig.* Your teacher can help you learn the steps.

Bagpipes ▶

REFRAIN

Tower - ing   in gal - lant fame,   Scot - land   my moun - tain hame,

High   may   your proud   stan - dards glo - rious - ly   wave for - ev - er.

Land   of   my high en - deav - or,   Land   of   the shin - ing   riv - er,

Land   of   my heart for - ev - er,   Scot - land   the brave.

Another Scottish Tune

Have you ever heard a Scottish person speak? Most Scots speak English, but two other languages are spoken there. One is Gaelic, and the other is Lowland Scots. Lowland Scots sounds a lot like English, but you may not recognize all the words.

Listen to "Loch Lomond." Find the unfamiliar Lowland Scots words, along with a new rhythm pattern.

CD 7–13

Loch Lomond

Folk Song from Scotland

1. By _____ yon bon - nie banks and by yon bon - nie braes,
2. 'Twas _ there that we part - ed in yon shad - y glen,
3. The _____ wee bird - ies sing and the wild flow - ers spring,

Where the sun shines bright on Loch Lo - mond,
On the steep, steep side of Ben Lo - mond,
While in sun - shine the wa - ters are sleep - in';

Where me and my true love were ev - er wont to gae,
Where pur - ple in hue, _____ the High - land hills we view,
The bro - ken heart kens nae sec - ond spring a - gain,

On the bon - nie, bon - nie banks of Loch Lo - mond.
An' the moon _ com - in' out in the gloam - in'.
Tho' the wae _____ fo' may cease frae their greet - in'.

REFRAIN

Oh, ye'll take the high road, and I'll take the low road,

And I'll be in Scot - land a - fore ye,

But me and my true love we'll nev - er meet a - gain

On the bon-nie, bon-nie banks of Loch Lo - mond.

Show What You Know!

Read these rhythm patterns from "Scotland the Brave" and "Loch Lomond," using rhythm syllables. **Identify** the line in the song that matches each rhythm pattern. Then, clap each pattern as you **sing** the words.

1.

2.

A NONSENSE RONDO

The lyrics of most songs are about people, places, or activities. Sometimes, though, the words of a song don't have a meaning. These are called "nonsense songs."

"Ama-Lama" is a nonsense song in **rondo** form.

Sing the song in Ⓐ Ⓑ Ⓐ ◬ Ⓐ form. Notice that this rondo adds a coda at the end.

> A **rondo** is a musical form in which the first section always returns. The most common rondo form is ABACA.

CD 7–15

AMA-LAMA

Traditional

Ⓐ Swing
F   C

do

A - ma - la - ma coo - ma - la - ma coo - ma - la piz - za.

F   C
2nd time to Section C
Last time to Coda ⊕

A - ma - la - ma coo - ma - la - ma coo - ma - la piz - za.

Ⓑ   (spoken)
F   C

Oh   no   no   no   no   a - piz - za.

(spoken)
F   C   D.C.

Oh   no   no   no   no   a - piz - za.

◬
F

A - chie ca - chie le - mon ra - chie oo - ah,   Thum - ba - li - na,

(spoken)
F   C   F   D.C. al Coda

A - nie ma - nie dix - ie pa - nie X   Y   Z.

142

A - ma - la - ma coo - ma - la - ma coo - ma - la piz - za.

A - ma-la - ma coo - ma-la - ma coo - ma-la piz - za!

Move to the Rondo

As you **listen** to "Ama-Lama," **move** to show the rondo form of the song.

A ▲ Walk around the circle with a step-touch movement while snapping on the off-beat (beats 2 and 4).

B ▲ Stop and face the center of the circle. Lean in and out of the circle while doing a "fist spin." Raise hands in the air on *a-pizza*!

C ▲ Using small steps, walk into the circle for four beats, out for four beats, and repeat.

Playing in Rondo Form

Clap the rhythm of each section of this rondo. **Perform** the rondo on percussion instruments to accompany "Ama-Lama." **Describe** the differences between the Ⓐ, Ⓑ, and Ⓒ sections.

Arranged by Julie Scott

Listen to a Rondo

This is the A section theme of a rondo by Mozart.

Listen to the beginning of *Rondo (Allegro)*.

Now, **listen** to the entire rondo. Raise your hand each time you hear the theme of the A section.

CD 7–17

Rondo (Allegro)

**from *Concerto No. 1 for Horn and Orchestra in D Major*
by Wolfgang Amadeus Mozart
as performed by Dennis Brain and the Philharmonia Orchestra**

This concerto was written in 1791, the year Mozart died.

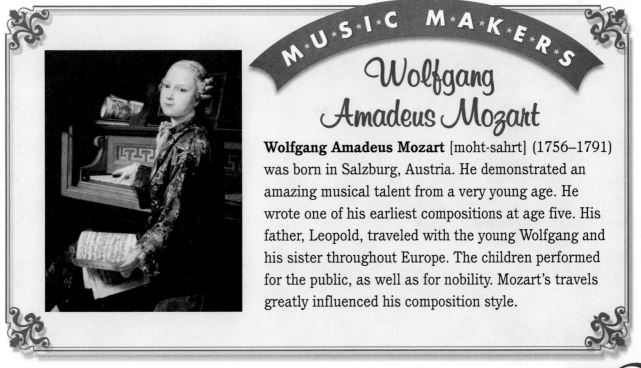

M·U·S·I·C M·A·K·E·R·S

Wolfgang Amadeus Mozart

Wolfgang Amadeus Mozart [moht-sahrt] (1756–1791) was born in Salzburg, Austria. He demonstrated an amazing musical talent from a very young age. He wrote one of his earliest compositions at age five. His father, Leopold, traveled with the young Wolfgang and his sister throughout Europe. The children performed for the public, as well as for nobility. Mozart's travels greatly influenced his composition style.

A Scale of Major Importance

Now that you know *ti*, you're ready for a new scale. This scale uses *do-re-mi-fa-so-la-ti-do^l* in an arrangement of whole and half steps. The half-steps occur between *mi* and *fa* and between *ti* and *do^l*. This pattern makes up a scale called the **diatonic major scale.**

A **diatonic scale** uses seven different notes. It is called "major" when the *tonic*, or home note, is *do*.

1		2		3	4		5		6		7	8
do		re		mi	fa		so		la		ti	do^l
	whole		whole		half	whole		whole		whole		half

Look at the pattern of whole and half steps. **Sing** the diatonic major scale.

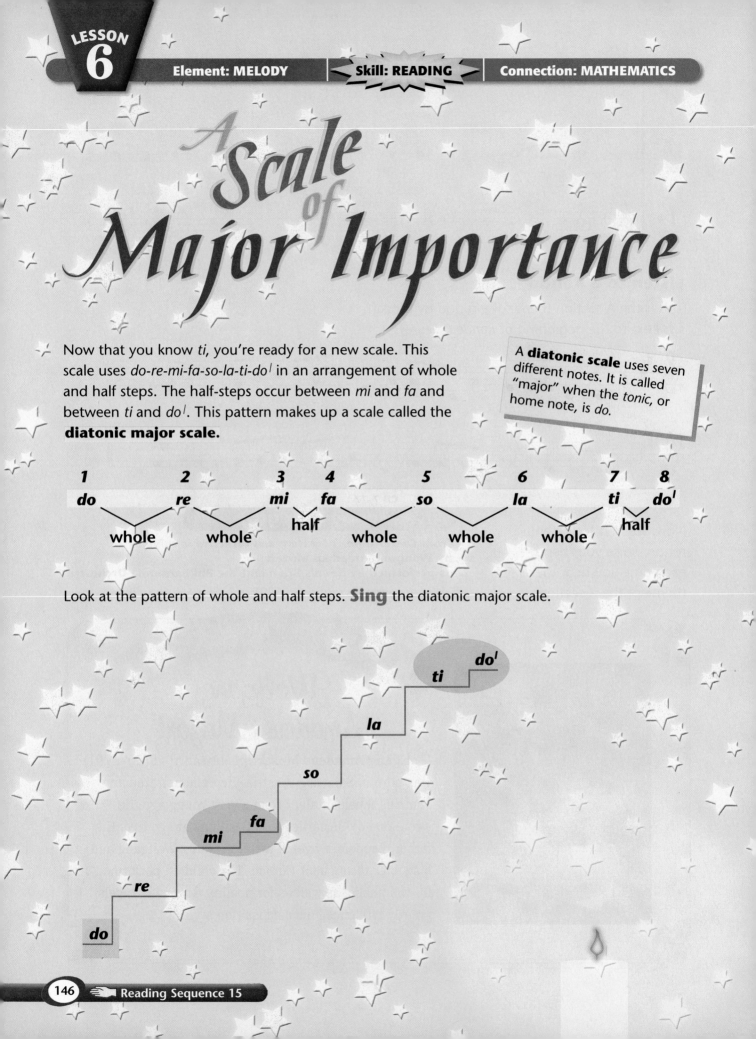

Read and Sing

"*Las velitas*" is based on the diatonic major scale. Does it use all the notes?

CD 7–18

Las velitas
(Candles Burning Bright)

English Words by Donald Scafuri

Folk Song from Mexico

Her - mo - sas ve - li - tas,   en la ob-scu - ri - dad.   Ha - blan de la es -
See the lit - tle   can - dles   shin-ing in the night,   Tell-ing of a

tre - lla   de la Na - vi - dad.   Ved nues-tras ve - li - tas,
star with   beams of ho - ly   light.   See our love - ly   can - dles,

ved que a-lum-bran bien.   Ha-blan de la es - tre - lla   que bri-lló en Be - lén.
let them lead the way   To a qui-et   vil - lage where a ba - by lay.

Show What You Know!

Do and *high do* are shown on the staff below.

Complete the scale. Write in the missing pitch syllables and add their letter names.

do   mi   fa   do¹
C   __   __   F   __   __   __   C

Sing the scale using pitch syllables.

A Song of Seasons

Have you ever heard a melody that reminded you of a story or a picture? To create a song, composers often begin with words or an idea. Sometimes a beautiful melody inspires a composer to create words to express the music.

Listen to "Autumn Canon." How do the words and the melody work together?

Sing "Autumn Canon" in unison. Then sing it as a canon.

CD 7–25

Autumn Canon

Words by Sean Deibler

Music by Lajos Bárdos

I

Fly,   fly,   fly, _____   the
Gone,   gone,   gone, _____   the

III

leaves   take   leave   of   the   branch.   Breez - es   are
leaves   are   gone   from   the   trees.   Soft   falls   the

IV

strong,   win - ter   is   com -   ing.
snow,   win - ter   is   here   now.

Follow the Contour

Read "Autumn Canon" from the staff and follow the shape of its melody with your finger. Look at the parts that are highlighted. How would you **describe** their shape, or melodic contour?

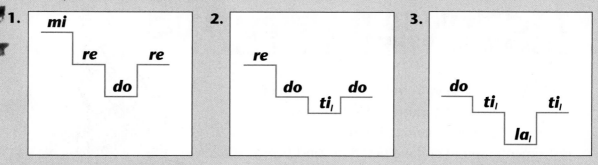

1. mi re re do

2. re do ti, do

3. do ti, ti, la,

The pattern above is an example of a melodic **sequence**.

Sing or **play** a sequence of each of these short melodies.

1. do re mi do

2. so la so mi

3. so fa mi re do

> A melodic **sequence** is a pattern of pitches that is repeated at a higher or lower pitch level.

Create a melody of your own for "Autumn Fires." Use a melodic sequence in your composition. Does your melody express the text of the poem?

Autumn Fires

by Robert Louis Stevenson

In the other gardens
And all up the vale,
From the autumn bonfires
See the smoke trail!

Pleasant summer over
And all the summer flowers,
The red fire blazes,
The grey smoke towers.

Sing a song of seasons!
Something bright in all!

Flowers in the summer
Fires in the fall!

LISTEN TO THE PATTERNS

"*Pollerita,*" a folk song from the Andes region of Bolivia, combines the music of South American Indian and Spanish cultures. The music has the instrumental sound of panpipes, flute, and *bomba* drums.

There are five different melodic patterns in "*Pollerita.*" Clap the rhythm of each pattern. Then **sing** each pattern using the syllable *loo.*

Siku (panpipes) ▲

Charango ▼

Patterns from Bolivia

Listen to "Pollerita" without looking at the music. **Identify** the patterns on page 150 as they occur in the song.

CD 7–30
MIDI 10

POLLERITA

English Words by Aura Kontra

Folk Song from Bolivia

Po - lle - ri - ta, po - lle - ri - ta de mi cho - li - ta,
Po - lle - ri - ta, po - lle - ri - ta that's what she's wear - ing,

Po - lle - ri - ta, po - lle - ri - ta co - lor ro - si - ta.
Po - lle - ri - ta, po - lle - ri - ta with none com - par - ing.

Que bien se bai - la, que bien se can - ta,
You're made for danc - ing, you're made for sing - ing

1.
con mi cha - ran - gui - to.
to my cha - ran - gui - to.

2.
con mi ___ cha - ran - gui - to.
to ___ my cha - ran - gui - to.

Sa - ra ma - la - gu ta tu ma - na tri - go pe - la - cu
Grind - ing corn is not for you, nei - ther cook nor boil a stew,

quena (flute) ▼

Unit 4   151

Ma - na chu - ño pun - ti - co.
Sing and dance the whole day through.

Que bien se bai - la que bien se can - ta
You're made for danc - ing, you're made for sing - ing

1.
con mi cha - ran - gui - to.
to my cha - ran - gui - to.

2.
con mi cha - ran - gui - to. _____
to my cha - ran - gui - to. _____

Listen to *Camino de piedra*, a piece inspired by music of the Andes. What instruments do you hear? What similarities can you hear between *Camino de piedra* and *"Pollerita"*?

CD 7–34
Camino de piedra

by Wilson López
as performed by Andes Manta

Camino de piedra means "the rocky road." The instruments and rhythm patterns are typical of Andean music.

Bolivian musicians, Carnival Tarabuco ▼

152

Map Out a Form

The listening map below shows the form of *Amores hallarás*.

Trace each section of the music as you **listen**.

by Victor M. Salgado
as performed by Inti-Illimani

Inti-Illimani is a Chilean ensemble whose members perform on more than 30 instruments. The group was formed in 1967 by engineering students at Santiago Technical University.

AMORES HALLARÁS
LISTENING MAP

Form:
- Ⓐ B interlude
- Ⓐ B interlude
- Ⓐ¹ B¹ interlude
- Ⓐ¹ B¹ *coda*

A Drum Roll, Please

All of us have an internal drum—our heartbeat!

Drumming can be soothing; drumming can stir us into action. Do you like to drum? Drums come in many different shapes. Even a tabletop can sound like a drum.

Listen to the Beat

Drums can be heard in all styles of music.

Listen to this selection featuring the sound of a drum and bugle corps. What specific instruments do you hear?

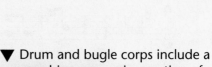

Tune In

Drums are found everywhere in the world. They have been in existence for at least 6,000 years.

CD 8–1
Malagueña

by Ernesto Lecuona
as performed by the Madison Scouts Drum and Bugle Corps

Malagueña is a style of music and dance from the region of Málaga in southern Spain.

▼ Drum and bugle corps include a marching percussion section of bass, tenor, and snare drums, as well as cymbals.

Listen to the sounds of a famous jazz band. How is the drum used in this song?

CD 8–2
Birdland

by Joe Zawinul
as performed by the Buddy Rich Big Band

Buddy Rich was a musician his entire life. At age four he was featured as a solo performer, nicknamed "Traps, the Drum Wonder."

The Buddy Rich Big Band was one of the best bands of the 1960s, and Rich himself is widely accepted as the greatest jazz drummer of all time. ▶

Listen to an exciting drum solo in this popular 1960s rock song, *Wipe Out*. Does the drum make you want to dance?

CD 8–3
Wipe Out

written and performed by the Surfaris

The Surfaris got their start as teenagers by playing dance music at local skating rinks and halls. *Wipe Out* is their best-known song.

The Surfaris got their name by combining the words "surfing safari," a common phrase used by surfers hunting good waves. Surf music was very popular in the early 1960s. ▶

Distant Drums

Drums are found everywhere in the world and are closely associated with ceremonies. Sometimes drums are housed in sacred places.

Listen to the Soh Daiko Taiko Drummers perform *Yaudachi*. They are playing traditional Japanese drums called *taiko*.

CD 8–4
Yaudachi

as performed by Soh Daiko Taiko Drummers

Soh means "peace, harmony, and working together." The Soh Daiko Taiko musicians needed all of these attributes when they started their careers using garbage cans, old tires, and barrels as practice instruments.

◄ *Taiko* means "big drum" in Japanese. These drums are traditionally used for ceremonies, but now are played also for entertainment.

Listen to these conga and bongo drums from Latin America.

CD 8–5
Conga Kings Grand Finale

Written and performed by the Conga Kings

The bongos are played with the fingers. Bongo players usually play a counter-rhythm to the main rhythm. Conga drums (shown below) are tall drums with high, medium, and low pitches.

Congas are played with the hands and palms. Since performances on congas and bongos are usually improvised, they are often included in jazz ensembles. ▼

A *bodhran* is a large Irish drum that is held by a crossbar under the drum's head. **Listen** to the *bodhran* in *O'Sullivan's March* by the Chieftains.

O'Sullivan's March

**Traditional Irish Tune
as performed by the Chieftains**

This song showcases the dark, low sound of the *bodhran* as it keeps the beat for the other musicians.

◄ The Chieftains are one of the best-known Irish music groups. They play many traditional Irish instruments, including the *bodhran*.

Rhythm and Improvisation

Play this percussion ensemble, adding one part at a time until all parts sound good together.

Then, **improvise** new solo parts to go with the ensemble. Use bells, talking drums *(dundun),* or other percussion instruments.

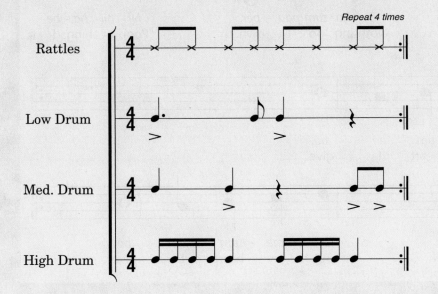

Where You Lead... I Will Follow

In a two-part **canon,** one part leads and the other part follows.

Listen to *"Ego sum pauper."* You will hear the voices sing the canon. You will also hear an instrumental canon. **Identify** the instrument.

Sing *"Ego sum pauper"* in unison. Then **perform** the song as a two-part canon.

> A **canon** is a musical composition in which the parts imitate each other. One part begins, or leads, and the other part follows.

CD 8–7
MIDI 11

Ego sum pauper

(Nothing Do I Own)

Traditional

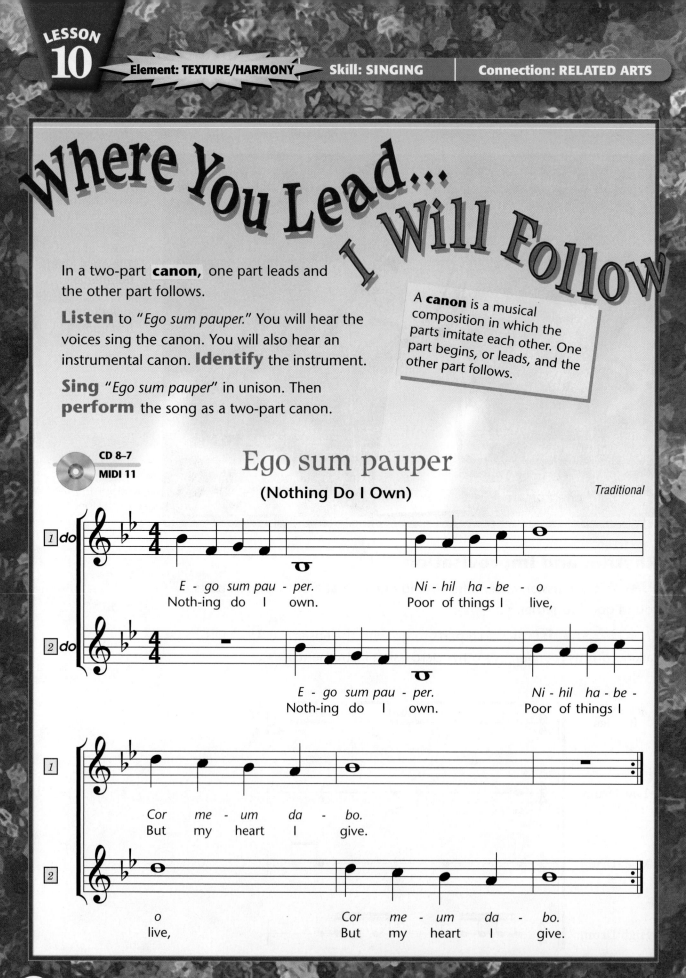

1 do

E - go sum pau - per.
Noth-ing do I own.

Ni - hil ha - be - o
Poor of things I live,

2 do

E - go sum pau - per.
Noth-ing do I own.

Ni - hil ha - be -
Poor of things I

1

Cor me - um da - bo.
But my heart I give.

2

o
live,

Cor me - um da - bo.
But my heart I give.

158

A Canon for Instruments

Listen to this selection and **identify** the instruments that play the leader and the follower.

CD 8–11

Allegretto poco mosso

from *Sonata in A Major*
by César Franck
as performed by Isaac Stern

Belgian composer César Franck [frahnk] (1822–1890) wrote this sonata for violin and piano at age 63.

M·U·S·I·C   M·A·K·E·R·S

Isaac Stern

Isaac Stern (1920–2001) was one of the leading violinists of our time. Stern was born in Russia and came to America when he was ten months old. He began playing the violin at the age of eight and made his recital debut at the age of thirteen. He has been recognized for his dedication to teaching young musicians all over the world. Stern was featured in the 1981 Academy Award-winning documentary *From Mao to Mozart*. He also appeared in the motion picture *Music of the Heart*, about a dedicated and determined violin teacher in Harlem. Stern served as president of Carnegie Hall. In 1960 he played a major role in saving Carnegie Hall from being demolished.

Isaac Stern is famous for his work with young musicians. *From Mao to Mozart* featured Stern using music to connect with people of all ages in China, "first as musicians, then as friends."

▼

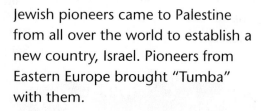

ROUND and ROUND and ROUND and ROUND and

Jewish pioneers came to Palestine from all over the world to establish a new country, Israel. Pioneers from Eastern Europe brought "Tumba" with them.

"Tumba" is a **round. Sing** the song in unison.

Next **sing** "Tumba" as a two-part or three-part round.

Rounds are compositions in which the parts enter in succession, singing the same melody.

Arts Connection   ▲ 15th Century Woodcut Mosaic of Jerusalem, by Gianni Dagli Orti

Tumba

Hebrew Melody

I Dm
Tum - ba tum - ba tum - ba tum, Tum - ba tum - ba tum - ba tum.

II Dm
La la la la la la, La la la la la, La la la la la la, La la la la.

III Dm
Tum - ba, Tum - ba, Tum - ba.

... and Round

Play the following accompaniment for "Tumba" to add more harmony to the song.

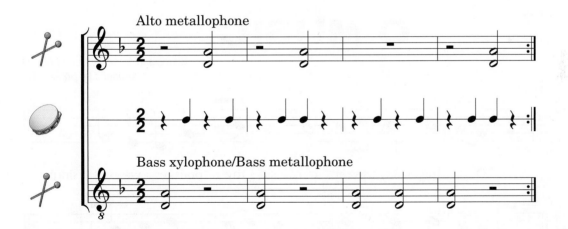

Alto metallophone

Bass xylophone/Bass metallophone

Dance A-Round

There is no traditional dance to "Tumba." You can form three circles; one circle within another circle, within another circle. Then **create** your own movements to dance a round.

ROOUNDS

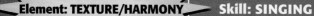

Lowell Mason, the composer of "O Music," was the first public school music teacher in the United States.

"O Music" is a three-part round. **Sing** it first in unison and then as three repeated phrases, sung by three groups.

After you know the song very well, sing it as a traditional round.

CD 8–15

O MUSIC

Words and Music by Lowell Mason
Arranged by Doreen Rao

O __ mu - sic, sweet __ mu - sic, thy __ prais - es we will sing;

We __ will __ tell of the __ pleas - ures and __ hap - pi - ness you __ bring.

Mu - sic, mu - sic, let the cho - rus sing.

In Music Meeting
by Victoria Forrester

Amid the sound,
the silent, unsung greeting:
we sing together
and our voices touch,
in music meeting.

M·U·S·I·C M·A·K·E·R·S

Lowell Mason

Lowell Mason (1792–1872) was born near Boston, Massachusetts, less than twenty years after the American Revolution. Mason was a performer, composer, and teacher. As a young man, he traveled by horse throughout the northeastern part of the United States teaching people how to sing and how to read music. Mason believed that everyone should learn to sing and read music. He proposed that music be taught in public schools as part of the curriculum. The School Committee of Boston accepted his proposal, and in 1838 music became a part of the curriculum in the public schools of Boston.

Review, Assess,

What Do You Know?

Match the Texture

Look at each type of song that is described on the left. Then point to the picture on the right that best represents the texture.

1. A three-part round   **a.**

2. A song with a countermelody   **b.**

3. A song sung in unison   **c.**

Fill in the Blanks

1. The music of the Irish group the Chieftains includes the _____ drum.

    a. snare   **b.** conga   **c.** bodhran

2. *Taiko* means _____ in Japanese.

    a. bass drum   **b.** big drum   **c.** snare drum

3. There are many styles of drumming. Drummer Buddy Rich's playing style would be classified as _____.

    a. jazz style   **b.** folk style   **c.** rock style

What Do You Hear? 4

CD 8–17

Look at the melody patterns on page 150. Point to the pattern that matches the one you hear.

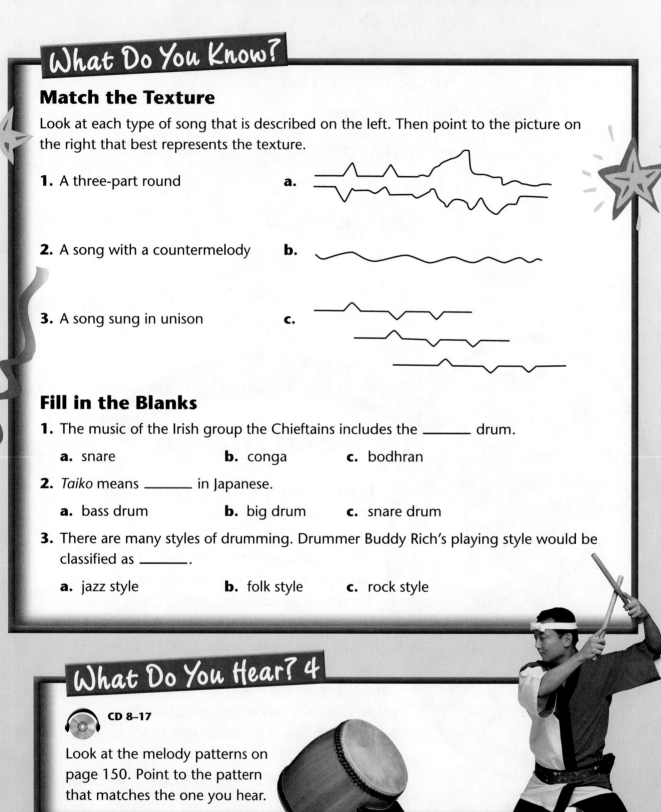

Perform, Create

Listen, Conduct and Sing

Listen to "Scotland the Brave," page 138, and conduct the beat while following the notation. Sing the song, using rhythm syllables and then the song text.

Create a Rondo

Use the two rhythm patterns below, plus a contrasting pattern of your own, to create a rhythm rondo.

To perform your rondo, choose rhythm instruments with contrasting timbres.

Immigrants who travel to the United States take a big step towards a new life. For many who arrived in the last century by boat, the first image of this new life was the inspiring sight of the Statue of Liberty. The poem "The New Colossus" is set on a tablet within the statue's pedestal. Read the poem and then **listen** to a choral setting of the text.

CD 8–22
The New Colossus

The New Colossus
by Emma Lazarus

Not like the brazen giant of Greek fame,
With conquering limbs astride from land to land;
Here at our sea-washed, sunset gates shall stand
A mighty woman with a torch, whose flame
Is the imprisoned lightning, and her name
Mother of Exiles. From her beacon-hand
Glows world-wide welcome; her mild eyes command
The air-bridged harbor that twin cities frame.
"Keep, ancient lands, your storied pomp!" cries she
With silent lips. "Give me your tired, your poor,
Your huddled masses yearning to breathe free,
The wretched refuse of your teeming shore.
Send these, the homeless, tempest-tost to me,
I lift my lamp beside the golden door!"

Setting Poetry to Music

The Mormon Tabernacle Choir is one of the best-known and loved choral organizations in the United States. **Listen** as they perform Irving Berlin's setting of Emma Lazarus' poem.

CD 8–23
Give Me Your Tired, Your Poor

by Emma Lazarus and Irving Berlin
as performed by the Mormon Tabernacle Choir

The Mormon Tabernacle Choir has toured all over the world and has released more than 130 recordings.

Discovering New Musical Horizons

From Sea to Shining Sea

Sing "This World." In what ways might the lyrics reflect the thoughts and feelings of a new immigrant to this country?

LESSON 1

Expression Takes Flight

You can do anything! You can accomplish things that may seem impossible at first. The key to success is believing in yourself. "I Believe I Can Fly" is a song that expresses this belief.

Musicians communicate by performing with expression. They use their own ideas, and they follow expression marks in the music. One type of expression mark is called a **slur.**

Identify all the slurs that occur in "I Believe I Can Fly." Then **sing** the song.

A **slur** indicates that a syllable is sung on more than one pitch.

CD 8–26

I Believe I Can Fly

Words and Music by R. Kelly

1. I used to think that I could not go
I was on the verge of break - ing

on, And life was noth - ing but an aw - ful
down. Some - times si - lence can seem so

song. But now I know the mean - ing of true
loud. There are mir - a - cles in life I must a -

love. I'm lean - ing on the ev - er - last - ing
chieve, But first I know it starts in - side of

Playing with Expression

Slurs can be sung or played on instruments. **Play** the recorder part below. Experiment by playing *staccato* (detached) and then *legato* (smoothly), with slurs. **Play** during the verses of "I Believe I Can Fly."

Play eight times

Another Mark of Expression

Another way to communicate expression is through the use of **accents.**

Listen for accents in this piece by Igor Stravinsky.

An **accent** (>) indicates that a note should be sung or played with more emphasis than the other notes.

Infernal Dance

from *The Firebird*
by Igor Stravinsky
as performed by the New York Philharmonic; Pierre Boulez, conductor

The Firebird was written as ballet music. It was first performed on June 25, 1910, in Paris, France.

Infernal Dance
LISTENING MAP

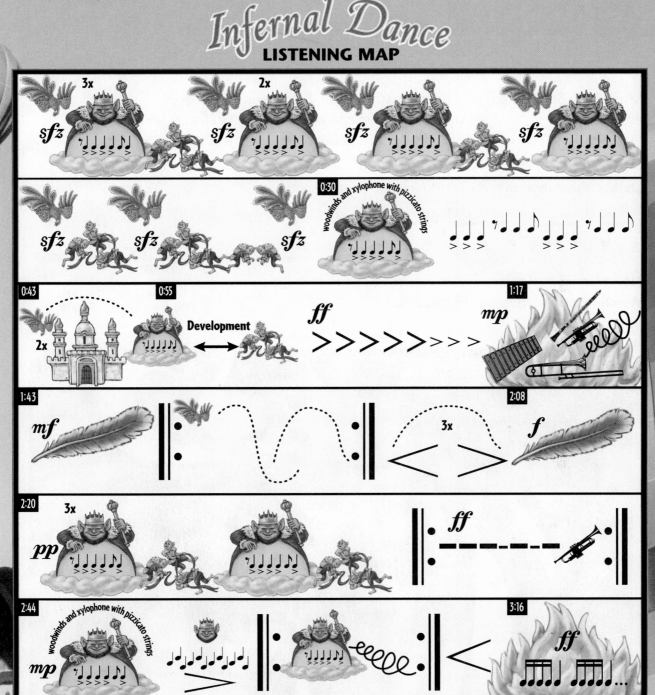

Simple or Compound

Music from Spain often has a gentle, swaying feel. Before you sing "*Las estrellitas del cielo*," **listen** to the recording and keep a steady beat. Can you feel the strong and weak beats? Pat the strong beats on your knees and softly clap the weak beats.

Look at these rhythm patterns. Which one fits the song?

Now clap each of these rhythm patterns as you **sing** the song. Which pattern feels more comfortable?

Arts **Connection**

Creatures in the Night
by Joan Miro, 1950 ▼

Las estrellitas del cielo
(Stars of the Heavens)

English Words by Aura Kontra

Folk Song from Spain

Las es-tre-lli-tas del cie - lo, Bri-llan con su luz de
Stars of the heav-ens are wink - ing, With sil - v'ry light they are

pla - ta. San-tia-go las fué sem-bran - do
twin - kling. A heav-en-ly rid - er came jing - ling

Con sus es-pue-las de pla - ta.
With sil - v'ry spurs, star-light sprin - kling.

That Stubborn Ostinato

Ostinato is an Italian word that means "stubborn." And that's what an ostinato is!
It repeats and repeats throughout the music. As you sing "*Las estrellitas del cielo*"
again, add an ostinato by clapping or playing this rhythm.

Create another ostinato to **perform** with "*Las estrellitas del cielo.*"

Simple or Compound?

When the beat is subdivided into groups of two, the meter is
called **simple meter.** When it is subdivided into groups of
three, it is called **compound meter.**

Is the meter of "*Las estrellitas del cielo*" simple or compound?

> **Simple and compound meter** describes the way beats in music can be subdivided into groups of two and three.

More About Meter

"*Don Alfonso*" is another song from Spain. Like "*Las estrellitas del cielo*," it also has a swaying feel.

Listen to the recording and tap the steady beat. Is the beat subdivided into groups of two, or subdivided into groups of three?

Spanish Guitars

Listen to this selection by the Spanish composer Joaquín Rodrigo. When you hear a steady beat, tap along with the recording. In most measures, the beat is subdivided into groups of three, as in "*Don Alfonso*."

CD 9–1

Caccía a la española

from *Concierto Madrigal for Two Guitars and Orchestra* **by Joaquín Rodrigo as performed by Pepe and Angel Romero**

Joaquín Rodrigo became blind at the age of three, due to illness.

MUSIC MAKERS
The Romero Family

The Romero Family of Spain is known as the "Royal Family of the Guitar." Celin, Pepe, and Angel Romero carry on the teachings passed down to them by their father, Celedonio.

Celedonio Romero (1913–1996) was mostly self-taught on the guitar. He went on to study at the Conservatory of Málaga in Spain. He was not allowed to perform outside of Spain due to government regulations. In 1957, Celedonio and his family settled in the United States.

Celin Romero (born 1936) is the oldest of Celedonio's sons. His first professional concert was at age seven at the Radio National de España. Today, he continues to perform worldwide.

Pepe Romero (born 1944) has also performed worldwide. He was the recipient of the "Premio Andaluccia de Müsica," one of the most prestigious awards in Spain.

Angel Romero (born 1946), in addition to performing on the concert stage, has been involved in performing and composing music for film. In 1995, he received an Ariel, Mexico's equivalent of the American Academy Award, for his work in this genre.

◀ The Romero Family (clockwise from left): Angel, Pepe, Celin, and Celedonio (seated)

Sing *"Don Alfonso."* Is the song in simple meter or in compound meter?

CD 9–2
MIDI 13

Don Alfonso

English Words by Samuel Maquí   *Folk Song from Spain*

1. De los ár - bo - les fru - ta - les ____ Me gus -
2. "¿Dón - de vas, Al - fon - so Do - ce? ____ ¿Dón - de
1. Of the fruit trees, __ I pre - fer the ____ ros - y
2. "In your sad - ness, __ Don Al - fon - so, ____ may I

ta el me - lo - co - tón, Y de los rey - es ____ de Es -
vas, tris - te de ti?" "Voy en bus - ca ____ de Mer -
peach to oth - ers known; And of the kings of ____ Spain the
ask where you are bound?" "I must seek my __ dear Mer -

pa - ña, ____ Don Al - fon - so de Bor - bón. ____
ce - des ____ que ha - ce tiem - po no la vi." ____
best is ____ Don Al - fon - so de Bor - bon. ____
ce - des, ____ in Ma - drid she can be found." ____

3. Ya Mercedes está muerta, Muerta está que yo la vi,
   Cuatro duques la llevaban Por las calles de Madrid.

3. But Mercedes has departed, she is gone, no more to see.
   She was carried through the city by four dukes of high degree.

Play these chords on guitar to accompany *"Don Alfonso."*

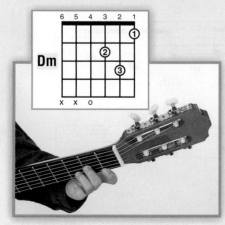
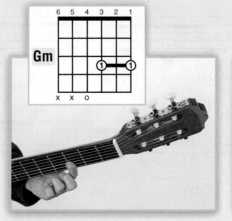
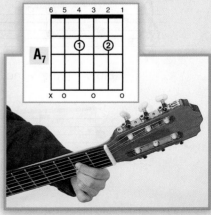

NAME A NEW METER

Every country that borders an ocean has songs and stories about the sea. "Blow the Wind Southerly" is one of many such songs. Can you think of others?

Identify the pattern of strong and weak beats as you **listen** to "Blow the Wind Southerly." Which rhythm pattern below fits best with the song?

simple   compound

Create an ostinato in $\frac{6}{8}$ compound meter and **perform** it as you **sing** the song.

CD 9–8 **BLOW THE WIND SOUTHERLY**

Folk Song from Northumbria

REFRAIN

Blow   the wind south - er - ly,   south - er - ly,   south - er - ly,

Blow   the wind   south   o'er   the   bon - ny   blue   sea;

Blow   the wind south - er - ly,   south - er - ly,   south - er - ly,

Blow   bon - ny   breeze ___   my   true   love   to   me.

G   D₇   G   D₇

1. He told me last night there were ships in the off - ing, And
2. I stood by the light-house that last time we part - ed, 'Til

G   D   A₇   D

I hur - ried down to the deep roll - ing sea; But my
dark - ness came down o'er the deep roll - ing sea; And no

C   G   D₇   G

eye could not see it, wher - ev - er might be it, The
long - er I saw the bright bark of my true love, Oh,

G   C   D₇   G   *D. C. al Fine*

bark that is bear - ing my true love to me.
blow bon - ny breeze __ and bring him to me.

Simple and Compound Meter

In simple meter, the bottom number of the time signature represents the beat. In $\frac{2}{4}$ the beat note is ♩. In compound meter the beat note is ♩.

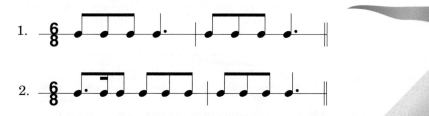

Clap these patterns in compound meter. Use the patterns to **create** a counter-rhythm. Then **perform** your counter-rhythm as you **sing** "Blow the Wind Southerly."

March To The Beat

The Civil War was a momentous event in American history. The war produced songs, such as "When Johnny Comes Marching Home," that have become part of our musical tradition.

Sing "When Johnny Comes Marching Home." **Move** to show its duple meter.

CD 9–13

When Johnny Comes Marching Home

Words and Music by Patrick S. Gilmore

1. When John-ny comes march-ing home a-gain,
2. Let love __ and friend-ship on the day, Hur - rah! ___ Hur - rah! ___
3. Get read - y for the ju - bi - lee,

We'll give him a heart - y wel - come then,
Their choic - est trea - sure then dis - play, Hur - rah! ___ Hur - rah! ___
We'll give __ the he - ro three times three,

The _ men will cheer, _ the boys will shout, The la - dies they _ will all turn out,
And _ let each one __ per-form some part, To fill with joy __ the war-rior's heart,
The _ laur - el wreath _ is read - y now To place up - on __ his roy - al brow,

And we'll shout "Hur - rah" when John-ny comes march-ing home! __

▲ Civil War Drum Corps. Photo
by Timothy H. O'Sullivan, 1863

Tune In

"When Johnny Comes Marching Home" was written by a Union army bandmaster, Patrick S. Gilmore, in 1863.

Percussion Patterns

Play these rhythm patterns on percussion instruments throughout the song.

Create a body percussion ostinato with a partner. **Perform** the ostinato as you **sing** the song.

Rhythm of the Rails

During the mid-1800s, railroads spread throughout the country. The coast-to-coast expansion was completed in 1869. A golden spike joined the Union Pacific and Central Pacific Railways at Promontory Summit, north of Salt Lake City.

"Pat Works on the Railway" is a humorous song that helped workers survive their strenuous labor. **Listen** to the song to hear how the music imitates the sound of building the railroad.

As you **sing** the song, **create** movements to show the meter.

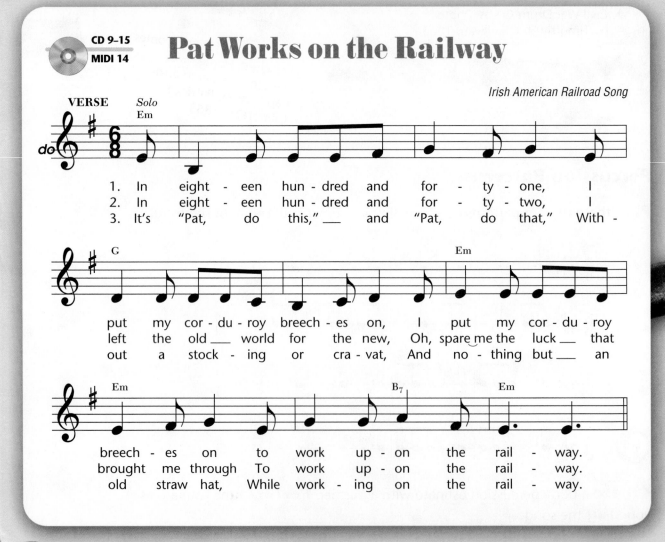

CD 9–15
MIDI 14

Pat Works on the Railway

Irish American Railroad Song

VERSE *Solo*

1. In eight - een hun - dred and for - ty - one, I
2. In eight - een hun - dred and for - ty - two, I
3. It's "Pat, do this," ___ and "Pat, do that," With -

put my cor - du - roy breech - es on, I put my cor - du - roy
left the old ___ world for the new, Oh, spare me the luck ___ that
out a stock - ing or cra - vat, And no - thing but ___ an

breech - es on to work up - on the rail - way.
brought me through To work up - on the rail - way.
old straw hat, While work - ing on the rail - way.

REFRAIN

Countermelody

Em

Fil - li - mee-oo _____ Fil - li-mee-oo - ree - oo - ree - ay,

G

Chorus

Fil - li-mee-oo - ree - oo - ree - ay, Fil - li-mee-oo - ree - oo - ree - ay,

Em

Fil - li-mee-oo _____ Fil - li-mee, fil - li-mee - oo - ree - ay.

B₇ Em

Fil - li-mee-oo - ree - oo - ree - ay, To work up-on the rail - way.

Play the score below to accompany
"Pat Works on the Railway."

Soprano/Alto glockenspiels *(Refrain only)*

Alto xylophone/Alto metallophone

Bass xylophone/Bass metallophone

(2nd. time)

A Musical Idea

People express ideas in many ways. You can ask, "How are you doing?" or "How are you feeling?" These are variations of "How are you?"

A musical statement or theme can do the same. How can music be varied, while keeping some elements the same? The idea is called **theme and variations.**

Let's use the song "Simple Gifts" as our musical "theme." **Sing** "Simple Gifts" to become familiar with the melody.

> **Theme and variations** is a musical form in which each section is a modification of the initial theme.

CD 9–17

Simple Gifts

Shaker Song

'Tis the gift to be sim-ple, 'Tis the gift to be free, 'Tis the gift to come down where we ought to be, And when we find our-selves _ in the place just _ right, 'Twill _ be in the val-ley of love and de-light.

Variations on a Theme

In his ballet *Appalachian Spring*, Aaron Copland used the theme of "Simple Gifts" to create a set of variations. **Listen** to the variations on this theme.

CD 9–19
Variations on Simple Gifts

from *Appalachian Spring*
by Aaron Copland

The ballet *Appalachian Spring* was choreographed by Martha Graham and premiered in 1944.

When true sim - pli - ci - ty is gained, To bow and to bend we ___

shan't be a-shamed, To turn, turn will be our de-light, Till by

turn - ing, turn - ing we come 'round right.

Same—but Different

Listen to *Variations on Simple Gifts* and follow the listening map below.

Variations on Simple Gifts **LISTENING MAP**

Introduction *pp*

Theme *mp*

Variation 1 *mf*

Variation 2 *mf–f*

Variation 3 *mf*

Variation 4 *mp*

Variation 5 *ff*

Sound Variations

What instruments did you hear in *Variations on Simple Gifts?* **Describe** at least one way the composer varied the theme.

Choreographer and dancer Martha Graham ▶

M·U·S·I·C M·A·K·E·R·S

AARON COPLAND

Aaron Copland [KOHP-land] (1900–1990) was a composer, an author, and a conductor. Although he never went to college, he became a respected instructor at Harvard University. Copland searched the musical and folk literature of America to find themes and story ideas for his compositions. His ballets *Rodeo* and *Billy the Kid* feature American folk tunes and jazz. "Simple Gifts," a Shaker hymn from Pennsylvania, was another source of inspiration. Copland used this melody in his ballet *Appalachian Spring*. This ballet became his most popular work and won him a Pulitzer Prize. Copland believed that classical music could express the spirit of America's beauty and historical traditions, and could be enjoyed by everyone.

CD 9–20

Interview with Aaron Copland

This historic interview with Copland was conducted in the mid-1960s.

A New Scale

Irish immigrants brought the melody of "Johnny Has Gone for a Soldier" to America. This version of the song comes from John Allison, whose family lived near Buttermilk Hill, on the west bank of the Hudson River, in New York. One of Allison's ancestors heard it sung as he marched with George Washington's army during the Revolutionary War.

Listen to "Johnny Has Gone for a Soldier" and notice the haunting quality of its melody.

CD 9–21

Johnny Has Gone for a Soldier

Song of the American Revolution
Collected by John Allison

1. There I sat on But-ter-milk Hill, Who could blame me
2. Me oh my, I loved __ him so, Broke my heart to
3. I'll sell my flax, I'll sell __ my wheel, Buy my love a

cry my fill; And ev - 'ry tear would __
see him go, And on - ly time will ____
sword of steel, So it in bat - tle ____

turn a mill; John - ny has gone for a sol - dier.
heal my woe; John - ny has gone for a sol - dier.
he may wield; John - ny has gone for a sol - dier.

Relative Scales

You know that the notes from *do* to *do*^l produce a scale called the diatonic major scale. The special sound of this scale comes from its pattern of whole steps and half steps. Let's learn a new scale, called the **natural minor scale.** It uses the same notes as the major scale, but they're arranged in a different pattern of whole steps and half steps.

> The **natural minor scale** is an arrangement of eight tones with a pattern of steps as follows: whole, half, whole, whole, half, whole, whole.

Identify where the half steps occur. **Sing** the natural minor scale, using pitch syllables. Because its tonic is *la,* it sounds different.

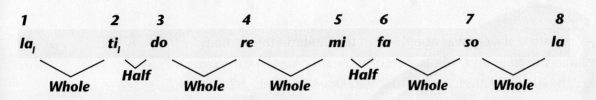

Read and **sing** "Johnny Has Gone for a Soldier." How many pitches of the natural minor scale can you find in this melody?

MELODY IN MINOR

In the years before slavery was abolished in the United States, many slaves related the trials and tribulations of biblical heroes to their own suffering. The African American spiritual "Go Down, Moses" tells about the ancient Hebrews held captive in Pharaoh's Egypt. But the song also had its own meaning for those under the bondage of slavery in America.

Listen to "Go Down, Moses." How many times do you hear the phrase *Let my people go?*

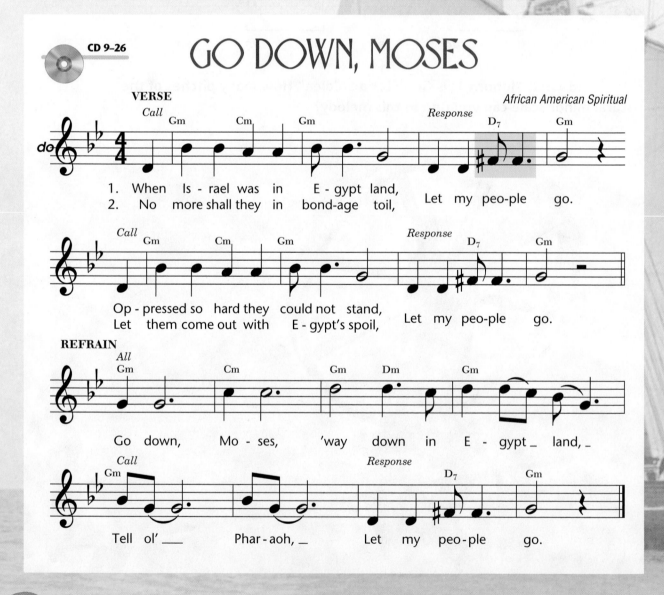

CD 9–26

GO DOWN, MOSES

African American Spiritual

Steps and Skips

Sing the phrase *Let my people go* each time it occurs in the recording. Use hand signs and pitch syllables for the notes you know. (Hum the new note).

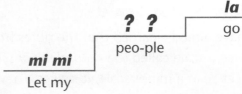

mi mi / Let my — ? ? / peo-ple — la / go

Now **analyze** the phrase by answering these questions.

• In what direction do the notes in this phrase move?

• How many *different* pitches did you sing?

• Where are the steps?

• Where are the skips?

The new note between *so* and *la* is called *si*. It is a half step higher than *so* and a half step lower than *la.* It shares a place on the staff with *so*, but you can tell them apart because *si* is always marked with an **accidental.**

Accidental signs are used to show altered pitches. The most common signs (which raise or lower a pitch by a half step) are sharps (♯), flats (♭), and naturals (♮).

Background photo: Replica of the nineteenth-century slave ship *Amistad*

▲ A family standing in front of the Civil Rights Memorial at the Southern Poverty Law Center, 1990

A New Minor Scale

You have already learned that the notes from *low la* to *la* produce a scale called the *natural minor scale*. But when *si* replaces *so* in a minor scale, it makes a new scale — the **harmonic minor scale.**

Look at the pattern of whole and half steps in the harmonic minor scale. **Sing** the scale, using pitch syllables.

1		2	3		4		5	6		7	8
la,		ti,	do		re		mi	fa		si	la
	Whole		Half	Whole		Whole		Half	Whole	Half	Half

Step Up to the Staff

Look at the staff below. This is the harmonic minor scale, in A -*la*. We can also call it the A-minor scale. (Remember that *si* will always be marked with an accidental.)

Read and **sing** the scale, using pitch syllables and hand signs. Can you **identify** the note name of *si?*

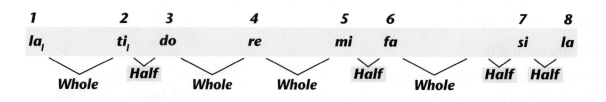

do   la,   ti,   do   re   mi   fa   si   la

Sing "Go Down, Moses." Then **identify** *si* each time it occurs in the music. (Its first appearance is shown in the color box.)

Group of freed slaves, 1862, who worked with the 13th Massachusetts Infantry Regiment during the American Civil War ▼

The Queen of Spiritual Singers

Listen to a performance of another African American spiritual that is based on the harmonic minor scale.

Sometimes I Feel Like a Motherless Child

African American Spiritual as performed by Mahalia Jackson

The African American civil rights leader and educator W. E. B. Du Bois (1868–1963) used the phrase "sorrow song" to describe emotionally poignant spirituals such as this.

MUSIC MAKERS

Mahalia Jackson

Mahalia Jackson (1912–1972) has been called "the true queen of spiritual singers." She was born in New Orleans, Louisiana, where, as a child, she sang in her father's church choir. A pioneer interpreter of gospel music, she insisted that gospel preceded jazz, affected jazz, and gave it inspiration and new forms. She sang only songs she believed in—positive anthems that reflected the spirit. The first gospel song she wrote and recorded was her personal statement: *I'm Going to Move on Up a Little Higher.* Her rich, deep contralto voice was one of the great voices of the century.

Jackson sang at the inauguration of President John F. Kennedy and for Dr. Martin Luther King Jr., when he delivered his "I Have a Dream" speech. She was inducted into the Rock and Roll Hall of Fame in 1997.

Show What You Know!

Using pitch syllables, **read** and **sing** each of these minor scales. Which scale is natural minor? Which one is harmonic minor?

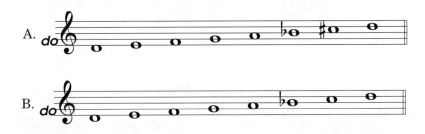

Searching For Scales

The song "*Meng Jian Nu*" is based on an old Chinese legend that tells the story of a devoted wife. Her husband, Wan Chi Liang, had gone away to help build the Great Wall. After many months with no word from him, Meng Jian Nu went to look for him. The song does not say if she ever found him.

Sing "*Meng Jian Nu*" and **listen** for the sound of a special five-tone scale.

 CD 10–1

Meng Jian Nu

English Words by Alice Firgau   *Folk Song from China*

Zheng yu _____ mei _____ hua, shi _____ xing _____
Blos - soms from cher - ries fall, Fra - grance fills _____ the

chung, _____ Jia jia _____ hu _____ hu
air; _____ Spring - time brings _ hap - pi - ness,

tian hon _____ deng, _____ Ran _____ jia
New Year _ with - out care. _____ But for me

zhang _____ fu _____ tuan _ yuan _____ ju, _____
there's _ no _ spring, _ Sad - ness _ fills my heart. _____

Meng _ Jian Nu de _ zhang _ fu _____ zou chan _____ cheng.
Wan _ Chi Liang has _ gone a-way And now we _ are _ a - part. _____

Play a Pentatonic Scale

The melody of "*Meng Jian Nu*" is built on a pentatonic scale — a scale that consists of only five notes. For a review, line up bells to form a G-major scale. **Play** the scale. It is the diatonic major scale.

Now remove the bells for C, F♯, and the high G.

Play the scale. It has a very different sound. The pentatonic scale is used in the folk music of many countries, not only in Asia, but in Europe and America as well. **Play** these pentatonic parts as others **sing** the song.

A String of Strings

All cultures have string instruments. Most string instruments are plucked. Some are struck with mallets, and a few are bowed like the violin. String instruments differ greatly from one country to another. They are thought to have evolved from an early instrument that resembled a hunting bow.

One group of string instruments is the zither family. In zithers, the strings are stretched over one or more bridges. Instruments in this group include the Japanese *koto*, the Vietnamese *dan tranh*, and the hammered dulcimer.

The *koto* and the *dan tranh* are similar in structure, with both instruments having up to 17 strings.

Koto ▶

▲ Hammered Dulcimer

Listen to these zithers and **describe** the sound of each.

CD 10–5
Zither Montage

This montage features the hammered dulcimer, the *koto*, and the *dan tranh*.

Keyboards

In the mid-1900s, musicians became interested in performing music from earlier eras on historic, or "period" instruments. This caused a revival of interest in the harpsichord.

Keyboard string instruments include the piano, clavichord, and harpsichord. The harpsichord was developed in the late 1400s and was the most widely used keyboard instrument until the piano was invented in the early 1700s.

▲ Clavichord

▲ Harpsichord

▲ Piano

Listen to these keyboard instruments and **compare** the sounds of each. What adjectives will you use?

CD 10–6
Keyboard Instrument Montage

This montage highlights the piano, clavichord, and harpsichord.

Strings Are for Picking

Harps and lyres are played by plucking the strings.

Other plucked instruments include the *sitar* of India, banjos, guitars, lutes, and the Arabic instrument called the *ud*.

▲ Banjo

▲ *Ud*

Listen to these string instruments. They are played by plucking the strings. **Analyze** and **describe** why they sound different.

CD 10–7
Plucked String Montage

Featured in this montage are the *sitar*, banjo, harp, guitar, lute, and *ud*.

▲ *Sitar*

Finnish Strings

The *kantele* is a small string instrument used for hundreds of years in Finland and still used today. The traditional *kantele* has five strings that are plucked. The modern version has 12 to 46 metal strings. The *kantele* is a national symbol of Finland.

Other instruments with four to six strings that are plucked are the psaltery and the lap dulcimer. If you have one of these instruments in your classroom, you can play this beautiful folk melody.

◀ Finnish girl playing the *kantele*

Traditional Kalevala Melody from Finland

Listen to the lyrical sound of Finnish *kanteles* as they accompany a solo singer in this selection.

CD 10–8

Eriskummainen kantele

by Kurki-Suonio
as performed by Loituma

The English title of this selection is *The Peculiar Kantele*. Both five-string and ten-string *kanteles* are heard in this performance.

Calypso Walk

Do you know where Jamaica is? You'll find this beautiful island in the Caribbean Sea. Jamaican musicians have given us a great deal of lively, danceable music. Some musicians, such as Bob Marley and his son, Ziggy, have achieved international fame.

This Jamaican calypso song can be accompanied by two chords: I and V_7. **Listen** to "Mango Walk" and **identify** the chord changes. Follow the chord symbols above the music as you listen.

CD 10–9

Mango Walk

Calypso Song from Jamaica

My bro - ther did - a tell me that you go man - go walk,

You go man - go walk, you go man - go walk.

My bro - ther did - a tell me that you go man - go walk

And steal all the num - ber 'lev - en.

Chords to Play

Play the F (I) and C₇ (V₇) chords on the marimba or other mallet instruments.

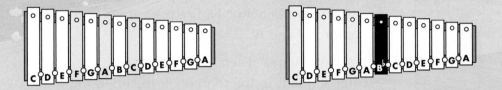

Use these chords to accompany "Mango Walk." **Play** a chord on the first beat of each measure. Which chord will you play first? When do you change chords? By accompanying the melody of "Mango Walk" with chords, you create a thicker texture. Next, **play** the following rhythm accompaniment with the chord accompaniment.

Sing "Mango Walk" with the chord and rhythm accompaniment.

Ready to Rumba

Arthur Benjamin borrowed the melody of "Mango Walk" for his composition *Jamaican Rumba*. **Listen** for the texture and chord changes.

CD 10–11
Jamaican Rumba

by Arthur Benjamin
as performed by the Cleveland Pops Orchestra

Much of the music of this composer was influenced by the sounds and rhythms of Latin America and the West Indies.

Element: TEXTURE/HARMONY | **Skill: SINGING** | **Connection: SOCIAL STUDIES**

Nothing More Than I and IV

Imbabura, a province in the South American country of Ecuador, is known for its beautiful lakes and mountains. The province is home to several volcanoes. The Pan-American Highway takes tourists through this beautiful area of the country. The song "Imbabura" praises the beauty of this area of South America.

Listen to "Imbabura." Notice the harmony uses only two chords: I and IV.

Sing "Imbabura." Then, **perform** an accompaniment to the song on keyboard, using the C (I) and F (IV) chords, as shown in the music.

Imbabura

English Words by Don Kalbach

Folk Song from Ecuador

1.,4. Im - ba - bu - ra de mi vi - da, tú se - rás la
1.,4. Im - ba - bu - ra, sing your prais - es, You're the best of

pre - fe - ri - da, por - que a to - dos das al - ber - gue
all the plac - es, For your shel - ter free - ly giv - en,

co - mo si fue - ran tus hi - jos.
As if we were all your chil - dren.

2. To - dos los e - cua - to - ria - nos te de - di - ca -
3. De mi co - ra - zón la due - ña has de ser, Im -
2. All the Ec - ua - do - rians love you, And they sing their
3. You have won my heart for - ev - er; It is yours, Im -

mos can - cio - nes pa - ra tus her - mo - sos
ba - bu - re - ña, por - que yo ad - mi - ro tus
prais - es of you, For the beau - ty of your
ba - bu - re - ña, For I love your lakes and

la - gos, que nos brin - dan sus ha - la - gos.
pren - das, tus mu - jé - res y tus flo - res.
wa - ters, And de - lights that they have brought us.
wa - ters, And your peo - ple and your flow - ers.

Too Much Talk

Rock 'n' roll, one of the most enduring styles in popular music, began in the 1950s. This music was usually accompanied by electric guitars and keyboards and had a driving percussion beat. Rock harmony was—and remains—simple, usually including only three basic chords: I, IV, and V_7.

Sing "Yakety Yak," an early rock 'n' roll hit. **Play** the C (I), F (IV), and G_7 (V_7) chords on keyboard or guitar to accompany the melody. The chord symbols in the music will tell you when to change chords.

M·U·S·I·C   M·A·K·E·R·S

The Coasters

The Coasters was a band that became very popular in the late 1950s. Using humor and upbeat rhythms, the group sang its way into the hearts of American teenagers. In 1957 the Coasters reached number one on the rhythm and blues charts with their hit songs *Searchin'* and *Young Blood.* Their other classics include *Charlie Brown, Poison Ivy,* and *Yakety Yak.* In 1987 they were inducted into the Rock and Roll Hall of Fame.

Listen to the "original artist " recording of *Yakety Yak.*

CD 10–16
Yakety Yak

by Jerry Leiber
and Mike Stoller
as performed by the Coasters

Yakety Yak

Words and Music by Jerry Leiber and Mike Stoller

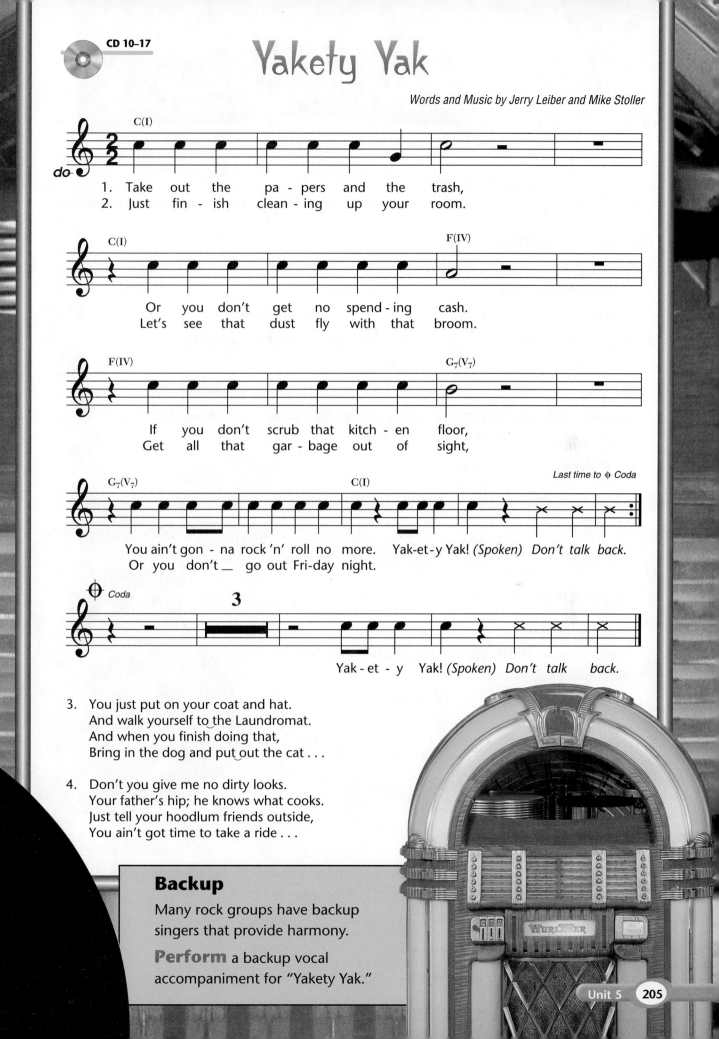

C(I)
1. Take out the pa - pers and the trash,
2. Just fin - ish clean - ing up your room.

C(I)   F(IV)
Or you don't get no spend - ing cash.
Let's see that dust fly with that broom.

F(IV)   G₇(V₇)
If you don't scrub that kitch - en floor,
Get all that gar - bage out of sight,

Last time to ⊕ Coda

G₇(V₇)   C(I)
You ain't gon - na rock 'n' roll no more. Yak-et-y Yak! *(Spoken) Don't talk back.*
Or you don't __ go out Fri-day night.

⊕ *Coda*

3

Yak - et - y Yak! *(Spoken) Don't talk back.*

3. You just put on your coat and hat.
   And walk yourself to the Laundromat.
   And when you finish doing that,
   Bring in the dog and put out the cat . . .

4. Don't you give me no dirty looks.
   Your father's hip; he knows what cooks.
   Just tell your hoodlum friends outside,
   You ain't got time to take a ride . . .

Backup

Many rock groups have backup singers that provide harmony.

Perform a backup vocal accompaniment for "Yakety Yak."

Review, Assess,

Fill in the Blanks

1. A mark that indicates to sing or play a note with more emphasis than the other notes is called _____.

   a. a tie   **b.** a slur   **c.** an accent

2. A musical form in which each section is a modification of the initial theme is called _____.

   a. verse and refrain   **b.** solo and chorus   **c.** theme and variations

3. The arrangement of eight tones with a step pattern of whole, half, whole, whole, half, whole, whole is a _____ scale.

   a. diatonic   **b.** major   **c.** natural minor

What Do You Hear? 5A

CD 10–19

Listen to the following musical excerpts as you conduct the meter. Identify the meter of each selection and point to your answer.

1. $\frac{4}{4}$ meter $\frac{6}{8}$ meter

2. $\frac{6}{8}$ meter $\frac{2}{4}$ meter

3. $\frac{6}{8}$ meter $\frac{4}{4}$ meter

What Do You Hear? 5B

CD 10–22

Listen to the following musical excerpts of string instruments and identify whether the instrument you hear is plucked, bowed, or struck.

1. plucked   bowed   struck

2. plucked   bowed   struck

3. plucked   bowed   struck

Perform, Create

Play Chords

As the group sings "Mango Walk," page 200, accompany the singers on Autoharp or keyboard. Be sure to play the I and V_7 chords at the appropriate time.

Create a Melodic Poem

• Read the poem *Who Has Seen the Wind?* by Christina Rossetti.

Who Has Seen the Wind?

by Christina Rossetti

Who has seen the wind?

Neither I nor you:

But when the leaves hang trembling,

The wind is passing through.

Who has seen the wind?

Neither you nor I;

But when the leaves bow down their heads,

The wind is passing by.

• Work together in two groups to create a melody. Group 1 should create a melody in C major, ending on C, to accompany lines 1–4 of the poem. Group 2 should create a melody in A minor, ending on A, to accompany lines 5–8.

• Play and sing your melodies for the other groups. Review each performance. Which melody did you like best and why? How could you improve it?

The British Are Coming

The musical blending of country, rhythm and blues, and folk styles produced many different types of rock. In the 1960s, bands from England launched a "British Invasion" of the American rock scene. Two legendary figures, John Lennon and Paul McCartney, were the main songwriting members of the most famous English rock group of all—the Beatles.

MUSIC MAKERS

John Lennon and Paul McCartney

John Lennon (1940–1980) and **Paul McCartney** (born 1942) took their love and knowledge of early rock (Elvis Presley, Buddy Holly, Chuck Berry, Little Richard, the Everly Brothers) and produced some of the most exciting and enduring rock songs ever written.

As both singers and composers, Lennon and McCartney were among the most expressive in rock music. Their harmonies were detailed and exciting. As performers, they were lively and photogenic. Lennon and McCartney constantly experimented with new styles and techniques. Each album they created broke new ground in rock music.

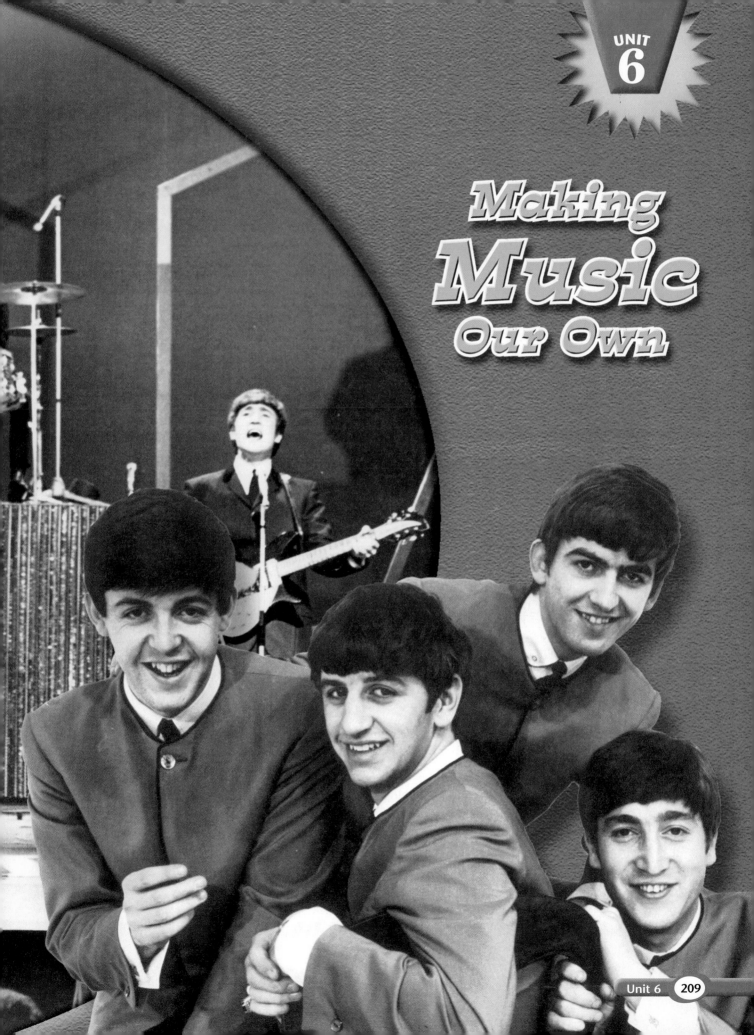

Making Music Our Own

A Place of Your Own

Sing this early Beatles song, written by John Lennon and Paul McCartney. Where is a place you can go when you feel sad?

CD 10–25

There's a Place

Words and Music by John Lennon and Paul McCartney

There, _____ there's a place where I can go when I feel low, when I feel blue, And it's my mind, _____ and there's no time. _____ When I'm a - lone, ____ I, _____ I think of you, and things you do go 'round my head. The things you've said, Like "I

Let's Rock!

The song most often associated with Elvis Presley, the "king" of rock 'n' roll, is "Hound Dog." It was popular in the 1950s.

Listen to "Hound Dog." What gives this song its energy?

CD 10–27
MIDI 15

Hound Dog

Words and Music by Jerry Leiber and Mike Stoller

You ain't noth-in' but a hound dog, __ cry - in' all the time.

You ain't noth-in' but a hound dog, __ cry - in' all the time.

Well, _ you ain't nev-er caught a rab-bit, and you ain't no friend of mine. _

When they said you was high-classed, _ well, that _ was just a lie.

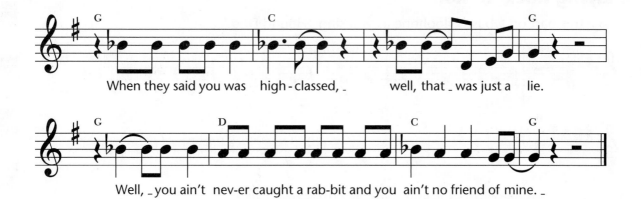

When they said you was high-classed, _ well, that _ was just a lie.

Well, _ you ain't nev-er caught a rab-bit and you ain't no friend of mine. _

Even a Hound Dog Can Be Expressive

How do you think "Hound Dog" would sound if you sang it very slowly? Try it and see how it works.

How does your musical expression change when you sing "Hound Dog" in different tempos?

When played and sung at a slow tempo, it sounds a little "bluesy," doesn't it?

These illustrations express different styles. What kind of music might go with each illustration?

Playing Rock 'n' Roll

Play this part on a bass xylophone as you sing "Hound Dog."

Next add these parts, using xylophones, as others sing.

Now add these percussion parts for a classroom rock-style sound.

High drum

Low drum

Cymbals

What Makes It Rock?

What makes rock music sound different from other kinds of music—jazz, folk, or a symphony? Rock is a *style* of music. It has a set of characteristics that makes it sound unique.

One of the most important characteristics of rock style is the *backbeat*.

Most music that is in $\frac{4}{4}$ meter has a stress on the first and third beats of the measure, with the third beat less accented than the first beat.

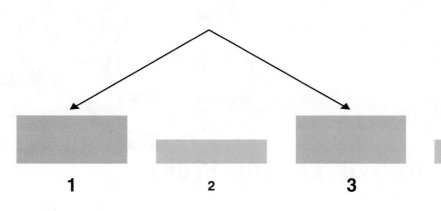

The backbeat in rock is on the second and fourth beats.

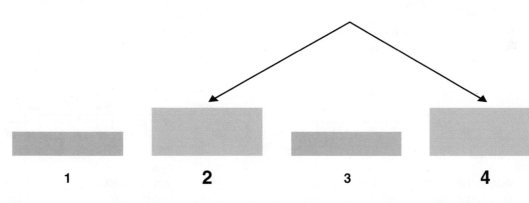

The percussion part you learned has a strong backbeat in the low drum.

 MIDI   Use the "Hound Dog" song file with sequencing software to experiment with a variety of tempos.

Musical Patterns

Did you ever sing a song about the sea and notice how just listening to the song paints a picture in your imagination? If you close your eyes, you can almost hear and see the water, feel the waves, and smell the salt air.

Listen to "Oh, Watch the Stars," a song from St. Helena Island, off the coast of South Carolina. What do you "see" when you close your eyes?

CD 10–29

oh, watch the stars

Folk Song from South Carolina

1. Oh, watch the stars, see how they run, Oh,
2. Oh, watch the sun, see how it sets, Oh,
3. Oh, watch the moon, see how it shines, Oh,

watch the stars, see how they run. ____ The _ stars run down _____ at the
watch the sun, see how it sets. ____ The _ stars rise up _____ at the
watch the moon, see how it shines. _ The _ sun runs down _____ at the

set-ting of the sun. Oh, watch the stars, see how they run.
set-ting of the sun. Oh, watch the sun, see how it sets.
ris-ing of the moon. Oh, watch the moon, see how it shines.

Conducting Patterns

Listen to the song again without looking at the music. Tap the beat and feel the pattern of strong and weak beats.

Conduct each pattern below to decide which pattern fits the song.

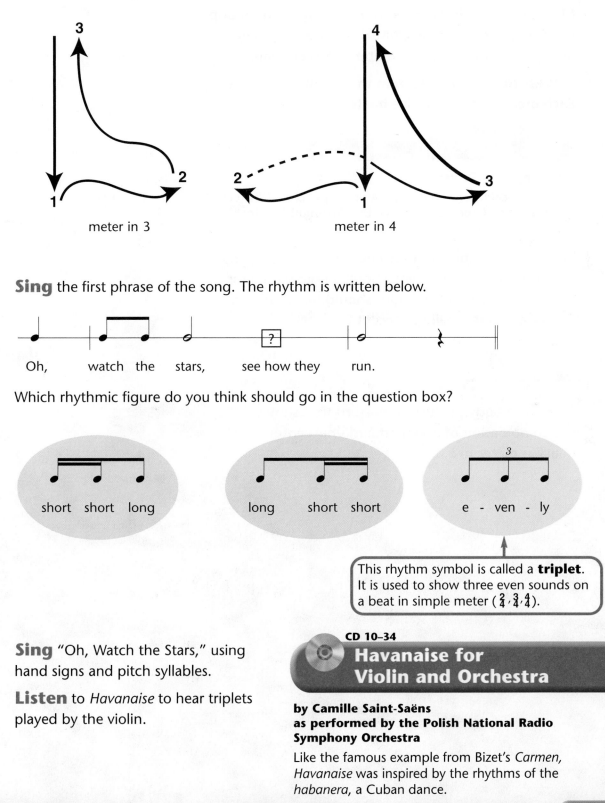

meter in 3

meter in 4

Sing the first phrase of the song. The rhythm is written below.

Oh, watch the stars, see how they run.

Which rhythmic figure do you think should go in the question box?

short short long

long short short

e – ven – ly

This rhythm symbol is called a **triplet**. It is used to show three even sounds on a beat in simple meter ($\frac{2}{4}, \frac{3}{4}, \frac{4}{4}$).

Sing "Oh, Watch the Stars," using hand signs and pitch syllables.

Listen to *Havanaise* to hear triplets played by the violin.

CD 10–34

Havanaise for Violin and Orchestra

by Camille Saint-Saëns
as performed by the Polish National Radio Symphony Orchestra

Like the famous example from Bizet's *Carmen*, *Havanaise* was inspired by the rhythms of the *habanera*, a Cuban dance.

A Different Meter

Most of the music we listen to is in some form of duple or triple meter. In some countries, especially in eastern and southeastern Europe, meter in 5 is common.

Listen to this example from the Republic of Turkey. Each measure contains five beats.

CD 10–35
Ali Pasha

Folk Song from Turkey

The historical figure Ali Pasha [PAH-shah] was an 18th-century governor of a Greek province of the Ottoman Empire.

Listen again and this time count out the meter by tapping each finger on your book. Begin with your thumb on 1. Your little finger should fall on beat 5. On which fingers will the accent fall?

1 2 3 **4** 5

Create a body percussion pattern that shows the combination of accented and unaccented beats in meter in 5.

Ali Pasha Folk Dance

People in Turkey have used these dance movements for hundreds of years. They still dance this way today.

▼ The leader on the end carries a handkerchief in her right hand. She uses it to signal changes in the steps.

▼ The *Ali Pasha* dance is performed in lines. Sometimes dancers hold each other's hands by hooking their little fingers together.

Another Take on Meter

Listen to the jazz piece *Take Five,* another "take" on meter in $\frac{5}{4}$. The percussion and piano introduction sets up the following five-beat pattern.

$\frac{5}{4}$ ♪♩ ♪♩ ♩ ♩ ‖

CD 10–37
Take Five

by Paul Desmond
as performed by the Dave Brubeck Quartet

This piece was made famous by the jazz quartet founded by pianist Dave Brubeck in the late 1950s. When first released, *Take Five* was at the top of the pop charts for months.

Although *Take Five* became Brubeck's signature tune, it was actually composed by saxophonist Paul Desmond. It uses drummer Joe Morello's idea of $\frac{5}{4}$ meter.

MUSIC MAKERS
Dave Brubeck

Dave Brubeck (born 1920 in Concord, California) is one of the 20th century's most important jazz composers and performers. In 1959 the Dave Brubeck Quartet cut its first album using experimental meters and rhythms. That album, *Time Out,* was the first jazz album to sell over one million copies. Brubeck has performed for four presidents (Kennedy, Johnson, Reagan, and Clinton) and was elected to the *Downbeat Hall of Fame.* Brubeck was one of the first musicians to have a star on the Hollywood Walk of Fame. He holds six honorary degrees and has appeared on the cover of *Time* magazine.

Moving in Five

Take Five follows this form:

1. Introduction: Percussion and piano set up the pattern of five beats.

2. Theme: a short **A** **B** **A** melody played by the saxophone.

3. The saxophone "takes a ride," or improvises a solo.

4. The drummer "takes a ride," improvising a solo.

5. The **A** **B** **A** theme returns in the saxophone.

Feeling an irregular meter is easy if you do it with motions. Try this movement with the saxophone theme. Each section lasts eight measures.

◀ **Count 1–2–3:**
Step forward on the right foot as you swing your arms upward.

Count 4–5: ▶
Step back on the left foot. Then swing your arms back as you bring your feet together.

(Repeat the entire five-beat pattern, beginning with the left foot.)

The LONG and SHORT of It

"Hey, Dad, can I have a raise in my allowance?"

"Sorry, son, we can't afford to *augment* your income right now."

"But, Dad, if I don't have a bigger allowance I'll have to *diminish* all my activities."

"Then I guess you'll just have to cut back on some things."

To "augment" means to make something larger or longer. To "diminish" means to make something smaller or shorter. How does that work in music?

Sing "Old Abram Brown" in unison. Then sing it as a round with your classmates.

CD 10–38

Old Abram Brown

Words by Walter de la Mare

Music by Benjamin Britten

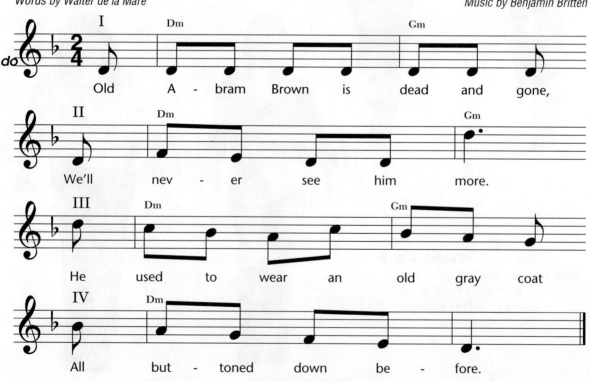

do

I Dm Gm
Old A - bram Brown is dead and gone,

II Dm Gm
We'll nev - er see him more.

III Dm Gm
He used to wear an old gray coat

IV Dm
All but - toned down be - fore.

Augmenting and Diminishing

If you augment the notes in "Old Abram Brown," they will become twice as long.

All the eighth notes ♪♪ will become quarter notes ♩ ♩ and the

dotted quarter ♩. will become a dotted half note ♩..

Sing "Old Abram Brown" in augmentation. Are the rhythms shorter or longer? Does this make the song seem faster or slower?

Perform "Old Abram Brown" again, this time diminish all the note values. You will have to cut all the note values in half.

Does this make the song seem faster or slower?

M·U·S·I·C M·A·K·E·R·S
Benjamin Britten

Benjamin Britten (1913–1976) was one of the most important British composers of the 20th century. While his style of composition seems clear and simple on the surface, it is actually very complex. Many of Britten's compositions require children performers. "Old Abram Brown" is from a song collection called *Friday Afternoons* that was written for children. Britten wrote in nearly every kind of musical form—opera, song, chamber works, oratorio, and cantatas.

Show What You Know!

Select any song from the ones you've learned in the book. **Play** it or **sing** it as you ordinarily would. Then **perform** the song in augmentation. Be sure to keep the beat the same. Did you perform it using longer notes or shorter notes? Now **perform** the song in diminution. Did you perform it using longer notes or shorter ones?

A Form of BLUES

What does it mean to have the blues? Did you know that this expression comes from an African American musical style that has been around for more than one hundred years?

How can we identify a blues song? One way is through the lyrics. Look at "Good Mornin', Blues" and **analyze** the form, or pattern, of the lyrics. Which lines are the same? How would you **describe** the form? Blues singers often improvise their lyrics on the spot. What do you think they do as they sing the second line? Of course! They think up the last line!

Sing "Good Mornin', Blues" with a "blues" feeling.

CD 11–7

Good Mornin', Blues

Edited with New Additional Material by Alan Lomax

New Words and New Musical Arrangement by Huddie Ledbetter

1. Good morn - in', blues, Blues, how do you do?

Good morn - in', blues, Blues, how do you do?

I'm do-in' all right, ____Good morn-in', how are you?

2. I sent for you yesterday, Here you come a-walkin' today. *(2 times)*
   Got your mouth wide open, You don't know what to say.

Country Blues

The blues can be about anything that gets you down. **Listen** to *Country Blues* to discover why the singer is feeling blue.

Country Blues

written and performed by Muddy Waters

Muddy Waters was famous for his bottleneck guitar playing. He would play guitar using a steak bone, pocket knife, brass tube, or bottleneck. Can you hear any of these sounds in this recording?

MUSIC MAKERS

Muddy Waters

Muddy Waters (1915–1983) was one of the most influential guitarists of the 20th century. The city of Chicago is known for its special kind of blues music, and Waters was the musician who defined the Chicago blues. His first hit song, *I Can't Be Satisfied*, was so popular in Chicago that he had a hard time buying a copy for himself! He taught himself to play the guitar using a slide and became one of the best musicians in the city. When Waters and his band members challenged other bands to contests, they almost always won the contest!

Blues in F

Learn to **play** these chords on keyboard to accompany "Good Mornin', Blues."

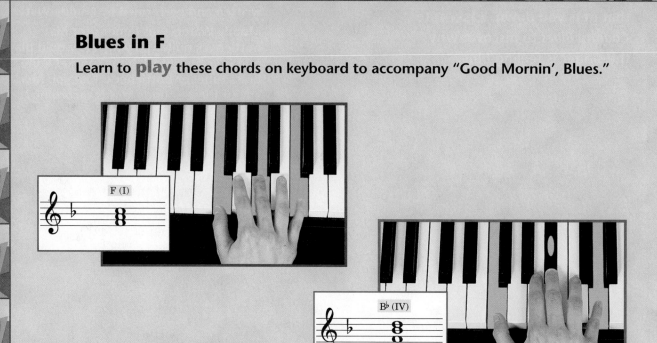

F (I)

B♭ (IV)

C₇ (V₇)

Create your own blues lyrics based on the rhyme scheme of "Good Mornin', Blues." Then **improvise** a melody to accompany your song.

Walkin' Blues

Listen to the blues sound of *Walkin' Blues*. How would you **describe** the feeling expressed in the music?

CD 11–10
Walkin' Blues

written and performed
by Robert Johnson

Robert Johnson (1912–1938) was one of the greatest of the Delta bluesmen. His guitar playing was legendary. Listen for the guitar solos at the beginning and end of *Walkin' Blues*.

Walkin' Blues LISTENING MAP

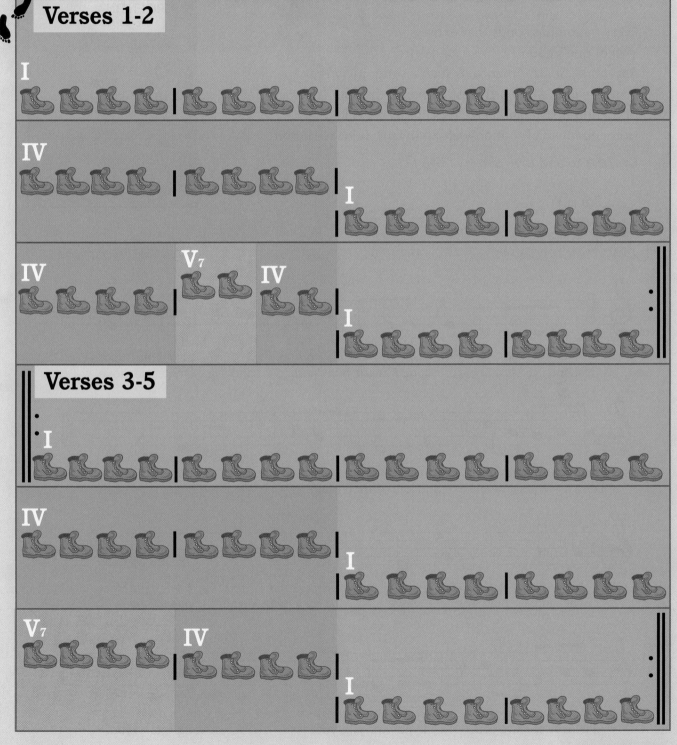

Love of Country

Every nation has songs that express love of one's country. *"Viva Jujuy,"* from Argentina, South America, is such a song. Jujuy is a province in the far northwest corner of the country, bordering Bolivia and Peru. A deep gorge, called Humahuaqueña [oo-mah-wah-KEH-nyah], is located there.

Listen to and then **sing** *"Viva Jujuy."*

CD 11–11
MIDI 16

Viva Jujuy

English Words by Aura Kontra

Folk Song from Argentina

Vi - va Ju - juy, ___ vi - va la pu - na, Vi - va mi a - ma - da.
Long live Ju - juy, ___ long live the high land, Long live my true love.

Vi - van los ce - rros pin - ta - rra - jea - dos De mi que - bra - da.
Long live the can - yon and loft - y moun - tains Soar - ing high a - bove.

De mi que - bra - da Hu - ma - hua - que - ña.
Soar - ing high a - bove Hu - ma - hua - que - ña.

No te se - pa - res De mis a - mo - res Tu e - res mi due - ña.
I'll nev - er leave you. I'll not for - sake you. I be - long to you.

Travel to a Different Tune

The two most common scales are major and minor. Every major scale has a relative minor scale with the same exact pitches. But the two scales start and end on different pitches. They share the same key signature. The major scale begins on *do;* the minor scale begins on *la.*

do	re	mi	fa	so	la	ti	do
C	D	E	F	G	A	B	C

la	ti	do	re	mi	fa	so	la
A	B	C	D	E	F	G	A

Sing the first two lines of *"Viva Jujuy."* Is the melody based on the major scale or the minor scale?

M·U·S·I·C M·A·K·E·R·S
Alberto Ginastera

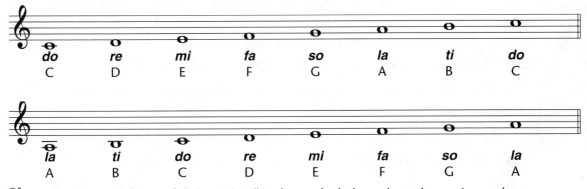

Alberto Ginastera [jee-nah-STEH-rah] (1916–1983) was a 20th century composer from Argentina. At age 7, he began studying the piano, and at age 12, he entered a music conservatory. Early in his career, Ginastera's music expressed strong feelings of Argentinian nationalism. In mid-career, his style changed and he began writing large, dissonant works that reflected the trends of the time.

Listen to *Danza del trigo*, one of Ginastera's earliest compositions. Can you **identify** which scale is used?

CD 11–15

⊙ Danza del trigo

from *Estancia*
by Alberto Ginastera
as performed by the Simón Bolívar Symphony Orchestra; Eduardo Mata, conductor

Estancia was a ballet written in 1941. The ballet includes dances showing Argentinian life. *Danza del trigo* is a wheat dance.

A SONG OF THE SEA

By the mid-1800s, whaling had become a vital industry in the New England states. Whale oil was used in lamps, lighthouse beacons and street lights, and in soap, varnish, and paint. Whalebone was strong and flexible. It was used to make canes, umbrellas, carriage springs, and shoehorns.

Whaling was a dangerous occupation. Many songs were written about the adventures of the whalers at sea.

Sing "The Greenland Whale Fishery," a whaling song that was first sung in Britain and then passed to Newfoundland sailors.

◄ Many sailors spent their spare time at sea doing scrimshaw. Scrimshaw involves engraving a design on polished ivory or whalebone with a sharp tool, and filling in the lines with ink. Today, a manufactured material called alabastrite is used as a substitute for whalebone.

CD 11–16

The Greenland Whale Fishery

Newfoundland Version of a British Sea Song

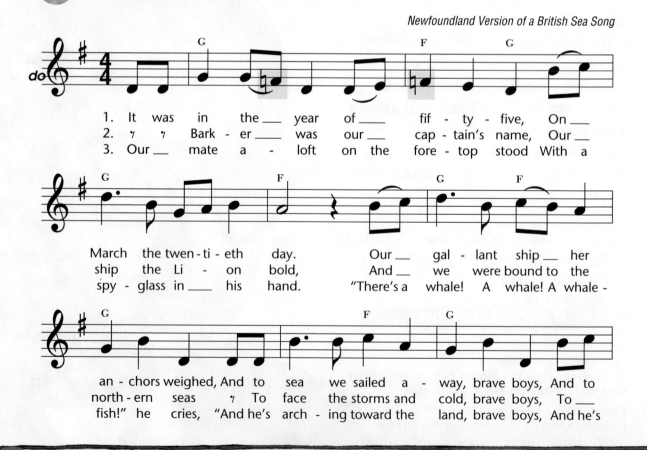

1. It was in the ___ year of ___ fif - ty - five, On ___
2. ⁊ ⁊ Bark - er ___ was our ___ cap - tain's name, Our ___
3. Our ___ mate a - loft on the fore - top stood With a

March the twen - ti - eth day. Our ___ gal - lant ship ___ her
ship the Li - on bold, And ___ we were bound to the
spy - glass in ___ his hand. "There's a whale! A whale! A whale -

an - chors weighed, And to sea we sailed a - way, brave boys, And to
north - ern seas ⁊ To face the storms and cold, brave boys, To ___
fish!" he cries, "And he's arch - ing toward the land, brave boys, And he's

	sea	we _____	sailed ___	a	-	way.
	face	the _____	storms ___	and		cold.
	arch	- ing _____	toward __	the		land."

4. We struck that whale and away he went
    With a flourish of his tail.
    He upset our boat, we lost one man,
    But did not gain that whale, brave boys,
    But did not gain that whale.

5. "My gallant crew, don't be dismayed
    By the losing of a man,
    For Providence will have its way
    That a man do all he can, brave boys,
    That a man do all he can."

A Whale of a Scale

You know about scales built on *do,* the major scale, and *la,* the minor scale.
Did you know that each of the other notes has its own scale?
These scales are called *modes.* The *so* scale is known as the mixolydian scale.

Sing *so* to *so¹* using hand signs. Start on G.

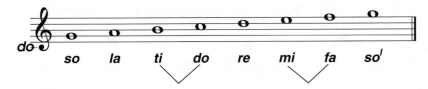

The mixolydian scale can also be sung from *do* to *do¹.* To keep the pattern of
whole and half steps, we need a new note, *ta,* in the place of *ti. Ta* is the note
between *la* and *ti.* It is a half step lower than *ti,* and a half step higher than *la.*

Sing this mixolydian scale both ways, first with G = *so,* then G = *do.* Which set
of pitch syllables will you use to sing "The Greenland Whale Fishery"?

Line up a set of resonator bells in a C-major scale pattern: C-D-E-F-G-A-B-C.

Next, rearrange the bells from A to A to show a natural minor scale. What
bells will you use to show a mixolydian scale? **Play** each scale.

A Song from Ireland

Connemara is a beautiful area in County Galway in the western region of Ireland. Connemara borders the Atlantic Ocean.

In "Connemara Lullaby" the gentle lilt of the rhythm suggests the rocking waves of the ocean. **Sing** "Connemara Lullaby."

CD 11–21

Connemara Lullaby

Words by Julie Scott

Folk Melody from Ireland

Now hush, my babe, now hush my dear one, The an - gels watch will keep o'er _ thy sleep. Now hear the wind blow o'er the o-cean, the gen - tle lull of the roll - ing deep. On wings of wind _ thy cra - dle is rock-ing, And safe - ly you will be drawn o'er the sea. Now slum-ber my babe _ and dream of the morn-ing, For soon, my dear one, you'll wake un - to me.

A New Mode

"Connemara Lullaby" is in the dorian mode. The dorian scale begins on *re*.

Sing from *re* to *re'* using hand signs. Start on D.

The dorian scale can also be sung from *la₁* to *la*. To keep the pattern of whole and half steps, we need a new pitch syllable, *fi*, in place of *fa*.

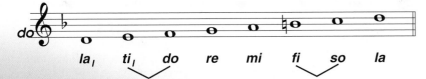

Sing this dorian scale both ways, first with D=*re*, then D=*la₁*. Which set of pitch syllables will you use to sing "Connemara Lullaby"?

Playing the Waves of the Sea

Perform this accompaniment with "Connemara Lullaby." Feel the steady beat as you **play**.

Listen for Dorian Mode

"Greensleeves" is an English folk tune that you might recognize.

Listen to *Fantasia on Greensleeves* by Ralph [RAFE] Vaughan Williams.
This piece is in ABA form. Listen for dorian mode in the B section.

CD 11–26
Fantasia on Greensleeves

by Ralph Vaughan Williams
as performed by the London Symphony Orchestra;
John Georgiadis, conductor

In addition to "Greensleeves," Vaughan Williams used
another English folk tune, "Lovely Joan," in this piece.

M·U·S·I·C M·A·K·E·R·S

Ralph Vaughan Williams

Ralph Vaughan Williams (1872–1958) was
born in Gloucestershire, England. As a young boy,
he studied piano with his aunt. He developed an
interest in composition and later went on to
attend the Royal College of Music in London.
During his education there, he formed a friendship
with fellow student and composer Gustav Holst.
The two offered each other constructive
comments on their compositions. In addition to
composing, Vaughan Williams collected over 800
English folk songs. He used many of them in
his own music.

Keyboard Technology

When composers wrote music hundreds of years ago, they wrote for instruments of their day. The technology of each era helped those historic instruments evolve into instruments we know today.

Listen to this short keyboard composition. It is performed on a harpsichord, the instrument for which it was originally composed.

CD 11–27
Two-Part Invention in A Major

by Johann Sebastian Bach as performed on harpsichord by Kathleen McIntosh

The harpsichord used for this recording is similar to the one Bach used when he composed this piece in 1723.

The strings on a harpsichord are plucked to make their sound. ▶

Bach Today

Although the harpsichord was the most popular keyboard instrument in Bach's time, the piano soon took its place.

Listen again to Bach's *Invention*, this time played on a modern piano.

CD 11–28

Two-Part Invention in A Major

by Johann Sebastian Bach as performed on piano by Glenn Gould

Gould specialized in playing Bach on the piano.

In the 20th century, Robert Moog [mohg], inventor and physicist, was one of the people who applied new technology to the keyboard. In 1964 he invented one of the first synthesizers.

Musicians representing styles from classical to rock quickly became interested in this new development.

Now **listen** to Bach's *Invention* played on a Moog synthesizer.

CD 11–29

Two-Part Invention in A Major

by Johann Sebastian Bach as realized on synthesizer

▲ The strings on a piano are struck to make their sound.

▲ Synthesizers generate sound by sending electronic impulses through a filter to an amplifier. Most synthesizers are controlled by a keyboard.

Listen to *Come Out and Play* played on a Moog synthesizer.

CD 11–30

Come Out and Play

by Brian Holland
as performed by Meco Eno and Uli Nomi

Come Out and Play is performed on a present-day synthesizer. The digital technology used is similar to that used in CD players and computers.

MUSIC MAKERS
Robert Moog

Before **Robert Moog** (born 1934) developed the first commercial synthesizer, these complex instruments were housed mainly in universities and electronic music centers. Early synthesizers were often so large that they occupied whole rooms. To use these synthesizers, each note and its tone color had to be manipulated separately. These notes then had to be recorded. Imagine how long it took to create an entire piece!

In 1964, Moog introduced his first synthesizer for the commercial market. Soon other companies began to compete with Moog. As a result, he developed the Minimoog, a small portable instrument that quickly became popular with rock groups. The Minimoog could play pre-set manufactured sounds. This encouraged more performers to use synthesizers.

In many ways, Robert Moog can be thought of as the father of the music synthesizer.

Impression: Snowflakes

Listen to this version of the piano piece *Snowflakes Are Dancing*, played on a Moog synthesizer. **Describe** how the tone colors of the synthesizer capture the image of snowflakes swirling in the wind.

CD 11–31

Snowflakes Are Dancing

**from *Children's Corner Suite*
by Claude Debussy
performed by Isao Tomita**

Snowflakes Are Dancing portrays the hypnotic effect that comes from watching the falling snow.

M·U·S·I·C M·A·K·E·R·S

Isao Tomita

Isao Tomita [toh-mee-tah], born in 1932 in Tokyo, Japan, first studied art history. He eventually chose music as his profession. While much of Tomita's music is written for television and films, he also wrote the theme music for the Japanese gymnastics team at the 1956 Olympics. Since 1973 his music has been created mostly for electronic instruments but also, on occasion, for traditional Japanese instruments.

HARMONIZING Folk Music

Each style of folk music appeals to the people who create, perform, and listen to it. It is usually simple enough that almost everyone can understand it.

Most folk music, whether it comes from Latin America, the Caribbean, or the United States, can be accompanied by three chords; I, IV, and V_7.

Sing "Linstead Market" and **listen** for the three chords used in the harmony. The three chords used are D (I), G (IV), and A_7 (V_7).

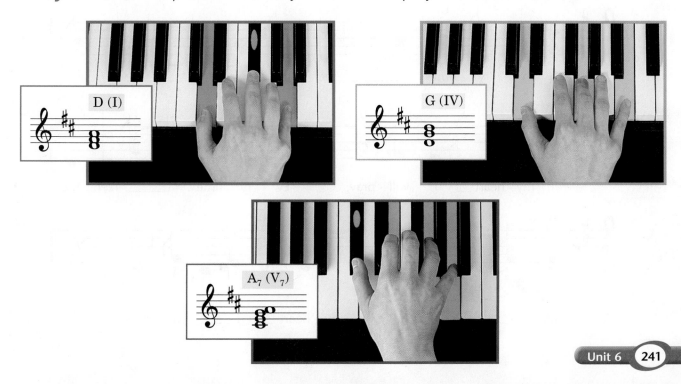

Linstead Market

Calypso Song from Jamaica

Playing I, IV, and V₇ chords

Play the D, G, and A₇ chords on the keyboard to accompany "Linstead Market."

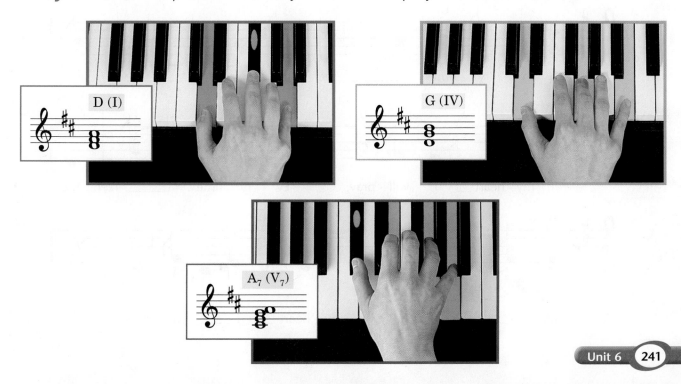

Two-Part Singing

In most traditional music, the human voice is the primary melody instrument. In this arrangement of "Ev'ry Time I Feel the Spirit," the voices sing in two-part harmony on the refrain. The verses are in unison. Learn both the harmony and melody parts. Then **sing** them together.

CD 11–34
MIDI 18

Ev'ry Time I Feel the Spirit

African American Spiritual

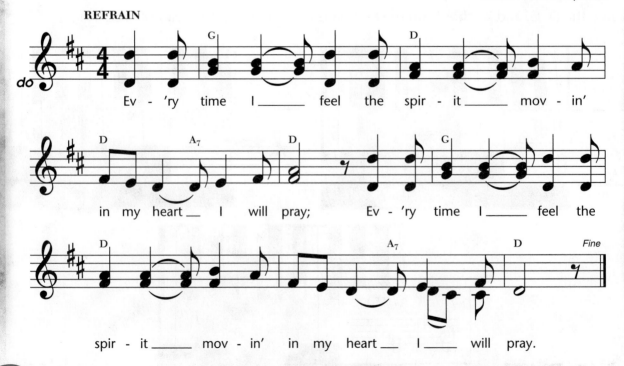

REFRAIN

Ev - 'ry time I _____ feel the spir - it _____ mov - in'

in my heart _____ I will pray; Ev - 'ry time I _____ feel the

spir - it _____ mov - in' in my heart _____ I _____ will pray.

1. Up on the moun - tain _____ when my Lord spoke,
2. I got a home in _____ the Prom - ised Land,

Out of His mouth came _____ fire and smoke,
Ain't gon - na stop till I shake His hand,

I looked a - round me, _____ It looked so fine,
Now Jor - dan riv - er _____ is chilly and cold,

I asked my Lord if _____ all was mine.
It chills the bod - y, _____ not the soul.

Three-Part Playing

During the refrain, **play** these parts on resonator bells to add more harmony.

Music in Three Parts

"Kum ba yah" is a long-time favorite song for singing around a campfire or in other social settings. The words have been translated as "come by you," "come by me," and "come by here." During the American Civil Rights movement of the 1960s, the song became a call for freedom and equal rights.

Sing the melody of *"Kum ba yah,"* then learn the harmony parts and **sing** it in three-part harmony.

CD 11–36

Kum ba yah

Traditional Song from Liberia

REFRAIN

Kum ba yah, my Lord, Kum ba yah! Kum ba yah, my Lord, Kum ba yah! Kum ba yah, my Lord, Kum ba yah! Oh, Lord, _____ Kum ba yah!

Play in Three Parts

When you've learned the song, **play** the chords on metallophones or resonator bells to accompany it.

Ladysmith Black Mambazo, a singing group from South Africa

1. Some - one's sing - in', Lord,   Some - one's
2. Some - one's pray - in', Lord, *Kum ba yah!*   Some - one's
3. Some - one's shout - in', Lord,   Some - one's

sing - in', Lord,   Some-one's sing - in', Lord,
pray - in', Lord, *Kum ba yah!*   Some-one's pray - in', Lord, *Kum ba*
shout - in', Lord,   Some-one's shout - in', Lord,

yah!   Oh,   Lord, _____   *Kum ba yah!*

Review, Assess,

What Do You Know?

1. Which of the following are expressive qualities?

a. form   **b.** tempo   **c.** dynamics

2. Meter in 5 means _____.

a. the music has only five measures   **b.** there is no such meter   **c.** there are five beats in a measure

3. In music, blues is an expression, a feeling, and a _____.

a. meter   **b.** form   **c.** verse

4. The dorian scale begins on _____.

a. *do*   **b.** *la*   **c.** *re*

What Do You Hear? 6A

CD 12–1

Listen to the following excerpts. Each time a number is called, point to the word that describes the tonality. Is it major or minor?

1. major   minor

2. major   minor

3. major   minor

4. major   minor

What Do You Hear? 6B

CD 12–5

Listen to the following excerpts. For each, point to the name of the instrument you hear.

1. harpsichord   piano   synthesizer

2. harpsichord   piano   synthesizer

3. harpsichord   piano   synthesizer

Perform, Create

Create a 12-bar Blues Song

• Compose your own 12-bar blues song (see the form of "Good Mornin', Blues," page 224, for an example).

• Notate your melody in the key of C.

Show the Meter

Listen to *Ali Pasha* and *Take Five*. Perform steady-beat movements that reflect the accent pattern of the meter in 5.

Sing in Harmony

Practice singing in two- and three-part harmony by reviewing these songs in Unit 6:

"Linstead Market," page 241

"Ev'ry Time I Feel the Spirit," page 242

"Kum ba yah," page 244

Working in small groups,

• Choose one song.

• Decide who will sing the melody and who will sing the harmony parts.

• Practice each part.

• Perform your song for the teacher and the other groups.

• Discuss how well each group was able to sing in two or three parts. Then offer suggestions that will help each group improve its performance.

PATHS TO Making Music

Singing Across the Country

Pack your bags for a musical journey across America. We'll start "Down by the Riverside," travel along the "Erie Canal," hop on "The Orange Blossom Special" for a fun time at "Camptown Races," and then move on to the "Colorado Trail." These are just a few of the songs that people sang as they built America.

Sing "Fifty Nifty United States" and add movement for a special performance.

Arts Connection

▼ *Map* by Jasper Johns, 1963. Encaustic and collage on canvas

Building America in Song

America has always been a singing country. In this unit, we will explore songs that tell the stories of America's history.

CD 12–8

Fifty Nifty United States

Words and Music by Ray Charles

Fif - ty nif - ty U - nit - ed States from thir-teen o-rig-i-nal col - o - nies;

Fif - ty nif - ty stars in the flag that bil-lows so beau-ti-f'ly in __ the breeze.

Each in - di - vid-u - al state con - trib-utes a qual-i - ty that is great.

Each in - di - vid-u - al state de - serves a bow, we sa - lute them now.

Fif - ty nif - ty U - nit - ed States from thir-teen o - rig - i - nal col - o - nies,

Shout 'em, scout 'em, Tell all a-bout 'em, One by one till we've giv-en a day to

ev - 'ry state in the U. S. A. Al - a -

bam - a, A - las - ka, Ar - i - zo - na, Ar - kan - sas, Cal - i -

for - nia, Col - o - ra - do, Con - nect - i - cut;

Del - a - ware, Flor - i - da, Geor - gia, Ha - wai - i, I - da -

ho, Il - li - nois, In - di - an - a;

I - o - wa, Kan - sas, Ken - tuck-y, Lou - i - si - an - a, Maine,

Mar - y - land, Mas - sa - chu-setts, Mich - i - gan; Min - ne -

so - ta, Mis - sis - sip - pi, Mis - sou - ri, Mon - tan - a, Ne -

bras - ka, Ne - vad - a;

New Hamp-shire, New Jer - sey, New Mex - i - co, New York,

North Car-o-li-na, North Da-ko-ta, O - hi - o; Ok-la-

ho-ma, Or-e-gon, Penn-syl-va-nia, Rhode Is-land, South Car-o-li-na,

South Da-ko-ta, Ten-nes-see, Tex-as; _____

U - tah, Ver-mont, Vir-gin - ia, Wash-ing-ton,

West Vir-gin-ia, Wis-con-sin, Wy - o - ming.

Spiritual STYLE

American spirituals were popular from 1820–1860 among both African and European Americans. The spiritual gave voice to enslaved African Americans who longed for the promised land of freedom.

Sing this spiritual and **identify** the syncopated patterns.

CD 12–10
MIDI 19

Down by the Riverside

African American Spiritual

1. Gon - na lay down my sword and shield, —
2. Gon - na join hands with ev - 'ry one, —
3. Gon - na ring out a song of joy, —

Down by the riv - er - side, —

Down by the riv - er - side, —

Down by the riv - er - side, —

Gon - na lay down my sword and shield, —
Gon - na join hands with ev - 'ry one, —
Gon - na ring out a song of joy, —

Down by the riv-er-side, ____
And stud-y ____ war no more. ____

REFRAIN

I ain't gon-na stud-y ____ war no more,

I ain't gon-na stud-y ____ war no more,

I ain't gon-na stud-y ____ war no

1.
more. ____ I ain't gon-na

2.
more. ____

Create new verses to "Down by the Riverside" by making up only one line of text.

- Start with the word *Gonna*.

- Make sure your line contains a total of eight syllables.

- Place your new text on lines 1 and 5 of the song.

- Write at least three new verses; then try them out by yourself and with your classmates.

The Sacred Harp

European Americans also created their own style of religious song that was different from the African American spiritual. Many of these spirituals, hymns, and anthems were collected in a book called *The Sacred Harp*.

Sing "The Promised Land," a well-known hymn from the early nineteenth century. The melody below is taken directly from *The Sacred Harp* collection.

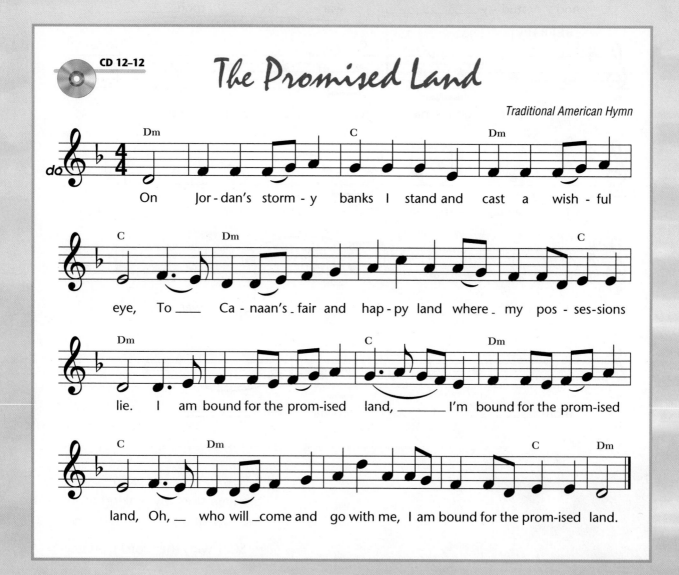

A Shape-Note Hymn

Listen to this performance of *Amazing Grace*, which is based on the shape-note arrangement shown below.

CD 12–14

Amazing Grace

Early American Hymn
as performed by the Sacred Harp Singers

This version of *Amazing Grace* is similar to the way you might hear the song sung today.

◀ The mountain dulcimer, from the Appalachian region of the United States, is often used to accompany folk and hymn singing. The strings are usually strummed with picks, quills, or the thumb.

The Sacred Harp hymns were notated using shape notes. Each shape stood for a tone syllable—*fa, so, la,* or *mi.* This is how "Amazing Grace" looks in the Sacred Harp book. The melody is in the tenor part, the third line down. ▼

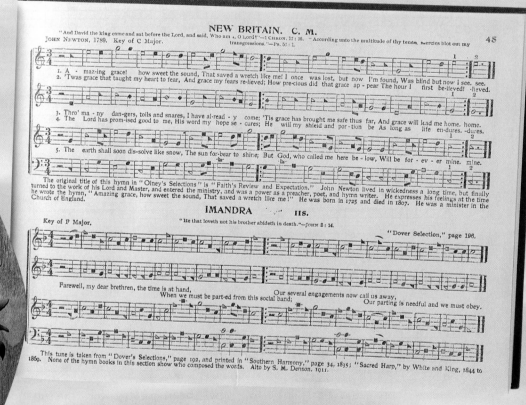

Dance to the Music

As Americans moved westward from the original thirteen colonies, they took their music with them. One of their favorite pastimes was dancing to the music of fiddles, harmonicas, and banjos. Mountain dulcimers were also used to accompany songs.

Sing "Shady Grove," an Appalachian song that was sung during the westward movement.

CD 12–15

Shady Grove

Folk Song from the United States

REFRAIN

Shad - y Grove, my lit - tle love, Shad - y Grove I know,

Shad - y Grove, my lit - tle love, Bound for the Shad - y Grove. *Fine*

VERSE

1. Cheeks as red as a bloom-in' rose, Eyes of the deep-est brown, You
2. Went to see my __ Shad - y Grove, Stand-in' __ in the door,
3. Wish I had a __ big fine horse, Corn to __ feed him on,

D. C. al Fine

are the dar - lin' of my __ heart, Stay till the sun goes down.
Shoes and stock-ings in her __ hand, Little bare __ feet on the floor.
Pretty little girl to stay at __ home, Feed him __ when I'm gone.

Accompany the Song

Play the Em and D chords on Autoharp or guitar to accompany the song.

Listen to *Cedar Swamp*, performed on the dulcimer.

CD 12–17
Cedar Swamp

Folk Song from the United States as performed by Jill Trinka, dulcimer

Cedar Swamp is included in the Jean Ritchie collection *Folk Songs of the Southern Appalachians.*

Jill Trinka playing the dulcimer. ▼

Miles and Miles

In the move westward, Americans frequently traveled along rivers and canals. Great cities often grew where the rivers came together. The Erie Canal, built in 1825, linked the Great Lakes and the Atlantic Ocean.

Sing "Erie Canal." **Identify** how the melody changes in the refrain.

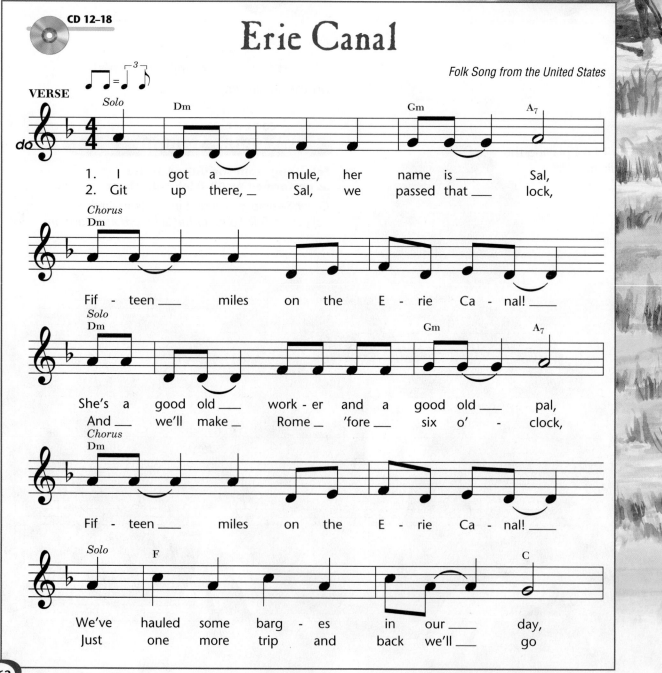

CD 12–18

Erie Canal

Folk Song from the United States

VERSE

Solo

1. I got a _____ mule, her name is _____ Sal,
2. Git up there, __ Sal, we passed that __ lock,

Chorus

Fif - teen ____ miles on the E - rie Ca - nal! ____

Solo

She's a good old ____ work - er and a good old ____ pal,
And __ we'll make __ Rome _ 'fore ___ six o' - clock,

Chorus

Fif - teen ____ miles on the E - rie Ca - nal! ____

Solo

We've hauled some barg - es in our ____ day,
Just one more trip and back we'll ___ go

The Erie Canal opened up the settlement of the Great Lakes states until 1850, when railroads became more widely used.

Songs of the Sea

The tradition of sea shanties began with sailors on the ocean. On board the tall ships, a shantyman was paid to lead the crew in singing to lighten the work. Sea shanties were sung to raise the anchor, hoist the sails, or pump out the ship. They were also sung in the crew's quarters for relaxation. As early Americans moved inland, many of the sea shanties became river songs.

Sing "Shenandoah," a well-known American sea shanty.

Identify the *call* (shantyman) and *response* (crew) form.

CD 12–21

Shenandoah

Capstan Sea Shanty

Call—Shantyman

1. Oh, Shen - an - doah, I long to hear you, ___
2. Oh, Shen - an - doah, I'm bound to leave you, ___
3. 'Tis sev'n long years since last I saw you, ___
4. When first I took a ram - bling no - tion ___

Response—Crew

And ___ see ___ you roll - in' riv - er, ___
A - way ___ you roll - in' riv - er, ___
And ___ heard ___ you roll - in' riv - er, ___
To ___ leave ___ you roll - in' riv - er, ___

Call—Shantyman

Oh, Shen - an - doah, I long to hear you, ___
Oh, Shen - an - doah, I'll not de - ceive you, ___
'Tis sev'n long years since last I saw you, ___
To sail a - cross the brin - y o - cean, ___

Response—Crew

A - way, ___ I'm bound a - way, 'Cross the wide ___ Mis-sou - ri.

Ship Ahoy!

Listen to Paul Robeson, a great African American bass, sing *Shenandoah*.

Shenandoah
CD 12–23

Capstan Sea Shanty
as performed by Paul Robeson

Capstan sea shanties were sung during the long tedious job of pulling the anchor in. Many of these shanties have long melodies and many verses.

Arts Connection

▲ *The Clipper Ship* by Alistair Ross. After the War of 1812, America became a major seafaring nation with large clipper ships trading in ports all over the world. All along the East Coast men shipped out of cities to go whaling, or to trade American textiles for goods in other seaports.

A SPECIAL RIDE

The Orange Blossom Special was Florida's "Distinguished Winter Train." It traveled the east coast to Florida from 1925 until 1953.

Listen as the harmonica and fiddle imitate the sound of a train. Then **sing** "Orange Blossom Special."

Orange Blossom Special, 1938 ▶

CD 12–24
MIDI 20

Orange Blossom Special

Words and Music by Ervin T. Rouse

1. Look - a yon - der com - in', _____
2. I'm go - in' down _____ to Flori - da _____
3. Talk a - bout _____ a - trav - 'lin', _____

com - in' down that rail - road _____ track!
and get some sand in my _____ shoes.
she's the fast - est train on the _____ line.

Hey, look - a yon - der com - in', _____
Or may - be Cal - i - for - nia _____
Talk a - bout _____ a - trav - 'lin',

com - in' down   that   rail - road   track!
and   get   some   sand   in   my   shoes.
she's   the   fast - est   train   on   the   line.

It's   the   Or - ange   Blos - som   Spe - cial
I'll   ride   that   Or - ange   Blos - som   Spe - cial
It's   that   Or - ange   Blos - som   Spe - cial

bring - in' my   ba - by ___ back.
and   lose ___ these   New ___ York ___ blues.
roll - in' down the   Sea - board _ line.

Souvenirs of the Orange Blossom Special

Playing cards ▼

Uniform ▲
lapel button

Luggage tag ▲

Sleeping car, 1951

SEABOARD
AIR LINE
RAILWAY

Stationery ▼

This map shows the railway system owned by the company that ran the Orange Blossom Special.

ORANGE BLOSSOM SPECIAL

All Aboard!

Listen to this bluegrass performance of *Orange Blossom Special* as you follow the listening map below.

CD 12–26

Orange Blossom Special

by Ervin T. Rouse
as performed by the Stanley Brothers

Carter and Ralph Stanley are well-known bluegrass musicians from the mountains of Virginia.

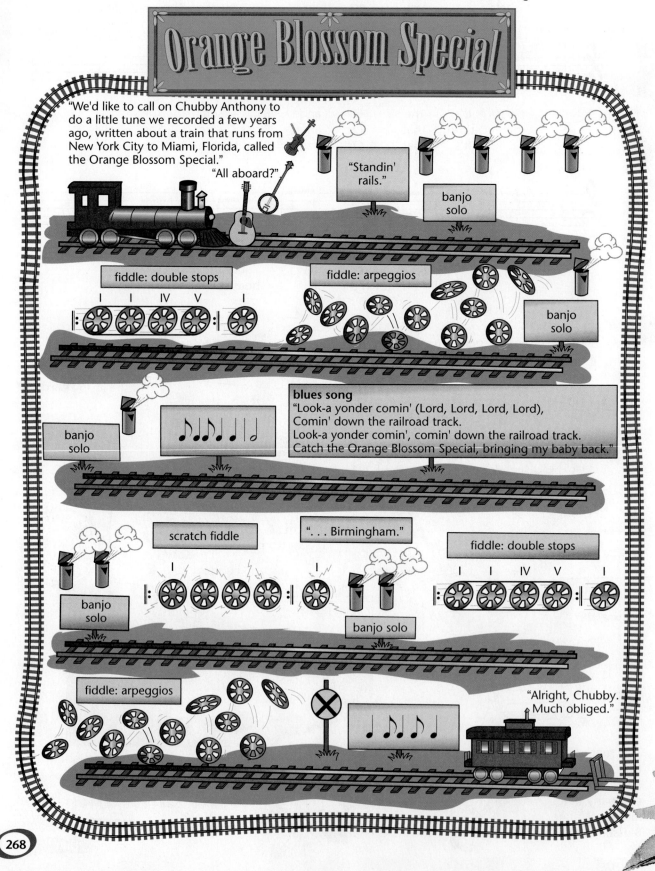

"We'd like to call on Chubby Anthony to do a little tune we recorded a few years ago, written about a train that runs from New York City to Miami, Florida, called the Orange Blossom Special."

"All aboard?"

"Standin' rails."

banjo solo

fiddle: double stops

fiddle: arpeggios

banjo solo

banjo solo

blues song
"Look-a yonder comin' (Lord, Lord, Lord, Lord),
Comin' down the railroad track.
Look-a yonder comin', comin' down the railroad track.
Catch the Orange Blossom Special, bringing my baby back."

scratch fiddle

". . . Birmingham."

fiddle: double stops

banjo solo

banjo solo

fiddle: arpeggios

"Alright, Chubby. Much obliged."

268

The *Orange Blossom Special* Dance

To **perform** this dance about a special train, **move** in a circle and then go through a "tunnel."

19ᵗʰ Century Pop

"Camptown Races" was written by Stephen Foster in 1850. It "topped the charts" in its day.

Listen to "Camptown Races" and **sing** along on the response part.

CD 12–29

Camptown Races

Words and Music by Stephen Foster

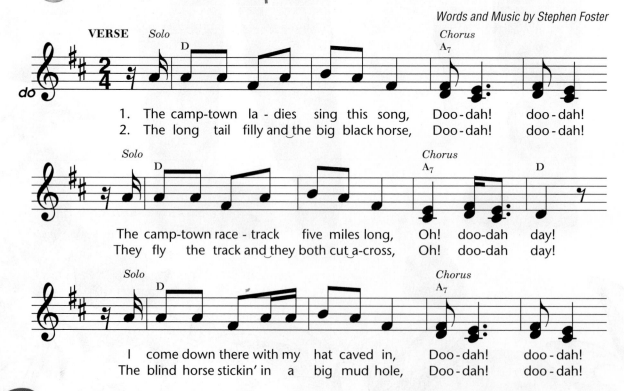

VERSE *Solo*   *Chorus*
D   A₇

1. The camp-town la - dies   sing this song,   Doo-dah!   doo-dah!
2. The long   tail   filly and the big black horse,   Doo-dah!   doo-dah!

Solo   *Chorus*
D   A₇   D

The camp-town race - track   five miles long,   Oh! doo-dah   day!
They   fly   the   track and they both cut a-cross,   Oh! doo-dah   day!

Solo   *Chorus*
D   A₇

I   come down there with my   hat caved in,   Doo-dah!   doo-dah!
The blind horse stickin' in   a   big mud hole,   Doo-dah!   doo-dah!

270

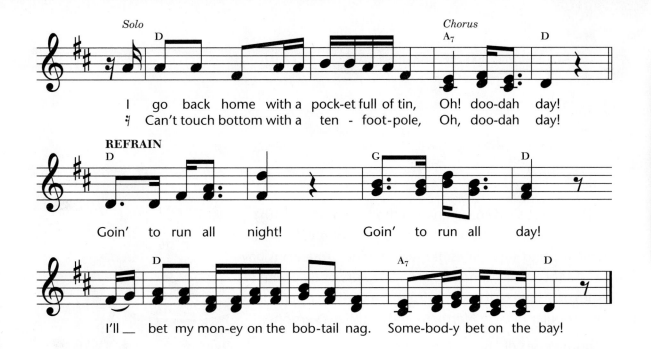

I go back home with a pock-et full of tin, Oh! doo-dah day!
Can't touch bottom with a ten - foot-pole, Oh, doo-dah day!

REFRAIN

Goin' to run all night! Goin' to run all day!

I'll __ bet my mon-ey on the bob-tail nag. Some-bod-y bet on the bay!

M·U·S·I·C M·A·K·E·R·S
Stephen Collins Foster

Stephen Collins Foster (1826–1864) added hit after hit to his long list of popular tunes. Steering away from the "conventional" songs of the day, Foster's new "minstrel" sound made him one of the most popular composers of the 19th century. In addition to his biggest hit, "Camptown Races," he wrote such favorites as "Oh! Susanna," "My Old Kentucky Home," "Jeanie with the Light Brown Hair," and "Old Folks at Home." Most of Stephen Foster's songs were about the South, even though he lived most of his life in Pennsylvania and New York.

Create an American song bag (a collection of your favorite songs) for your music class. Write the title, composer, origin, and a special fact about each song on a 3x5 card. Put the song in a bag decorated with symbols from America's history. Keep your song bag for review.

Comin' Home

The Civil War (1861–1865) between the Union (the North) and the Confederacy (the South) was a time of great upheaval and strife. During such times of great change, Americans have always produced new songs to lift their spirits or deal with their sorrow. Many of the songs from the Civil War period became popular in both Northern and Southern versions.

Sing both verses of "Battle Cry of Freedom."

CD 12–31

Battle Cry of Freedom

Northern Words by George F. Root
Southern Words by W. H. Barnes

Music by George F. Root

VERSE

(Northern) Yes, we'll ral - ly round the flag, boys, we'll ral - ly once a - gain,
(Southern) Our ___ gal - lant boys have marched to the roll - ing of the drums,

Shout - ing the bat - tle cry of free - dom,
Shout, shout, the bat - tle cry of free - dom,

We will ral - ly from the hill - side, we'll gath - er from the plain,
Be - neath it oft we've conquered and will con - quer oft a - gain,

Shout - ing the bat - tle cry of free - dom.
Shout, shout, the bat - tle cry of free - dom.

REFRAIN

The Un - ion for - ev - er, Hur - rah, boys, Hur - rah!
Our Dix - ie for - ev - er, she's never at a loss.

Down with the trai - tor, Up with the star;
Down with the eag - le and up with the cross;

While we ral - ly round the flag, boys, ral - ly once a - gain,
We'll __ ral - ly round the bonny flag, we'll ral - ly once a - gain,

Shout - ing the bat - tle cry of free - dom.
Shout, shout the bat - tle cry of free - dom.

Arts Connection

◀ "Drummer Jackson"

▲ *Yankee Volunteers Marching to Dixie*, 1862

Marching On

In the North, "Battle Hymn of the Republic" was the best-known song of the Civil War. Learn the descant part and **sing** it on the refrain.

"Battle Hymn of the Republic" has gone through many lyric changes and has been sung for various purposes. **Create** your own words to this melody.

CD 12–33

Battle Hymn of the Republic

Words by Julia Ward Howe

Music by William Steffe

VERSE

1. Mine __ eyes have seen the glo-ry of the com-ing of the Lord;
2. He has sound-ed forth the trum-pet that shall nev-er call re-treat;

He is tramp-ling out the vin-tage where the grapes of wrath are stored;
He is sift-ing out the hearts of men be-fore the judg-ment seat.

He hath loosed the fate-ful light-ning of His ter-ri-ble swift sword;
Oh, be swift, my soul, to an-swer Him! Be ju-bi-lant, my feet!

His truth is march - ing on.
Our God is march - ing on.

REFRAIN

Descant

Glo - ry, glo - ry, hal - le - lu - jah!

Melody

Glo - ry, glo - ry, hal - le - lu - jah!

Glo - ry, glo - ry, hal - le - lu - jah!

Glo - ry, glo - ry, hal - le - lu - jah!

Glo - ry, glo - ry, hal - le - lu! His

Glo - ry, glo - ry, hal - le - lu - jah! His

truth is march - ing, march - ing on.

truth is march - ing on.

Listen to Morton Gould's *American Salute*. What familiar Civil War melody do you hear?

CD 12–35

American Salute

by Morton Gould
as performed by the Philadelphia Orchestra; Eugene Ormandy, conductor

Morton Gould was a Pulitzer Prize-winning composer who used American themes in much of his music.

Singing on the Trail

The heyday of the American cowboy was the period following the Civil War until 1885. Many war veterans went West in search of adventure or work opportunities. Many ended up as cowboys, often working for less than a dollar a day.

Sing "Colorado Trail." Which phrases use the same melody?

CD 12–36

Colorado Trail

Cowboy Song

Eyes like a morn-ing star, cheeks like a rose,

Lau - ra was a pret-ty girl, ev - 'ry - bod - y knows.

Weep all ye lit - tle rains, wail winds, _ wail,

All a - long, a - long, a - long the Col - o - ra - do Trail.

Strumming Cowboys

Learn to **play** one of the chords below to accompany "Colorado Trail" on guitar.

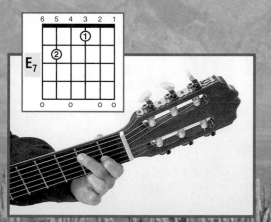

Sounds of the Trail

Listen to this recording of *Colorado Trail* and **compare** it to the version of the song on page 276. How is it the same? How is it different?

CD 13–1
Colorado Trail

**Cowboy Song
arranged by Matthias Gohl**

This rendition was featured in the film *The West*.

Arts Connection

◀ This hand-colored engraving by American artist and sculptor Frederic Remington (1861–1909) depicts cowboys trailing cattle.

Send the Word

America entered World War I (1914–1918) in 1917. In order to stir American patriotism and support, vaudeville songwriters like George M. Cohan wrote songs such as "You're a Grand Old Flag" and "Over There."

Sing "Over There," and share in the enthusiasm of the lyrics and the upbeat rhythm. Then **identify** the part of the melody that repeats throughout the song.

I WANT YOU
FOR U.S. ARMY
NEAREST RECRUITING STATION

MUSIC MAKERS

George M. Cohan

George M. Cohan (1878–1942)— American musical theater actor, composer, singer, dancer, playwright, director, and producer—added his support of the war with his hit "Over There." The song was as popular as his other show stoppers, "You're a Grand Old Flag, "I'm a Yankee Doodle Dandy," and "Give My Regards to Broadway."

Listen to another spirited patriotic favorite from George M. Cohan.

CD 13–2
I'm a Yankee Doodle Dandy

by George M. Cohan

I'm a Yankee Doodle Dandy, from the musical *Little Johnny Jones,* premiered on November 17, 1904. This song was one of Cohan's early successes.

CD 13–3

Over There

Words and Music by George M. Cohan

do

G
O - ver there, o - ver there,

G
Send the word, send the word o - ver there

D₇ **G**
That the Yanks are com-ing, the Yanks are com-ing, The

D₇ **A₇** **D₇**
drums rum tum - ming ev - 'ry - where.

G
So pre - pare, say a pray'r,

G
Send the word, send the word to be - ware

G **D₇**
We'll be o - ver, we're com-ing o - ver, And we

G **C** **D₇** **G**
won't come back 'till it's o - ver o - ver there.

Visit **Take It to the Net** at
www.sfsuccessnet.com to learn more
about George M. Cohan.

Gospel Calling

In the late 1920s, a blues pianist named Thomas A. Dorsey added elements of blues and jazz to the African American spiritual and hymn tradition. He helped create a style that became known as gospel music.

Listen to "Twelve Gates to the City," a traditional spiritual that is arranged here in gospel style.

Describe the voices and the accompanying instruments on the recording.

CD 13–5

Twelve Gates to the City

African American Spiritual

REFRAIN

Oh, _____ what a beau-ti-ful ci-ty; _____ Oh, _____ what a
beau-ti-ful ci-ty; _____ Oh, _____ what a beau-ti-ful ci-ty; _____

*Fine
2nd time to Refrain
3rd time to verse 2*

Twelve gates to the ci-ty, a-hal-le-lu. _____

VERSE

1. My Lord built _____ the ci-ty, _____ Ci-ty was just _____ four
square, Said he want-ed his child-ren _____ to
meet him in _____ the air, And there's twelve gates _ to the

ci - ty, a - hal - le - lu. ___

2. Three gates in - a the East, ___ Three gates in - a the West, ___

___ Three gates in ___ the North, ___

Three gates in - a the South, _ That makes twelve gates _ to the

ci - ty, a - hal - le - lu. ___

A Gospel Performance

Listen to *What Could I Do*, a gospel song written by Thomas A. Dorsey. **Compare** the vocal and instrumental timbres with those heard on the recording of "Twelve Gates to the City."

CD 13–7
What Could I Do

by Thomas A. Dorsey
as performed by Marion Williams

Gospel singer Marion Williams's career spanned more than 40 years. She was a Kennedy Center Honoree in 1993.

MUSIC MAKERS

Thomas A. Dorsey

Thomas Andrew Dorsey (1899–1993) is known as the "father of gospel music." He was born in Georgia and began his career playing in theaters and clubs. He later played with legendary blues vocalist Ma Rainey. After the deaths of his wife and son, Dorsey wrote "Precious Lord, Take My Hand," one of the best-loved gospel songs of the twentieth century. He founded the first independent publisher of African American gospel music.

Better Times Ahead . . .

The stock market crash of 1929 brought a decade of hardship to many Americans. The severe drought of the 1930s added to this misery by creating the Dust Bowl. Thousands of people suffered as the land dried up. Many were forced to migrate to other parts of the country.

Sing this song about the feelings of many Americans at this very difficult time.

CD 13–8

Goin' Down the Road Feelin' Bad

Words and Melody Adapted and Arranged by John A. Lomax and Alan Lomax

1. I'm go-in' down the road feel-in' bad,
2. I ain't got but one old lous-y dime,
3. I'm go-in' where the cli-mate suits my clothes,

Lord, I'm go-in' down the road feel-in' bad,
Lord, I ain't got but one old lous-y dime,
Lord, I'm go-in' where the cli-mate suits my clothes,

Well, I'm go-in' down the road feel-in' bad, Lord,
Well, I ain't got but one old lous-y dime, Lord,
Well, I'm go-in' where the cli-mate suits my clothes, Lord,

Lord, And I ain't gon-na be treat-ed this-a-way.
Lord, But I'll find me a new dol-lar some old day.
Lord, 'Cause I ain't gon-na be treat-ed this-a-way.

Folk Guitar Chords

Play the following chords on guitar to accompany "Goin' Down the Road Feelin' Bad."

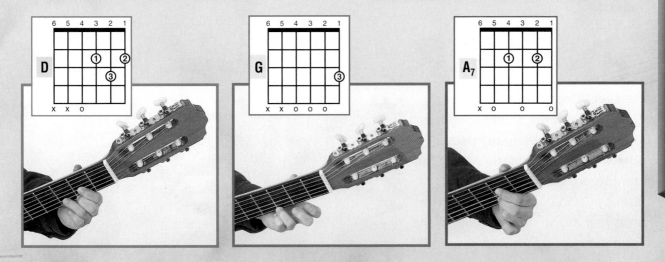

Listen to Woody Guthrie's performance of *Goin' Down the Road Feelin' Bad.*

CD 13–10

Goin' Down the Road Feelin' Bad

**adapted, arranged, and performed by
Woody Guthrie and Lee Hays**

This song was sung by many Dust Bowl farmers
as they left their devastated homes and fields in
hope of finding a better life.

M·U·S·I·C M·A·K·E·R·S

Woody Guthrie

Woody Guthrie (1912–1967) was one of the most
important American folk music artists of the 20th
century. He was born in Oklahoma, one of the
hardest-hit states during the Dust Bowl
years. Along with other folk music
legends like Pete Seeger and
Leadbelly, Guthrie had a major
influence on the next generation
of folk artists, such as
Bob Dylan and Joan Baez.

ANOTHER CHALLENGE

The Great Depression of the early 1930s brought mass unemployment and long food lines. Many people looked to popular entertainment for a temporary escape from their hardships. One song, written in the same year as the stock market crash, gained unexpected popularity. With its catchy, syncopated rhythms, and optimistic lyrics, "Happy Days Are Here Again" expressed new hope for better days. It went on to become the theme song of President Franklin D. Roosevelt's efforts to lead the country out of the Depression.

Listen to and then **sing** "Happy Days Are Here Again." Can you **identify** the repeated syncopated rhythm pattern?

▲ Food line on East 25th St., New York City, 1931

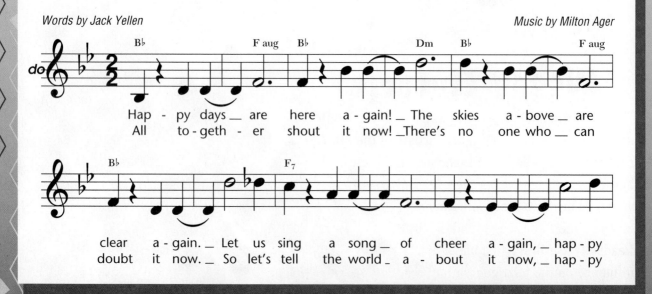

CD 13–11

HAPPY DAYS ARE HERE AGAIN

Words by Jack Yellen

Music by Milton Ager

Hap - py days __ are here a - gain! __ The skies a - bove __ are
All to - geth - er shout it now! __ There's no one who __ can

clear a - gain. __ Let us sing a song __ of cheer a - gain, __ hap - py
doubt it now. __ So let's tell the world __ a - bout it now, __ hap - py

▲ Ticker tape parade,
November 28, 1931,
Los Angeles, California

Franklin Delano Roosevelt ▶

Element: RHYTHM | **Skill: CREATING** | **Connection: SOCIAL STUDIES**

THE Sign OF THE Times

On November 22, 1963, President John F. Kennedy was assassinated. This tragic event launched a decade of social triumphs and tragedies that deeply affected our nation. As always, America's folk music voiced the feelings, hopes, and dreams of the American people. Songs about civil rights, equality for all, environmental concerns, and peace echoed throughout the country.

"Ask not what your country can do for you—ask what you can do for your country."
— JFK Inaugural address, January 20, 1961

"If I Had a Hammer" is a song that raised a few warnings. **Sing** it and then **create** other verses that might reflect the concerns of the present decade.

WAR IS NOT HEALTHY FOR CHILDREN

IF I HAD A HAMMER

Words and Music by Lee Hays and Pete Seeger

do

1. If I had a ham - mer, __ I'd ham - mer in the morn - ing, __
2. If I had a bell, _____ I'd ring it in the morn - ing, __
3. If I had a song, _____ I'd sing it in the morn - ing, __
4. Well, I got a ham - mer, __ And I ____ got a bell, _____

I'd ham-mer in the eve - ning __
I'd ring it in the eve - ning __
I'd sing it in the eve - ning __   All o - ver this land,
And I ____ got a song to sing.

I'd ham-mer out dan - ger, _   I'd ham-mer out a warn-ing, __
I'd ring __ out dan - ger, _   I'd ring __ out a warn-ing, __
I'd sing __ out dan - ger, _   I'd sing __ out a warn-ing, __
It's the ham-mer of jus - tice, _ It's the bell __ of __ free - dom, _

I'd ham-mer out
I'd ring __ out
I'd sing __ out   love be-tween my broth-ers and my sis-ters,
It's the song a - bout

All _____ o - ver this land. _____

"If I Had a Hammer" (The Hammer Song) TRO–© Copyright 1958 (Renewed) 1962 (Renewed) Ludlow Music, Inc., New York, NY. Used by Permission.

Building America in Song

The song *Where Have All the Flowers Gone?* expresses many of the social concerns of the 1960s. **Listen** to Pete Seeger's performance.

Where Have All the Flowers Gone?

written and performed by Pete Seeger

Where Have All the Flowers Gone?, written in 1961, was inspired by the novel *And Quiet Flows the Don.*

A King's Dream

The latter part of the 1960s was a difficult time. The Vietnam War was still raging, and cries for freedom and peace continued to echo across the nation. A song of hope became a moment of silence when another leader was taken away. On April 4, 1968, Martin Luther King, Jr. was assassinated, and another dream remained unfulfilled.

"Woke Up This Morning" is an older African American song that was revived during the Civil Rights movement.

Sing this song and **create** additional verses that reflect King's dream.

CD 13–16   WOKE UP THIS MORNING

African American Freedom Song

1. Woke up this morn - ing with my mind (my mind it was) stayed _____ on
3. Sing - in' and pray - in' with my mind

free - dom, (oh, well I) Woke up this morn-ing with my mind _____
Sing - in' and pray - in' with my mind _____

stayed _on free - dom, (oh, well I) Woke up this morn-ing with my mind (my mind it was)
Sing - in' and pray - in' with my mind

stayed _____ on free - dom, Hal - le - lu, hal - le - lu, hal - le -

lu, hal - le - lu, hal - le - lu - jah! _____

Fine

288

2. Walk   walk (doo doo doo) walk   walk   walk   walk with my mind on free-dom, _

Walk   walk   walk   walk   (a-well-a) walk   walk   with my mind on   free-dom,

Ah _____ walk   walk   walk   walk

Distant Lands

Let's travel beyond our borders—around the world.
We'll sing folk songs in Spanish, dance a few
Middle Eastern dances, play an African game,
visit an Indonesian shadow puppet play, and
listen to a world-renowned sitarist from India.

▼ Bagpiper

Israeli Folk dancers dressed
in traditional costume
▼

▲ Accordion (left) and
maraca players

Music Around the World

Performer at the ▶
Festival of Our Lady
of Guadalupe,
Mexico City

Let us travel to new places
and explore new musical
traditions. We will
celebrate the things
that make us different,
and focus on what
brings us together
through music.

Ravi Shankar
performing on
the *sitar* ▼

Many Voices Singing

Sing "Beyond Borders," a song that describes the power of music to unite people across time and distance.

CD 13–18

Beyond Borders

Words and Music by Christopher Landriau

1. In the still and calm __ of long a - go, __ there were
2. They're sing - ing now __ in dis - tant lands __ where they

man - y voi - ces sing - ing. __ Who they were, __ we'll
watch our sun __ and moon. _____ Can we touch __ their

nev - er know, __ but you can hear their ech - oes ring - ing. __
reach - ing hands, _____ and to their hearts at - tune? _____

And when you an - swer the an - cient call, __ to the
Be - yond the bor - ders of na - tions, __ feel the

mus - ic we'll all __ be - long. __ Do you ev - er won - der af - ter
beat - ing hu - man heart. __ In the com - mon choir __ of cre -

Last time to Coda D. C.

we have __ gone, __ who will hear our song? _____
a - tion, __ will you sing your part? _____

Element : **RHYTHM** | Skill: **MOVING** | Connection: **CULTURE**

Move to the Music

All around the world, people clap interesting rhythms as they sing. Clapping or tapping your fingers is like dancing with your hands—something you can do even when you can't get up and move around.

Clap the strong beats as you **sing** "*¡Qué bonita bandera!*", a lively song about the flag of Puerto Rico.

CD 13–20

¡Qué bonita bandera!
(What a Beautiful Banner!)

English Words by Samuel Maqui

Folk Song from Puerto Rico

VERSE

A - zul, blan - ca   y ____ co - lo - ra - da,   y en el
Blue and white and   red __ are the   col - ors,   with a

me - dio tie - ne un es - tre - lla.   Bo - ni - ta, se -
pure white star   in the   cen - ter.   A beau - ti - ful

ñor - es,   es   la   ban - de - ra Puer - to - ri - que - ña.
ban - ner   is   the   flag   of our Puer - to   Ri - co!

REFRAIN

¡Qué bo - ni - ta ban - de - ra!   ¡Qué bo - ni - ta ban - de - ra!
What a beau - ti - ful   ban - ner!   What a beau - ti - ful   ban - ner!

¡Qué bo - ni - ta ban - de - ra es   la   ban - de - ra Puer - to - ri - que - ña!
What a beau - ti - ful   ban - ner is   the   flag of our Puer - to   Ri - co!

294

Fun with Rhythm

"*¡Qué bonita bandera!*" features a lively Puerto Rican rhythm typical of the islands of the Caribbean. The underlying eighth notes in this piece are grouped as 3 + 3 + 2, instead of the usual 4 + 4. Pay special attention to the accents as you **perform** these patterns.

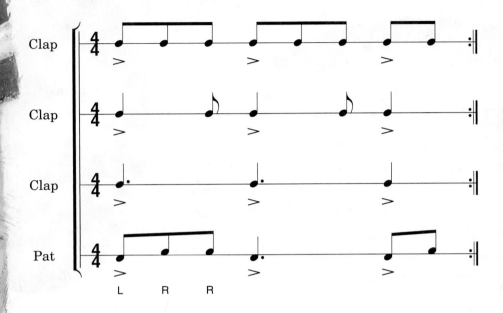

Perform this rhythm with the refrain of "*¡Qué bonita bandera!*"

Play these 3 + 3 + 2 rhythms on either guitar or keyboard.

A typical rhythm played by Latin American claves starts with this 3 + 3 + 2 pattern. **Play** this rhythm pattern on claves with the recording of "*¡Qué bonita bandera!*"

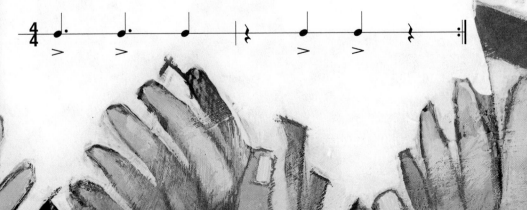

Fiery Footwork

The flamenco dance is one of Spain's best-known cultural traditions. Clapping is an important element. **Listen** to this exciting flamenco performance of *Río de la miel*. Do you hear the overlapping rhythms of the clapping hands and stomping feet?

M·U·S·I·C M·A·K·E·R·S

Francisco Sánchez Gómez

Francisco Sánchez Gómez (born 1947), better known as Paco de Lucía, is considered to be one of the greatest living flamenco guitarists. Introduced by his father to the flamenco guitar style, he showed an early understanding of the music. Gómez began to play professionally at the age of thirteen. By the beginning of the 1970s, he was known the world over. In 1975 he gave a famous concert at the Royal Theater in Madrid.

CD 13–25
Río de la miel

written and performed by Francisco Sánchez Gómez

Río de la miel (River of Honey) has earthy, exciting rhythms that accompany the dancers' rapid heel-tapping footwork and complicated clapping rhythms.

▲ Originating in the Andalucian region of Spain, *flamenco* refers as much to music as to dance. In addition to native Spanish elements, it has its roots in the Gypsy and Arabic cultures that influenced Spain over the centuries.

A Different Rhythm

This lively dance song from Cairo, Egypt, includes a simple clapping pattern performed at face level.

Sing *"Ah ya Zane."*

CD 13–26

Ah ya Zane
(Zane from Abedeen)

English Words by Harovnel-Dabh

Arabic Folk Song

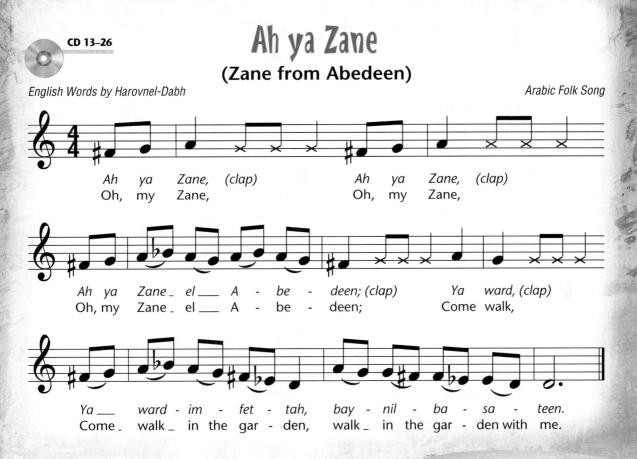

Ah   ya   Zane,   (clap)   Ah   ya   Zane,   (clap)
Oh,   my   Zane,   Oh,   my   Zane,

Ah   ya   Zane _ el ___ A - be - deen; (clap)   Ya   ward, (clap)
Oh,   my   Zane _ el ___ A - be - deen;   Come   walk,

Ya ___ ward - im - fet - tah,   bay - nil - ba - sa - teen.
Come _ walk _ in the gar - den,   walk _ in the gar - den with me.

The Arabic *doumbek* part in *"Ah ya Zane"* is named *baladi*. **Play** this drum part to accompany the song.

High
Low

The *doumbek* (also spelled *dumbek*) can be heard in the recording of *"Ah ya Zane."* The instrument gets its name from the low tone ("doum") in the center of the drum and the high sharp tone ("bek" or "tek") played on the edge of the drum. ▶

Element: MELODY | **Skill: SINGING** | **Connection: RELATED ARTS**

Dancing in Friendship

In 1998, in anticipation of the fiftieth anniversary of the birth of Israel, the well-known song "*Tzena, tzena*" was remade to promote peace in the Middle East by changing the English verse and adding verses in both Hebrew and Arabic.

Sing "*Tzena, tzena*" in English. Then learn both the Hebrew and the Arabic verses.

CD 13–30
MIDI 21

TZENA, TZENA

Hebrew Words by Yehlel Haggiz
Arabic Words by Salman Natour

English Words by Gordon Jenkins
(with one line altered by Pete Seeger)

Music by Issachar Miron

Hebrew: Tze - na, tze - na, tze - na, tze - na, ha - ba - not ur - e - na cha - ve -
Arabic: Zei - na, zei - na, zei - na, zei - na, ma - had yuw - kaf bei - ni w'be - na
English: Tze - na, tze - na, tze - na, tze - na, can't you hear the mu - sic play - ing

rim _____ ba - im la - ir. Al - na, al - na,
b'lel _____ let t'wa - ad na. Yal - la ma'a - na
in _____ the cit - y square? Tze - na, tze - na,

al - na, al - na, al - na, teet - cha - be - na u - miz - mor
ma'a - na yal - la nyd - buk deb - ka nur - kus ho - ra ma -
tze - na, tze - na, come where all our friends will find us with

Two Cultures Shake Hands . . .

The *hora* and the *debky* are dances that come from people who live in the Middle East. The steps are quite similar, but there are some interesting differences in style.

Listen to "*Tzena, tzena*" and dance the *hora*.

How to Dance the Hora

The *hora* came to Israel in the early twentieth century when the land was called Palestine. The word *hora* means "circle dance"; the traditional *hora* moves to the left (clockwise). The steps are high and joyous, with leaps and kicks.

1. Step left.
2. Step right (in front or in back of left foot).
3. Step left.

4. Lift right foot and swing it slightly to the left.
5. Step right.
6. Repeat step 4. Then repeat steps 1–6.

. . . and Dance

The *debky,* which means "line dance," is one of the most common dances of the Arabic people.

Listen to *Ala Da'lona,* form a line, join hands, and dance!

CD 14–1
Ala Da'lona

Arabic Folk Song

This recording also features the *oud* [ood], a string instrument that has been used in the Middle East for more than 1,000 years.

How to Dance the Debky

The *debky* is often performed in short lines. Hands are generally joined down at the side, with dancers moving shoulder to shoulder in a tight formation to the right. The *debky* steps are up-and-down, with stamps and knee movements.

1. Step right.

2. Step left (in front or in back of right foot).

3. Step right.

4. Step right foot (in place) and stamp left foot (next to right).

5. Step left.

6. Repeat step 4.
   Then repeat steps 1–6.

Singing Stories

The legends of many cultures are often about heroes, ways of learning how to live, or a moment of history. When stories are set to song, they become more powerful and more memorable.

The "Haliwa-Saponi Canoe Song" is a dance song about traveling in a canoe. The song uses **vocables** instead of words. Vocables have no specific meaning, but among the Haliwa-Saponi, the meaning of this song is clear. It is about teaching the young the importance of canoeing and how this ties into the history of their people.

> **Vocables** are sung or spoken syllables that do not have a specific meaning.

CD 14–3

Haliwa-Saponi Canoe Song

Native American Song of the Haliwa Saponi
Transcribed by J. Bryan Burton

Drums
(continue throughout)

We ya we we ya we we ya we,

Ya we __ ya o - we; Ya we ya we we ya we we ya we,

Fine
Ya we __ ya o - we. Ya we ha ya we ha yo - we;

Ya we __ ya o - we. Ya we ha ya we ha yo - we;

1.
Ya we __ ya o - we. Ya

2.
D.S. al Fine
we __ ya o - we.

Listen to this performance of *Haliwa-Saponi Canoe Song* as you follow the music. Find the lowest and highest notes. Is the range of the music narrow or wide?

CD 14–5
Haliwa-Saponi Canoe Song

Native American Song of the Haliwa-Saponi as performed by the Haliwa-Saponi Singers

This recording features Native American drums and bells.

M·U·S·I·C M·A·K·E·R·S
Haliwa-Saponi Singers

The Haliwa-Saponi Singers are a group of Native Americans from the Saponi people. The Haliwa portion of their name comes from the place in which they live—Halifax and Warren Counties of North Carolina. The Haliwa-Saponi hold a big pow-wow every year in April. A pow-wow is a celebration with music, dancing, and food—something like a family reunion.

Ballads

Venezuela is a beautiful country with dramatic scenic contrasts: the snowcapped Andes in the west, the Amazonian jungles in the south, the Gran Sabana plateau with its flat-topped mountains in the east, and white-sand beaches along the Caribbean coast. This is a perfect setting for singing and telling stories.

Stories are a way of passing on our values—what we believe. When stories are set to song, they are called ballads.

Sing *"El carite,"* a ballad that describes a very successful fishing expedition.

Choose one of the parts below to **perform** a Latin rhythm with *"El carite."*

El carite
(The Kingfish)

Folk Song from Venezuela
Arranged by Jerry Silverman

VERSE

A - yer sa - lió la lan - cha Nue - va Es - par - ta.
The Nue - va Es - par - ta set sail yes - ter - day, ___

Sa - lió con - fia - da a re - co - rrer los ma - res.
Set out so brave - ly to sail a - cross the o - cean.

En - con - tró un pez de fuer - zas muy li - je - ro.
It met a fish that was so ver - y trick - y.

Que a - ga - rra los an - zue - los y re - vien - ta los gua - ra - les.
It grap - pled with our fish - hooks and it smashed up our fish box - es.

REFRAIN

Co - mo la cos - ta es bo - ni - ta, Yo me ven - go di - vir - tien - do;
Oh, the coast - line is so pret - ty, As I sailed __ a - long for pleas - ure;

Pe - ro ___ me vie - ne si - guien - do de fue - ra u - na pi - ra - gui - ta.
But I saw ap - proach - ing swift - ly a ca - noe off in the dis - tance.

Music Around the World

Another Singing Tale

Colombia is located in northwestern South America. It is bordered by Ecuador and Peru on the south, Brazil and Venezuela on the east, and Panama on the northwest.

With its snowcapped peaks (in the Andes mountains) and tropical regions, Colombia is another perfect setting for story-telling. **Sing** the Colombian song "*Se va el caimán*," which tells a wonderful, exaggerated story. As you sing, notice the many repeated patterns. How many different patterns can you **identify**?

CD 14–10
MIDI 22

Se va el caimán
(The Alligator)

English Words by Aura Kontra　　　　　　　　　*Dance Song from Colombia*

VERSE

1. Voy a em-pe-zar mi re-la - to ___ con a - le-grí-a y con a-fán. ___
2. Lo que co-me es-te cai-mán _____ yo le ten-go ad-mi - ra-ción, ___
1. Let me tell a sil-ly sto - ry ___ on a light and hap-py note, ___
2. What this ga-tor has for din - ner ___ is a won-der to be-hold, ___

Voy a em-pe-zar mi re-la - to ___ con a - le-grí-a y con a-fán, ___
Lo que co-me es-te cai-mán _____ yo le ten-go ad-mi - ra-ción, ___
Let me tell a sil-ly sto - ry ___ on a light and hap-py note. ___
What this ga-tor has for din - ner ___ is a won-der to be-hold, ___

Por el rí - o Mag-da - le - na ___ se vol-vió un hom-bre cai - mán, ___
Co-me que-so y co-me pan _____ con re-fre - scos de li - món, ___
On the riv-er Mag-da - le-na, ___ a ga-tor likes to float, ___
There is cheese and there is bread _____ and lem - on-ade served cold. ___

Por el rí - o Mag-da - le - na ___ se vol-vió un hom-bre cai - mán.
Co-me que-so y co-me pan _____ con re-fre - scos de li - món.
On the riv - er Mag-da - le-na, ___ a ga - tor likes to float.
There is cheese and there is bread _____ and lem - on-ade served cold.

306

REFRAIN

C   G   G₇ 3   C

Se va el cai - mán, se va el cai - mán,   *Se   va pa - ra Ba - rran - qui - lla,*
Oh, there he   goes, oh, there he   goes;   He's   leav-ing for Ba-ran - qui - lla;

C   G   1.   G₇ 3   C

Se va el cai - mán, se va el cai - mán,   *Se   va pa - ra Ba - rran - qui - lla.*
Oh, there he   goes, oh, there he   goes;   He's   leav-ing for Ba-rran - qui - lla.

2.   G₇ 3   C   to verses 2 and 3 | last time   3   C

va pa - ra Ba - rran - qui - lla.   *va   pa - ra Ba - rran - qui - lla.*
leav-ing for Ba-rran - qui - lla.   leav-ing for Ba-rran - qui - lla.

3. *Al otro lado del río*
   pescaron una mojarra, (2 times)
   Y del buche le sacaron
   él que toca la guitarra. (2 times)
   Refrain

3. On the far side of the river,
   fishermen reeled in a perch, *(2 times)*
   It had swallowed the guitarist,
   now they've called off the search. *(2 times)*
   Refrain

MIDI Create new rhythm patterns and add them to the "*Se va el caimán*" song file.

Singing GAMES

All over the world, both children and adults love to pass the time playing musical games. These singing games often include moving or dancing, passing something, complicated clapping patterns, or just singing the right thing at the right time. How many games can you remember that include music?

Sing "*Bantama kra kro,*" a game song from Ghana about delicious pastries made in the town of Bantama.

CD 14–14

Bantama kra kro

English Words by George Nkwame

Song from the Akan People of Ghana

Call
Ban - ta - ma kra kro,   meh yeh den na m'an - ya bi ma - dzi
Ban - ta - ma's the town where all the most de - li - cious pas - tries are,

Call
Kra kro __ deh deh iyi, meh yeh den na m'an - ya bi ma - dzi
Sweet treats __ to try and buy, it real - ly is - n't ve - ry far;

Call
Kra kro __ kra kro,   meh yeh den na m'an - ya bi ma - dzi
If I've __ no mon - ey for the sweets a - top the pas - try cart,

Call
me nyi __ si - ka meh yeh den na m'an - ya bi ma - dzi.
How can __ I buy that de - li - cious look - ing hon - ey tart?

Playing Games

In Ghana, West Africa, as in other parts of the world, stone-passing games are common. People sit in a circle and pass smooth stones in rhythm while they sing.

Play the stone-passing game for *"Bantama kra kro"* by forming a circle and following this simple plan.

Tap, tap—Hold stone in right hand and tap it on the ground in front of you.

Pass—Right hand passes stone to right in front of the next person, and drops the stone on word *pass.*

Grab—On the word *grab,* right hand grabs the stone the person to left has passed you.

Follow the rhythm pattern below and play this game while you **sing** *"Bantama kra kro."* As the game proceeds, gradually speed up the tempo.

Fiddle RELATIVES

Musical instruments have relatives around the world. A common relative of the violin is the spike fiddle. Spike fiddles are played with a bow, in a vertical position.

▲ Spike fiddles are made of a stick or pole and a resonator box, with one or more strings. This example is a *rebab* from Java.

Listen to the sound of the Chinese *erhu*.

▲ The *erhu* is played in a vertical position. There are two strings with the bow hair inserted between them.

CD 14–19

Picking Red Chestnuts

Traditional Folk Music from China as performed by Lei Qiang

The *erhu* is thought to be at least 1,000 years old.

A New Sound

The entire European violin family (violin, viola, cello, string bass) is related to the spike fiddle. Their four strings are stretched over hollow, rounded bodies of different shapes. They are usually bowed, but can be plucked and struck in various ways to make interesting sounds.

Read about the Turtle Island String Quartet. Then **listen** to the group's cellist perform *Julie-O.* **Describe** the sounds of the cello. How do you think the performer produces them?

CD 14–20

Julie-O

written and performed by Mark Summer, cellist, the Turtle Island String Quartet

The Turtle Island String Quartet took its name from creation stories found in Native American folklore.

The Turtle Island String Quartet

The Turtle Island String Quartet is a traditional type of chamber music group with a very different sound. The members play the traditional string quartet instruments (violin, viola, and cello), but arrange and perform music in a wide variety of styles. These include folk, bluegrass, jazz, Indian music, funk, New Age, hip-hop, and Latin music, in addition to the usual classical string repertoire. The musicians even improvise while playing classical music, bringing back a practice that is over 200 years old.

Music Around the World

The Fiddle Goes Digital

The new digital Zeta MIDI violin is capable of sounding like any instrument—an organ, a brass instrument, a drum, or an electric guitar.

The MIDI violin does this by using digital sounds stored in a synthesizer. Because the resonator box is no longer important (as in the solid-body electric guitar), the shape of the body of the MIDI violin can be very different from that of a regular violin.

Listen to Susie Hansen play the Zeta MIDI violin. How can you tell that this is not a regular acoustic violin?

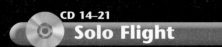

CD 14–21
Solo Flight

written and performed by Susie Hansen

Susie Hansen is a rising star in the field of Latin jazz. This selection also features Mark Gutierrez on piano.

Rodeo Strings

Listen to *Hoedown* from Aaron Copland's ballet *Rodeo*. The listening map on page 313 shows how the composer combined string instruments with other sections of the orchestra.

CD 14–22
Hoedown

from *Rodeo*
by Aaron Copland
as performed by the London Symphony Orchestra

Copland based the music for *Hoedown* on a square dance tune. At the time this music was written (1942), it was unusual for a composer to make violins in an orchestra sound like country fiddles.

Midi violins ▼

Hoedown
LISTENING MAP

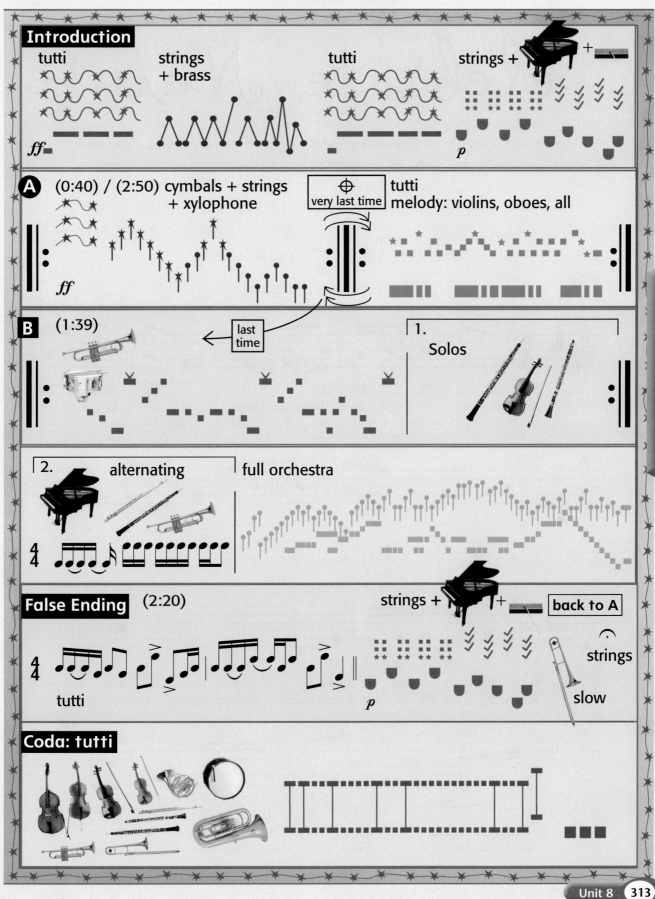

Introduction

tutti strings + brass tutti strings + +

ff p

A (0:40) / (2:50) cymbals + strings + xylophone   very last time tutti melody: violins, oboes, all

ff

B (1:39) last time 1. Solos

2. alternating full orchestra

False Ending (2:20) strings + + back to A

tutti p strings slow

Coda: tutti

Celebrate Nature

Songs and paintings that celebrate nature are common throughout the world. In China the image of the moon in its different phases has been the source of much musical inspiration. **Sing** "Yüe liang wan wan," a song that symbolizes new hope for a better life. How many different notes are used in the melody?

CD 14–23

Yüe liang wan wan
(Crescent Moon)

English Words by Elaine Nienow

Folk Song from China

跑 马 溜 溜 的 山___ 上 一 朵 溜 溜 的
Pao ma liu liu di shan___ shang yi duo liu liu di
Cres - cent moon float-ing on a cloud O'er the crest of the

云 哟 端 端 溜 溜 的 照___ 在
yün yo Duan duan liu liu dee zhao___ zai
moun - tain. Sil - ver gem in a sat - in crown,

康 定 溜___ 溜 的 城 哟 月 亮 弯___
Kang ding liu - liu di cheng yo. Yüe liang wan___
Rest - ing on the roy - al moun-tain. Pale moon, new moon,

弯___ 康 定 溜 溜 的 城 哟
wan___ Kang ding liu - liu di cheng yo.
cres - cent moon___ Shin - ing bright-ly o - ver K'an - ting.

"Crescent Moon" Ostinato

Play this pattern on a mallet instrument to accompany *"Yüe liang wan wan."*

(last measure)

Choose two or more of the following notes and **improvise** your own part to play with the song.

𝒜rts Connection

▲ Chinese ink painting of a panda by Wu Zhoren.
Paintings made of or depicting bamboo are common throughout East and Southeast Asia, because bamboo is so abundant in this part of the world. Painters work for many hours to produce just the right brush strokes in a painting of a bamboo plant.

Flowers of the Moon

This folk song, originally from southern China, is about a girl who compares herself to jasmine flowers. **Listen** to the lyrics to discover what the young girl is asking for.

CD 14–27

Jasmine Flowers

Words by Rebecca Schwan

Folk Song from Taiwan

1. White jas-mine flow-ers of the Sixth Moon are fair,
2. White jas-mine flow-ers of the Sixth Moon are fair,
3. White jas-mine flow-ers of the Sixth Moon are fair,

And there's a young lad who's no-ble and fine.
Love-ly _____ lass _____ has nev-er been found.
Lass-es a-lone _____ are sor-ry and sad.

Love-ly flow-ers rare-ly ev-er grow _ all a-lone;
Flowers and lass-es should nev-er be _____ a-lone;
Love-ly flow-ers should be bloom-ing side _____ by _____ side.

Fair lone-ly lass can _ be _____ sad, _____ so _____ sad.
Sad is the love-ly _____ lass who's nev-er, _ nev-er _____ found.
When will the lass be _ found and nev-er _ be a-lone?

Play the following parts on glockenspiel or resonator bells, finger cymbals, and woodblock to accompany "Jasmine Flowers."

Play 3 times

*Play once
Entire pattern
repeats*

316

Spring Flowers

This folk song from Taiwan celebrates the beauty of nature. **Listen** to the notes used in this song and compare the melody to that of "Jasmine Flowers."

CD 14–29

Lahk gei mohlee

Words by Hsy Ping-Ting
Transliterated by Han Kuo-Huang

Folk Song from Taiwan

六　　月　　茉　　莉　　真　　正　　美
Lahk　gei ___　moh　lee ___　jeen　jeeahn __　shwee,

郎　　君　　生　　著　你　都　真　　古　　椎
long　goon ___　sheen　jway　lee　go　jeen ___　go　jwee.

好　　花　　難　　得　　成　　雙　　對
Hoh　hway　lahn ___　dee ___　sheen __　shiong __　dwee,

身　邊　哪　沒　娘　啊　你　都　上　　刻　　虧
sheen　bean　nah　moh　new ah　lee - goh　shiong ___　keh ___　kwee.

MUSIC AND THEATER

Theater is a way of presenting a story. The combination of music and theater can have a powerful effect. There are many types of musical theater throughout the world, such as opera, Broadway musicals, Kabuki, and Indonesian shadow puppet theater. Can you think of others?

Sing *"Cho'i hát bội,"* a Vietnamese song about a theater game.

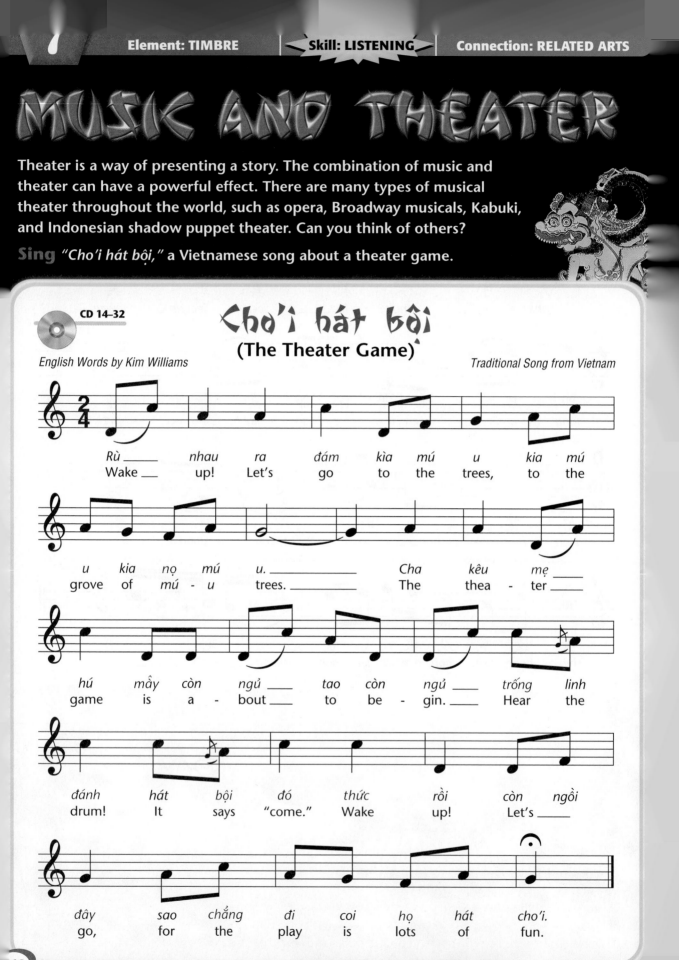

CD 14–32

Cho'i hát bội
(The Theater Game)

English Words by Kim Williams

Traditional Song from Vietnam

Rù _____ nhau ra đám kìa mú u kia mú
Wake _____ up! Let's go to the trees, to the

u kia nọ mú u. _____ Cha kêu mẹ _____
grove of mú - u trees. _____ The thea - ter _____

hú mấy còn ngủ _____ tao còn ngủ _____ trống linh
game is a - bout _____ to be - gin. _____ Hear the

đánh hát bội đó thức rồi còn ngồi
drum! It says "come." Wake up! Let's _____

đây, sao chẳng đi coi họ hát cho'i.
go, for the play is lots of fun.

◯Arts Connection

A *wayang kulit,* or shadow puppet, performance on the Indonesian island of Java usually takes place in the evening, out of doors, and may last all night long. The puppets are made of brightly painted leather and are held up with sticks against a white screen. ▶

A Gamelan

The music of *wayang kulit* is provided by a gamelan, a small orchestra of gongs, xylophones, metallophones, drums, flutes, zithers, and a *rebab.*

Listen to the Javanese gamelan piece *Patalon.*

CD 14–36
Patalon

**Traditional Song From Indonesia
as performed by the Hardo Budoyo Ensemble of Central Java**

In a shadow puppet performance the gamelan sits behind the white screen and is not normally seen. The puppeteer not only works the puppets, but also sings and speaks the roles.

Musical Feelings

Music expresses what words cannot. People of all countries and cultures around the world use music in many different ways.

In India, music is sometimes used as an accompaniment to meditation or devotional activities.

Listen to "*Ragupati Ragava Raja Ram*," a Hindu song that is well known in India.

M·U·S·I·C M·A·K·E·R·S

Ravi Shankar

Ravi Shankar (born 1920) is considered one of the world's greatest sitar players. He rocketed to international stardom during the 1960s when George Harrison of the Beatles helped to popularize the sitar in the West. Shankar performs traditional Indian classical music and has experimented with using the sitar in other styles of music.

Listen to Ravi Shankar's performance of *Sindhi-Bhairavi*. How would you **describe** the sound of the sitar?

CD 15–1
Sindhi-Bhairavi

**Traditional Raga from India
as performed by Ravi Shankar**

The sitar is associated with the sound of India, and used mainly for playing classical Indian music.

Ragupati Ragava Raja Ram

CD 15–2

Traditional Hindu Song

Traditional Melody

REFRAIN

Ra - gu - pa - ti   ra - ga - va   ra - ja ____ Ram ____

Pa - ti - ta   pa - va - na   Si - ta ____ Ram.

VERSE

1. Si - ta   Ram   jai   Si - ta ____ Ram,
2. Ish - ware   Al - lah   te - re ____ nam,

Pa - ti - ta   pa - va - na   Si - ta ____ Ram.
Sub - be - ko   sun - mut - ti   de   bha - ga - wan.

Dance of Joy

"*La Jesusita*" is a Mexican song that describes a courtship.
The first phrase in the lyrics is an invitation to dance.
Enjoy the *mariachi* style of the recording as you sing.

CD 15–5
MIDI 23

La Jesusita

English Words by Aura Kontra

Folk Song from Mexico

VERSE

G   D₇

Va - mos al bai - le y ve - rás que bo - ni - to _____
Will you go danc - ing with me, how de - light - ful, _____

D₇   G

_____ Don - de se a - lum - bran con vein - te lin - ter - nas. ____
_____ Where twink - ling lights fill the air with their bright - ness. ___

G   D₇

_____ Don - de se bai - lan las dan - zas mo - der - nas, ____
_____ Where those who go know the steps to the mu - sic, ____

D₇   G   Fine

_____ Don - de se bai - la de mu - cho va - ci - lón. _____
_____ Let's join our friends as they dance the night a - way. _____

Y quié-re-me, Je - su - si - ta, Y quié-re-me, por fa - vor;
Be true to me Je - su - si - ta, be true to me if you please

Y mi - ra que soy tu a - man - te y se - gu - ro ser - vi - dor.
Re - mem-ber how much I love you, my heart you must nev - er tease.

Strumming Strings

Throughout Latin America, songs of friendship and love are frequently accompanied by the sound of lightly strummed string instruments. One such guitar-like instrument is the *vihuela* from Mexico.

Listen to the sound of the *vihuela* in *"La Jesusita."*

"La Jesusita" uses just two different chords: G and D⁷. (The photos below show how these chords are played on guitar.) Follow the music and **create** your own guitar strumming pattern to accompany *"La Jesusita."*

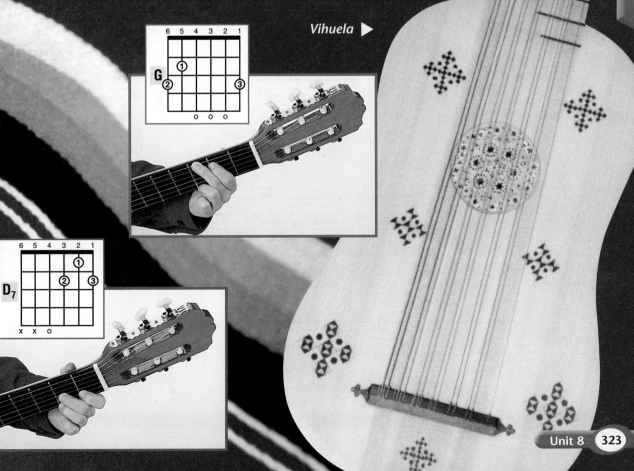

Vihuela ▶

Family and Friends

Sing "Love Is on Our Side," a popular song about family and friends. What feeling do you get from the rhythm of the music? What meaning do you get from the lyrics?

CD 15–9

Love Is on Our Side

Words and Music by Tish Hinojosa

1. Show me some-one helping out a friend. Show me a bro-ken man standing up a-gain. Show me a smile in an-cient eyes. I'll say love is on our side.

2. See the lit-tle ba-by in her moth-er's arms. Dad-dy wants a shel-ter keep-ing her from harm. When the storm gets clos-er, we re-al-ize that love is on our side.

We're ___ all ___ on that ___ train, _____

D. C. (verse 2) al Coda

There's ___ where ___ hope be - gins. ____

Coda

side, _____ That ___ love _____

_____ is on ____ our side.

Mexican family making a *piñata* ▼

Love for the Homeland

Have you ever thought about what it would be like if you left your home and moved away to a distant country?

What would you miss about the United States if you moved to a different country? What would you miss about your state?

Listen to *"Canción Mixteca,"* a song about leaving Mexico and feeling homesick.

As you **listen**, find where the voices sing in two-part harmony.

CD 15–11

Canción Mixteca
(Mixteca Song)

English Words by Don Kalbach

Words and Music by José López Alavés

¡Que le - jos es - toy del sue - lo don - de he na - ci - do! ___
I've come ver - y far, so far from my na - tive home - land! _

In - men - sa nos - tal - gia in - va - de mi
And my heav - y heart re - mem - bers how

pen - sa - mien - to. _____
much I love you. _____

Y al ver - me tan so - lo y
I'm sad and a - lone, I'm

tris - te cual ho - ja al vien - to,
just like a leaf that's blow - ing,

qui - sie - ra llo -
And I want to

Sing of Mexico

Sing "*Canción Mixteca*" in harmony. First, **sing** the melody. Then sing the harmony, which begins on line *3* of the song. Finally, divide into two groups and **sing** both parts together.

Popular Music Sweeps the Nation

New styles of popular music began to sweep across the country in the twentieth century. Music played an important role in expressing society's happenings, hopes, dreams, and feelings. Almost every style of music had a dance to go with it— from the cakewalk to the jitterbug to rock 'n' roll.

75c. in U. S. A.

Livery Stable

Comp

Original

In the
Pop
Style

There was a song about everything and for everyone. Society was changing and so was its music. Music makes history, and the history of each era is told through songs.

Music for Dancing

Roll up the rug and get ready to dance! After Chubby Checker created "The Twist" in the 1960s, lots of new dance crazes swept the country. "Land of a Thousand Dances" mentions many of those dances, such as "the mashed potato."

Sing this flashback favorite with its popular "na-na" chorus.

CD 15–16

Land of a Thousand Dances

Words and Music by Chris Kenner and Antoine "Fats" Domino

1. You got-ta know how to po - ny _____ like
2. Dance with me hon - ey _____ like

Bo - ny Ma-ro - nie,   Mashed po - ta - ta _____   Do _____
Long _ Tall Sal - ly,   Twistin' with Lu - cy, _____   Do _____

_____ the al - li - ga - ta,   Put your hands on your hips, yeah,
_____ the wa - tu - si,   Put your hands on your hips, yeah,

Let your back-bone slip,   Do the wa-tu - si _____
Let your back-bone slip,   Do _ the jerk, _____

like _ my _ lit-tle Lu - cy.
watch _____ me work. _____

330

Element: **RHYTHM** | Skill: **LISTENING** | Connection: **STYLE**

RAGTIME AND THE NEW CENTURY

At the turn of the twentieth century, there were no radios and no CDs. Most musicmaking took the form of singing or playing the piano. Many people also played piano rolls at home when they wanted to listen to music.

The musical rage at the time was **ragtime**, a style created or composed mostly for the piano.

Ragtime is a form of jazz popular from about 1890 until World War I. With their steady beat in the left hand and syncopated melodies in the right hand, piano rags influenced much of the popular music that followed.

▲ Player piano, above. Piano rolls, top left.

Ragtime Piano

Listen to *Cotton Boll Rag*. As you listen, find the symbol in the listening map that shows the steady beat in the left hand. Next, follow the symbols that represent the melody played by the pianist's right hand.

Charles Hunter (1876 - 1906), almost totally blind from birth, learned piano tuning at a school for the blind.

CD 15–18

Cotton Boll Rag

by Charles Hunter

Cotton Boll Rag was published in 1901—two years after Scott Joplin's first big sheet music hit, *Maple Leaf Rag.*

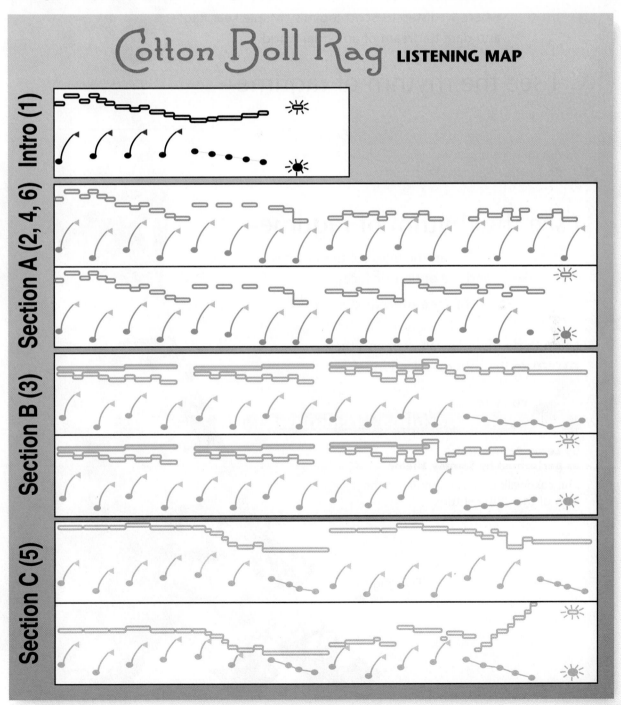

In the Pop Style

Ragtime

by Toyomi Igus

I see the rhythm of ragtime.

In our fine top hats and gowns,
we celebrate our newfound freedom
at ballroom dances and festive jubilees
where we listen to Scott Joplin's "Maple Leaf Rag"
and dare to dream of an equal world.

I see the rhythm of ragtime–

the music of the cakewalk,
the happy, high–steppin' dance of former slaves,
mimicking the high–steppin' dances of their masters,
now danced by everyone.

I see the rhythm of ragtime–

in the fine, cultured places
and the optimistic faces

of free men and women.

Learn to do the cakewalk step and then
move to this musical selection.

CD 15–19

North Carolina Breakdown

by Leroy Arthur Smith
as performed by Sammy Shelor

The cakewalk became popular at the
turn of the 20th century.

Dancing the
cakewalk ▶

During the 1920s through 1940s, the legendary Cotton Club, in Harlem, New York City, showcased many jazz greats who started their careers playing ragtime.

MUSIC MAKERS

SCOTT JOPLIN

Scott Joplin (1868–1917) was one of the greatest ragtime composers. He was born into a musical family and learned to play the guitar and cornet as a young boy. Later he taught himself to play his neighbor's piano. Joplin left home at age eleven to pursue a career as an entertainer. He published his first and most popular rag, "Maple Leaf Rag," in 1899. ("Maple Leaf" was the name of the Club where Joplin played the piano.) Joplin also wrote a ballet and two operas, but he is best known for his piano rags.

CD 15–21

Scott Joplin's New Rag

by Scott Joplin

This rag was written in 1912, the same year the *Titanic* made its fateful voyage.

Listen to one of Joplin's later pieces, *Scott Joplin's New Rag*. Why do you think most rags were written for the piano?

In the Pop Style

SWING with the BIG BANDS

In 1931, big bands began sweeping the country. The style of music these big bands played became known as "swing." Many of these bands featured a singer or an instrumentalist as a soloist. These soloists were known as "sidemen."

Sing "It Don't Mean a Thing (If It Ain't Got That Swing)," which was popular during the swing era.

Tune In

A typical big band of the 1930s featured saxophones, trumpets, trombones, piano, guitars, and drums.

CD 15–23

It Don't Mean A THING
(If It Ain't Got That Swing)

Words by Irving Mills

Music by Duke Ellington

It makes no dif-f'rence if ___ it's sweet or hot. ___

Just give that rhy-thm ev - 'ry - thing you got,

Call

Oh, _ it don't mean a thing, _ if it ain't got that swing, _

Response

Doo wah, _ doo wah, doo wah, doo wah, doo wah, _ doo wah, doo wah, doo wah.

Reprinted with permission of the publisher, Children's Book Press, San Francisco, CA. Art copyright © 1998 by Michele Wood

In the Pop Style

▲ Artist Michele Wood's illustration (from the book *i see the rhythm*) captures the rhythmic excitement of swing music in the 1930s.

Play that Swing

Using a keyboard or another instrument of your choice, learn to play the chords shown below. These are the chords used in the response part of "It Don't Mean a Thing," on pages 336–337.

Now, follow the chord symbols in the music and **improvise** rhythm patterns along with the recording, each time the response is sung.

Hear that Swing

Listen to a recording of *It Don't Mean a Thing (If It Ain't Got That Swing)* by one of the great jazz singers of the twentieth century.

CD 15–25

It Don't Mean a Thing If It Ain't Got That Swing

by Irving Mills and Duke Ellington as performed by Ella Fitzgerald

This Ellington song also appeared in the Broadway musicals *Bubbling Brown Sugar* and *Sophisticated Ladies.*

Duke Ellington (1899–1974) helped to popularize scat singing in 1926 while performing "Heebie Jeebies." He dropped his music and couldn't remember the words. Rather than stop singing, Ellington sang the melody, using nonsense words. Jazz singers have been scatting ever since. In 1928, Ellington organized his band and performed at the Cotton Club, a famous dance club in Harlem, New York City. Ellington's band was the most popular of all swing bands.

In the Pop Style

Scat Singing

During the 1930s, radio and phonograph records made it possible for swing to expand its boundaries from the dance hall to homes all across America.

Sing this popular swing song from that era. Can you **identify** a phrase in the song that duplicates the effect of scat singing?

CD 15–26

Sing, Sing, Sing!

Words and Music by Louis Prima

REFRAIN

Sing, sing, sing, sing, __ ev - 'ry-bod - y start to sing like __

dee dee dee, bah bah bah dah. Now __ you're sing - in'

1. with a __ swing. __ 2. Now __ you're sing-in' like ev-'ry - thing. __ *Fine*

VERSE *Call*

When the mu-sic goes a - round, __ *Response* ev - 'ry-bod-y's gon-na go to __ town. __

Call

But here is one thing you should __ know; __ *Response* sing __ it high and sing it __ low! Oh, __ *D.C. al Fine*

Sing and Swing

Scat singing can be used to express a variety of emotions and musical effects. In this example, **listen** to the wide range of dynamics and pitches performed by the soloist.

🔵 CD 15–28
How High the Moon

**by Nancy Hamilton and Morgan Lewis
as performed by Ella Fitzgerald**

In describing her scat singing skills, Ella Fitzgerald said, "I just tried to do what I heard the horns in the band doing."

M·U·S·I·C M·A·K·E·R·S
Ella Fitzgerald

Ella Fitzgerald (1917–1996) is considered one of the finest jazz singers of the 20th century. She had a special gift for singing in the "swing style." Her ability to swing eighth notes and her perfect timing for singing syncopated rhythms made her the envy of other performers. One of the best scat singers of her time, Fitzgerald was able to make her voice sound like an instrument.

Create your own scat singing. Experiment with a song you already know. Use your voice as an instrument and scat the song on nonsense syllables instead of the words. "This Train," on page 27, would be a good song for scat singing.

In the Pop Style

◀ Benny Goodman and his orchestra

▲ The Glenn Miller Orchestra

Trombonist and big band leader Tommy Dorsey ▶

And the Bands Played On

Not all of the big bands played swing or had a vocalist. Each band had a particular sound, depending on the instrumentation of the band.

Listen to *Pennsylvania 6-5000,* performed by the Glenn Miller Orchestra, as you follow the listening map on page 343. What instruments can you **identify**?

CD 16–1

Pennsylvania 6-5000

by Carl Sigman and Jerry Gray
as performed by the Glenn Miller Orchestra

The title of this selection is the phone number for Manhattan's Hotel Pennsylvania, located near Penn Station. This spot was a prime location in New York for big bands.

Pennsylvania 6-5000

Penn-syl-van-ia   six five thou-sand.

Penn-syl-van-ia six five   0 - 0 - 0. __

In the Pop Style

ON THE LONE PRAIRIE

Cowboys expanded our western boundaries as they drove cattle in search of grazing land. They sang songs while out on the range. These songs were the inspiration for many later country pop ballads.

Feel the meter in 3 as you **sing** "Cattle Call."

CD 16–3

CATTLE CALL

Words and Music by Tex Owens

VERSE

1. The cat - tle are prowl - in', the coy - otes are
2. For hours he would ride on the range far and

howl - in' way out where the do - gies bawl.
wide when the night winds blow up a squall.

Where spurs are a - jing - lin', the cow - boy is
His heart is a feath - er; In all kinds of

sing - in' ___ his lone - some cat - tle call.
weath-er ___ he sings his cat - tle call.

REFRAIN

Ooh, _ ooh, _ do - gie,

Ooh, _ ooh, _ doo doot doo doo doo doo

doo _ doo _ do - gie.

1. To next stanza 2. Fine

Oh, oh - dl - oh dee dee dee. dee.

In the Pop Style

He rides in the sun 'til his day's work is done, and he
rounds up the cat - tle each fall. Ooh, __ ooh, __
do - gie. Sing-in' his cat - tle call.

Playing Cowboy

Choose a mallet instrument or a keyboard and **play** the following part along with the refrain of "Cattle Call." How does this part stress the feel of meter in 3?

REFRAIN:
Lines 1 and 3 *(play 4 times)*

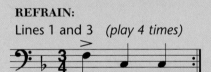

Line 2 *(play 4 times)*

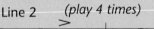

Line 4

A Shining Star

Just as some swing singers sing scat, some country and western singers **yodel**. **Listen** to this duet by country singers Eddy Arnold and LeAnn Rimes. What familiar vocal style can you **identify** in this version of *Cattle Call?*

Yodeling is rapid shifts between a lower full voice and a high voice type of singing called *falsetto.*

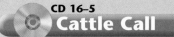

CD 16–5
Cattle Call

by Tex Owens
as performed by Eddy Arnold and LeAnn Rimes

LeAnn Rimes was a fan of Eddy Arnold. In time, the two became great friends.

M·U·S·I·C M·A·K·E·R·S

LeAnn Rimes

LeAnn Rimes (born 1982) is a shining star of country music. Her albums have soared to multiplatinum status. The album *You Light Up My Life: Inspirational Songs* made her one of the first country artists to achieve number one status on three of the Billboard charts (country, pop, and contemporary Christian). Rimes has received two Grammy awards and was the first country artist to be named Best New Artist. Since Rimes recorded her first album at age eleven, she has indeed become a shining star.

Tune In

Eddy Arnold was the first country music performer to add an orchestra and strings to his music. He was also the first country singer to appear at Carnegie Hall in New York City.

Home Sweet Home

In the seventeenth and eighteenth centuries, British settlers came to the New World. Many settled in the mountains of Appalachia. They brought with them their folk songs. Many of these songs tell of heartaches. Accompanied by fiddles and guitars, they became the root of country music.

The lyrics for the song "Rocky Top" are typical of country music. The singer has moved to the city but misses the old homestead in Rocky Top, Tennessee. As you **sing** the song, notice that the lyrics are sad but the music is upbeat.

Ozark folk art:
Wood carving
by Mike Kotz ▶

CD 16–6

Rocky Top

Words and Music by Boudleaux Bryant and Felice Bryant

VERSE

Wish that I was on ol' Rock-y Top, down in the Ten-nes-see hills;

Ain't no smog-gy smoke on Rock-y Top, Ain't no tel-e-phone bills.

Once I knew a girl on Rock-y Top, Half bear, oth-er half cat;

Wild as a mink, but sweet as so-da pop, I still dream a-bout that.

The country group **Alabama** was formed in 1973 in Myrtle Beach, South Carolina. The members of the group are songwriter/guitarist Randy Owen; his cousin, songwriter/bass player Teddy Gentry; their distant cousin songwriter/instrumentalist Jeff Cook; and drummer Mark Herndon. Throughout the group's career, Alabama has tried to present a good role model for young people, singing about the joys of loving relationships and family life. In 1998, Alabama got its own star on the Hollywood Walk of Fame.

My Country Home

From the cowboys to bluegrass to honky-tonk, country music has gone through many changes over a long period of time and is still being defined.

Listen to the popular country music group Alabama sing a song about their home.

CD 16–8
Tennessee River

**by Randy Owen
as performed by Alabama**

This song combines country-rock and honky-tonk styles.

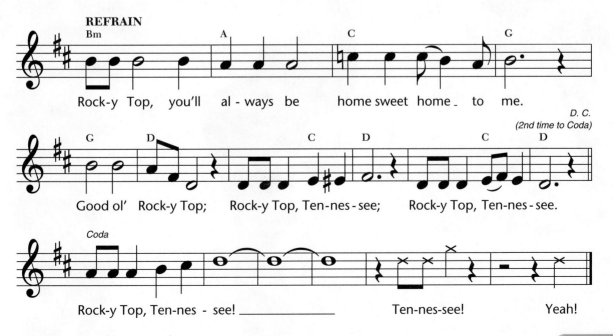

REFRAIN

Rock-y Top, you'll al-ways be home sweet home to me.

D. C.
(2nd time to Coda)

Good ol' Rock-y Top; Rock-y Top, Ten-nes-see; Rock-y Top, Ten-nes-see.

Coda

Rock-y Top, Ten-nes - see! _____ Ten-nes-see! Yeah!

In the Pop Style

"Rocky Top" Rhythms

Play these rhythm patterns to accompany "Rocky Top."

A Country Line Dance

Older generations "two-stepped" to songs like "Rocky Top." Line dances are popular today. **Perform** a line dance to *I Love a Rainy Night.*

CD 16–9

I Love a Rainy Night

by Eddie Rabbitt, Even Stevens, and David Malloy
as performed by Eddie Rabbitt

Country's Finest

The Grand Ole Opry in Nashville, Tennessee, is the home of country music. The Opry House provides a stage for performance, radio broadcasting, and recording studios. All of this helped popularize the country music style, and produced many recording stars. ▼

Hank Williams

Ernest Tubb

Patsy Cline

In the Pop Style

The Carter family, Jimmie Rodgers, Roy Acuff, Patsy Cline, and Hank Williams were some of the early country recording artists. Alan Jackson, Dolly Parton, Patty Loveless, Willie Nelson, George Strait, and Reba McEntire are just a few of the many performers who carry on the country music tradition today.

Singing THE BLUES

The ancestors of many African Americans came to America against their will. Life in America was hard. Denied their freedom, many slaves found an emotional escape through singing. Their songs were often sad, and they would **improvise** on the spot. This tradition eventually led to a musical style called the blues.

> **Improvise** means to make up the music while performing.

"St. Louis Blues" is a 12-bar blues song with three phrases, each phrase being four measures long. The lyrics of the first and second phrases are the same. The third phrase is different.

Read the words of "St. Louis Blues" before you **sing** the song.

Create lyrics for a 12-bar blues. Make your phrases rhyme.

CD 16–11

St. Louis Blues

Words and Music by W. C. Handy

Swing

1. I hate to see __ the ev-'nin' sun go down. _
2. Feel-in' to-mor-row, _ like _ I feel to-day. __

Hate to see __ the ev-'nin' sun go down. _
Feel to-mor-row, _ like _ I feel to-day. __

'Cause my ba-by, __ he done left this town. _
I'll pack my trunk, _ make my get-a-way. __

Blues Harmony

A blues harmony frequently has only three chords: I, IV, and V. Using a keyboard, **play** these chords in the key of F: F, B♭7, C.

Now practice this chord progression:

F — B♭7 — F — F

B♭ — B♭7 — F — F

C7 — B♭7 — F — F

Perform this progression as you **sing** "St. Louis Blues."

Using your blues lyrics, **create** a melody for a 12-bar blues.
Listen to the great blues artist Bessie Smith sing *St. Louis Blues.*

CD 16–13
St. Louis Blues

by W. C. Handy
as performed by Bessie Smith

It's been said that Smith's performance of *St. Louis Blues* expresses the essence of the blues.

MUSIC MAKERS
Bessie Smith

Bessie Smith (1894–1937) sang many kinds of music, from vaudeville to blues. In 1923, she was the first major blues and jazz singer to make widely-distributed recordings. She is famous for her passionate and powerful voice that overcame the primitive recording quality of that era. The older blues style lost its popularity by the end of the 1920s and Smith's career declined, but she kept on working. Near the time of her death, she was starting to explore swing music, but Bessie Smith will always be known as the "Empress of the Blues."

CD-ROM Use *Band in a Box* to create your own song in blues style.

UPBEAT BLUES

Not all blues songs are sad, a point proven by "Basin Street Blues." In what other ways is this song different from the "standard" blues song "St. Louis Blues"?

Listen for this syncopated rhythm as you **sing** this blues song.

CD 16–14

BASIN STREET BLUES

Words and Music by Spencer Williams

Swing
VERSE

Won't-cha come a-long with me, to the Mis-sis-sip-pi?

We'll take the boat _ to the land of dreams, _ Steam down the riv-er, down to

New Or-leans; _ The band's there to meet us, old friends to greet us,

We'll see the place the folks all meet, _ This is Ba-sin Street. _

Tune In

"Basin Street Blues" is about a special street in New Orleans, Louisiana, where blues can be heard almost 24 hours a day.

REFRAIN

Ba - sin Street _ is the street _ where the e - lite _

al - ways meet _ in New Or - leans, _ Land of dreams, _ you'll

nev - er know how nice it seems or just how much it real - ly means.

Glad to be, _ yes, sir - ee, _ where wel - come's free, _

Dear to me, _ Where I can lose _ My Ba - sin Street blues. _

Rock 'n' Roll 'n' Sing

The differences between rhythm-and-blues and country music faded during the mid-1950s. Elvis Presley, Chuck Berry, Bill Haley, Buddy Holly, Fats Domino, and many others blended blues elements with country-western music to create a unique style called "rock 'n' roll."

With his group, called the "Downhomers," Bill Haley played local amusement parks that featured live entertainment. Even then he wanted to combine country and pop music. When he left this group he formed a new band, "Bill Haley and the Comets"— the first rock 'n' roll band in history.

Listen to Bill Haley's *Rock Around the Clock*, one of the first rock 'n' roll hits of the 1950s.

▲ Bill Haley and the Comets

CD 16–16

Rock Around the Clock

by M. Friedman and J. DeKnight
as performed by Bill Haley and the Comets

Since its release in 1955, *Rock Around the Clock* has sold over 16 million copies.

Another group to popularize country and rock was Phil (born 1937) and Don (born 1939), better known as the Everly Brothers. Using two-part harmony, and elements of bluegrass country sounds and pop music, they became one of the most influential rock 'n' roll duos across the decades.

Listen to their first hit, *Bye Bye Love*.

CD 16–17

Bye Bye Love

**by Felice and Boudleaux Bryant
as performed by the Everly Brothers**

Bye Bye Love launched a three-year string of classic hit singles for this duo.

THE PLATTERS

The Platters were one of the most popular singing groups of the 1950s. The group consisted of four male singers and one female singer. Tony Williams was the lead tenor. Other members of the group were David Lynch, Herb Reed, Paul Robi, and Zola Taylor. The group performed mostly slow rock 'n' roll tunes. The Platters toured the world as "international ambassadors of musical goodwill," and appeared in several movies, including *Rock Around the Clock* and *The Girl Can't Help It*. They are remembered for their crisp, impeccable harmonies and their string-laden accompaniments.

Triplets in the Background

Softer, slower rock 'n' roll songs divide the beat in three, resulting in triplets.

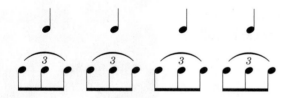

Listen to the Platters sing *The Great Pretender*. Tap the triplets as you listen.

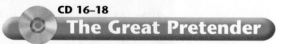

CD 16–18
The Great Pretender

by Buck Ram
as performed by the Platters

The Great Pretender was one of four number one singles from the Platters in the late 1950s.

American Bandstand

Dick Clark was neither a composer nor a performer, but was still very influential in the promotion of early rock 'n' roll. He was the host of *American Bandstand*, a TV show in Philadelphia that showcased local high school students dancing to popular hit records. Clark transformed the local show into a national phenomenon. He often interviewed recording artists on his show, which helped many of these young performers become stars. Clark was responsible for the popularity of Frankie Avalon, Bobby Rydell, Fabian, and Chubby Checker.

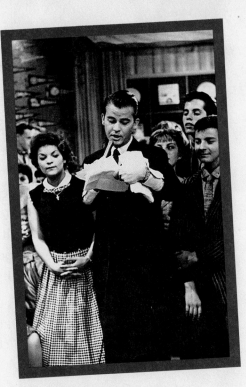

Move to a New Beat

Many new dance steps were introduced on *American Bandstand* — the Hucklebuck, the Pony, the Fly, and the Mashed Potato — but none became as popular as the Twist.

Learn to do the Twist, then **move** as you **listen** to Chubby Checker's performance.

Put one foot out and pretend you're crushing a bug with your big toe. At the same time, move your hands and body as though you're drying your back with a towel. Now, twist!

▲ Dick Clark from *American Bandstand*

CD 16–19
The Twist

**by Hank Ballard
as performed by Chubby Checker**

The Twist dance craze went international and inspired a whole series of new songs, such as "Twist and Shout," "Twistin'," and "Twist Polka."

▲ It's 1960 and Chubby Checker introduces a new dance craze — the Twist — at the Peppermint Lounge in Manhattan.

The Soul of the Music

Black gospel music crossed the boundaries of the church in the early 1960s to blend with rhythm and blues. The result was called *soul*. As in most styles of rock music, the backbeat is important in soul.

Martha Reeves and the Vandellas are the original soul artists who sang "Dancin' in the Street." **Sing** the song and clap to the backbeat rhythm.

Now **listen** to the original soul artists sing *Dancin' in the Street.*

CD 16–20

Dancin' in the Street

by Marvin Gaye, Ivy Hunter, and William Stevenson as performed by Martha Reeves and the Vandellas

The Vandellas were one of the favorite groups for dance music in the 1960s.

▼ Rosalind Ashford, Martha Reeves, and Annette Sterling

Tune In

"A song has to become a part of you. It's something in you that you'll have for the rest of your life."

Martha Reeves

Dancin' in the Street

CD 16–21

Words and Music by Marvin Gaye,
Ivy Hunter, and William Stevenson

Call - in' out ___ a - round ___ the world, _ are you

read - y for a brand new beat? ___ Sum-mer's here _ and the

time is right ___ for danc - in' in the street. _

___ They're danc - in' in Chi - ca - go, ___

down in New Or - leans, _ in New York _ Cit-

- y; All ___ we need _ is mu - sic, sweet _ mu -

- sic, There'll be mu - sic ev - 'ry - where. _ There'll be

In the Pop Style

The Queen of Soul

Soul music can express a performer's strong emotions. Some of the special musical techniques that singers use include repetition of short phrases; improvisation; loud, intense singing; and call-and-response form.

Listen to one of Aretha Franklin's soul classics. Which musical techniques listed above can you identify in this performance?

CD 16–23

Soulville

by T. Turner, M. Levy, R. Glover, and D. Washington
as performed by Aretha Franklin

Franklin recorded *Soulville* as part of a tribute to the great blues singer Dinah Washington.

M·U·S·I·C M·A·K·E·R·S

Aretha Franklin

Aretha Franklin (born 1942), known as the "Queen of Soul," is a member of the Rock and Roll Hall of Fame. She sang at the Inaugurations of Presidents Carter and Clinton, and also at the memorial service for Martin Luther King Jr. In 1999, VH1 named her one of the top 100 musicians of the twentieth century.

In the Pop Style

Friends Forever

Friends like to share important moments with each other. Feelings about friendship can be expressed through music or poetry.

..."And the song from beginning to end, I found again in the heart of a friend."

Henry Wadsworth Longfellow

▲ Willie Nelson and friends

MUSIC MAKERS

Carole King

Carole King (born 1942) is one of the most successful singers and songwriters in our country's history. She is noted for her ability to express her genuine emotions through her songs. King co-wrote songs recorded by artists such as the Beatles, Aretha Franklin, the Monkees, and several "girl groups" of the 1960s. In 1971, after several unsuccessful albums, she released her own solo album, *Tapestry.* It sold over 13 million copies and secured King's place in music history as an important singer and songwriter.

Listen to *You've Got a Friend* as performed by Carole King.

CD 17–1

You've Got a Friend

by Carole King
You've Got a Friend also became a top hit for singer James Taylor.

Crosby, Stills, and Nash ▲

364

◀ Neil Young

▲ Kris Kristofferson (left) performing at a Farm Aid Concert

Keepers
of the
Earth

Time spent with friends makes things around us special. Friends share in our joys and sorrows and stand by us when we need them the most. They are indeed the keepers of the earth.

▼ Willie Nelson (left) and Woody Harrelson

When You Need a Helping Hand

Some people express their feelings about friendship through music. **Sing** Carole King's song about friendship and think of someone you consider a friend.

CD 17–2

You've Got a Friend

Words and Music by Carole King

VERSE

When you're down __ and trou-bled, And you need __ some love and care, __
__ a-bove __ you grows __ dark __ and full of clouds, __

And noth-in' __ noth-in' is go-in' right, __
And that ol' __ north wind be-gins __ to blow, __

Close your eyes __ and think of me, and soon I __ will be there __ To
Keep your head __ to-geth-er, and call my __ name out loud; __

bright-en up __ e - ven your dark - est night. __
Soon you'll hear __ me __ knock-in' at __ your door. __

REFRAIN

You just call __ out my __ name, __ and you know __ wher-ev-er I am, __

I'll come run - nin' __ to see you a - gain. __

last time to Coda

Win-ter, spring, sum-mer or fall, __ All you have to do is call, __ and I'll be __

WATCH THE STARS

We miss our friends when they are far away, but we can stay in touch. We can share letters and phone calls. We can send them small gifts. Watching the sun and moon and stars reminds us that our friends are watching, too.

Listen to the song "Somewhere Out There."
Describe how the composers use words and melody expressively.

CD 17–4

Somewhere Out There
(from *An American Tail*)

Words and Music by James Horner, Barry Mann, and Cynthia Weil

Some-where _ out there be - neath the pale moon - light, _

some - one's think-in' of me and lov - ing me to - night. _

Some-where out ___ there _ some-one's say-ing _ a prayer ___ that

we'll find one an - oth-er ___ in that big some-where _ out _ there.

And e - ven though I know how ver - y far a - part _ we are, ___ it

Music of the Heart

Music can be comforting. In the movie *An American Tail*, two characters who are separated by a great distance sing this song as a duet. Through the song, they are united in their hearts. **Listen** to another version of *Somewhere Out There*.

CD 17–6

Somewhere Out There

**by James Horner, Barry Mann, and Cynthia Weil
as performed by James Galway**

Somewhere Out There was nominated for a Golden Globe award and won two Grammy awards in 1986.

helps to think we might be wish - in' on the same bright star. And

when the night wind starts to sing a lone - some lul - la - by, it

helps to think we're sleep-ing un - der - neath the same big sky.

Some-where out there if love can see us through,

then we'll be to - geth - er some-where out there, out

where dreams come true. _____

Where on Earth?

The South American country of Chile is made up of many different landscapes. The Atacama Desert is located in the north, while the Andes Mountains serve as the eastern border with Argentina. Other features of the land include rivers, lakes, and glaciers.

The Chilean song "Río, río" shows how emotions can sometimes be expressed through images of nature—in this case, a swiftly-flowing river.

SOUTH AMERICA
Atacama Desert
Andes Mountains
Chile

CD 17–7

Río, río
(River, River)

English Words by Alice Firgau

Traditional Song from Chile

do

Qué gran - de que vie - ne el rí - o, _____ qué
How wide __ and deep is the riv - er, _____ How

gran - de se va a la mar. _____ Si lo au - men - ta el __ llan - to
swift - ly it flows to the sea. _____ Rí - o, rí - o, ___ rí - o,
If my tears should __ meet its
Riv - er, riv - er, ___ flow - ing

Sing of South America

Follow the notation as you **listen** to *"Río, río."*
Sing the melody part. Then learn to sing the
harmony part. You'll be singing harmonies
that are typical of Spanish music. What
interval is used the most?

Play these parts on mallet instruments to accompany *"Río, río."*

Alto Metallophone

Bass Metallophone

mí - o _____ co - mo gran - de _____ no ha de es - tar, _____ Si lo au -
rí - o, _____ De - vol - ved - me el _____ a - mor mí - o. De - vol -
wa - ters, ___ Oh, how deep it _____ then would be. _____ If my
riv - er, _____ Please re - turn my ___ love to me. _____ Please re -

men - ta el ___ llan - to mí - o _____ co - mo gran - de ___ no ha de es - tar.
ved - me el ___ a - mor mí - o _____ que me can - so ___ de llo - rar.
tears should ___ meet its wa - ters, ___ Oh, how deep it _____ then would be.
turn my ___ love to me, Oh, ___ from my sor - row ___ set me free.

Undersea Worlds

Scientists now know about animals and plants that live miles beneath the ocean. Some of them even thrive on volcanic heat. "Under the Sea" describes an imaginary world where the creatures yearn for a different home. **Listen** for calypso sounds and instruments as you **sing.**

CD 17–12

Under the Sea
(from Disney's *The Little Mermaid*)

Words by Howard Ashman   Music by Alan Menken

The sea - weed is al - ways green - er
Down here ___ all the fish is hap - py

in some - bod - y el - se's lake.
as off ___ through the waves they roll.

You dream _ a - bout
The fish _ on the

go - ing up there, but that _ is a big mis - take.
land ain't hap - py, they sad ___ 'cause they in the bowl.

Just look _ at the world a - round you, right here _ on the
But fish _ in the bowl is luck - y, they in ___ for a

Undersea Ostinatos

After you learn to sing "Under the Sea," choose percussion instruments and then **improvise** your own parts.

Out _ in the sun they slave _ a - way, ___ while _ we de -
Un - der the sea we off _ the hook. ___ We _ got no

1.

vo - tin' full _ time to float - in' un - der the sea.
trou - bles, life _ is the bub - bles un - der the

2.

sea. Un - der the sea! Since _ life is

sweet here we _ got the beat here nat - u - ral - ly.

E - ven the stur-geon and _ the ray ___ they _ got the

urge 'n start _ to play. ___ We _ got the spir - it, you _ got to

-fish she sings. The smelt ___ and the sprat they know ___

___where it's at, an' oh, that blow-fish blow.

Un - der the sea. Un - der the

sea. When ___ the sar - dine be - gin ___ the be -

guine it's mu - sic to me. What ___ do they

got, a lot ___ of sand. We ___ got a hot crus-ta - ce - an

Water Music

Listen to this musical description of aquatic life.
Compare the composer's use of rhythm with that of "Under the Sea."

CD 17–14

Aquarium

**from *Carnival of the Animals*
by Camille Saint-Saëns**

Other animals depicted in Saint-Saëns' [san(n)-sa(hn)] musical "carnival" include birds, elephants, lions, tortoises, kangaroos, and even practicing pianists.

band. Each lit - tle clam here know how to jam here un - der the

sea. Each lit - tle slug here cut - tin' a

rug here un - der the sea. Each lit - tle

snail here know how to wail here that's why it's

hot - ter un - der the wa - ter. Ya we in

luck here down in the muck here un - der the sea.

Tune In

"Under the Sea" won an Academy Award in 1989 for best song of the year. *The Little Mermaid* won a Golden Globe Award for best original score.

SEASONS OF LIFE

Change is a part of life. Everyone at some point makes new friends, moves to a new school, or changes an address. "Turn, Turn, Turn" reminds us that every change has its purpose.

Look at any object around you. You'll see it has a shape, a form. A song has form, too. **Identify** the musical symbols that guide you through the song. Then follow the symbols as you **sing** "Turn, Turn, Turn."

CD 17–15

TURN, TURN, TURN
(To Everything There Is a Season)

Words Adapted from the Book of Ecclesiastes

Adaptation and Music by Pete Seeger

PETE SEEGER

Pete Seeger (born 1919) is one of the leaders of the folk-music revival in the 1940s and 1950s. He sang on college campuses, at folk concerts and festivals, radio, and television shows. Seeger is a folk musician who uses music to express his political views. His musical style and concern with ordinary working people, war, and social issues influenced many other folk singers. In 1948, he was one of the founders of the Weavers, a folk music group, and performed with them throughout the United States. Seeger loves and collects folk songs and performs many of them at concerts all over the world.

CD 17–17

Interview with Pete Seeger

Tune In

Pete Seeger helped create a group dedicated to cleaning up the Hudson River. The group's symbol is the *Clearwater*, a boat that monitors water quality on the Hudson.

CHILDREN LEARN WHAT THEY LIVE

CD 17–18

by Dorothy Law Nolte

If children live with criticism, they learn to condemn.

If children live with hostility, they learn to fight.

If children live with fear, they learn to be apprehensive.

If children live with pity, they learn to feel sorry for themselves.

If children live with ridicule, they learn to feel shy.

If children live with jealousy, they learn to feel envy.

If children live with shame, they learn to feel guilty.

If children live with encouragement, they learn confidence.

If children live with tolerance, they learn patience.

If children live with praise, they learn appreciation.

If children live with acceptance, they learn to love.

If children live with approval, they learn to like themselves.

If children live with recognition, they learn it is good to have a goal.

If children live with sharing, they learn generosity.

If children live with honesty, they learn truthfulness.

If children live with fairness, they learn justice.

If children live with kindness and consideration, they learn respect.

If children live with security, they learn to have faith in themselves and in those about them.

If children live with friendliness, they learn the world is a nice place in which to live.

A BETTER WORLD

Some songs make us aware of the needs of others. The music of the 1960s reflects the people's yearning for social progress and world harmony.

"Blowin' in the Wind" asks many questions. Does the refrain have the answers? As you **sing** the song, focus on the meaning of the words.

Arts Connection

Friends by Diana Ong, 1940 ▶

CD 17–19

Blowin' in the Wind

Words and Music by Bob Dylan

VERSE

1. How man-y roads must a man walk __ down be - fore they
2. How man-y years must a moun-tain ex - ist be - fore it is
3. How man-y times must a man look __ up be - fore he can

call him a man? ____ How man-y seas must a white dove __ sail be-
washed to the sea? ____ How man-y years can some peo-ple ex - ist be-
see the __ sky? ____ How man-y ears must __ one man __ have be-

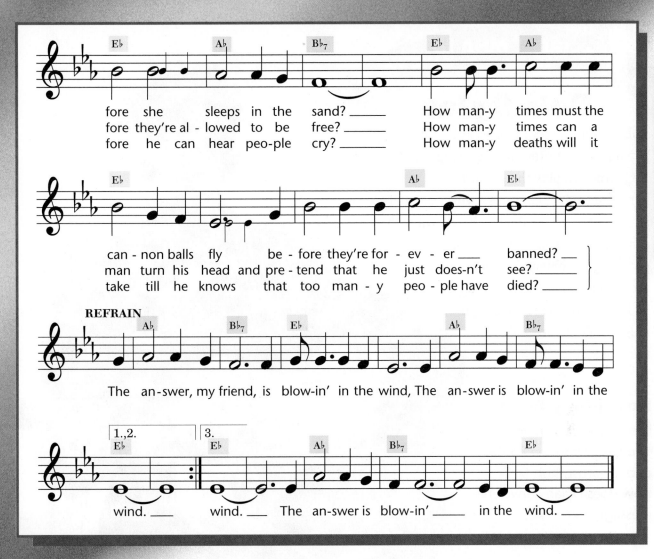

fore she sleeps in the sand? _____ How man-y times must the
fore they're al - lowed to be free? _____ How man-y times can a
fore he can hear peo-ple cry? _____ How man-y deaths will it

can - non balls fly be - fore they're for - ev - er ____ banned? __
man turn his head and pre - tend that he just does-n't see? _____
take till he knows that too man - y peo - ple have died? _____

REFRAIN

The an-swer, my friend, is blow-in' in the wind, The an-swer is blow-in' in the

1.,2. | 3.

wind. ____ wind. ____ The an-swer is blow-in' _____ in the wind. ____

How Many Chords?

You can **play** these chords to add harmony to "Blowin' in the Wind."

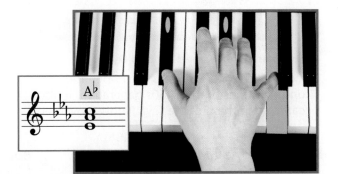

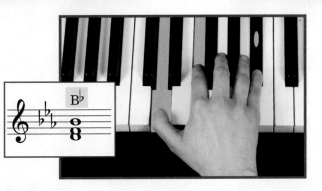

Bob Dylan

Bob Dylan [DIH-lan] (born 1941) is a popular song writer and recording artist. He learned to play the guitar and harmonica when he was six years old and started his first band when he was in high school. Dylan started writing songs to protest governmental policies and social problems. His music is influenced by his love of country-western music, folk music, and the blues.

How Many Roads?

Listen to *Blowin' in the Wind* as performed by the original artist, Bob Dylan. How does Dylan convey his message?

CD 17–21
Blowin' in the Wind

written and performed by Bob Dylan

Blowin' in the Wind expresses the hopes and strong emotions of the 1960s generation. It also became an anthem of the Civil Rights movement.

Listen to *The Times They Are A-Changin'* by Bob Dylan. What is the message?

CD 17–22
The Times They Are A-Changin'

written and performed by Bob Dylan

Dylan wrote this song in 1963, the same year President John F. Kennedy was assassinated.

Joni Mitchell

Joni Mitchell (born 1943) is a visual artist turned folk singer. She is considered one of rock music's best songwriters. Mitchell's music career spans over three decades. Her work includes folk, pop, and jazz. Her music has both emotional and intellectual appeal.

Listen to *Both Sides Now*. How would you **describe** Joni Mitchell's music?

CD 18–1

Both Sides Now

by Joni Mitchell as performed by Judy Collins

Many famous singers, such as Judy Collins, Willie Nelson, and Pete Seeger, have performed Mitchell's songs.

Same but Different

Every person has unique gifts, but we all share things that are the same. Our differences, though, are what often make us interesting.

Read the lyrics of "A World of Difference." What gifts do you have to offer?

CD 18–2

A World of Difference

Words by Joseph and Pamela Martin

Music by Joseph M. Martin

1. It takes the sun-shine and the rain _ to help a gar-den grow. _
2. Moun-tains need the val - leys, _____ the wa - ter needs the sand, _

The sun and moon _ to - geth - er work _ to make the o - cean flow. _
And we all need each oth - er _____ to lend a help - ing hand. _

Our strength is in our dif - f'ren - ces, _ the gifts we have to share, _
So we must work to - geth - er; __ we can't do it a - lone. _

And to - geth-er we can build a bet - ter world _ for peo - ple ev - 'ry - where. _
Yes, _ we _ all _ need each oth - er __ to make this house a home. _

REFRAIN

We're the col-ors of the rain - bow; we're the stars up in the sky.

No _ two of us _ are quite the same _ and _ here's the rea - son why: _

We all have a pur - pose and a spe - cial place to serve, _

For it takes a world of dif-f'ren-ces _ to make a dif-f'rence in our world. _____

It Takes Syncopation

The syncopated rhythm of "A World of Difference" adds interest to the song. **Perform** the first phrase without syncopation.

1. It takes the sun-shine and the rain to help a gar-den grow.

Now **perform** the same phrase as written. **Describe** the difference.

2. It takes the sun-shine and the rain _ to help a gar-den grow. _

As you **sing** the entire song, notice how syncopation is used in other phrases.

People in Harmony

In many ways, people are the same all over the world. There are some differences in culture, music, art, and language, but basically people have the same needs, hopes, and dreams. They are the keepers of the earth, and of themselves. Where does this all start? Read the poem and find out.

You and I

by Mary Ann Hoberman

Only one I in the whole wide world
And millions and millions of you,
But every you is an I to myself
And I am a you to you, too!

But if I am a you and you are an I
And the opposite also is true,
It makes us both the same somehow
Yet splits us each in two.

It's more and more mysterious,
The more I think it through:
Every you everywhere in the world is an I;
Every I in the world is a you!

What's the Difference?

Listen to and **compare** *Everyday People* and "A World of Difference."

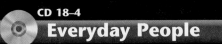

CD 18–4

Everyday People

by Sylvester Stewart
as performed by Sly and the Family Stone

With its message promoting the brotherhood of all people, *Everyday People* became a number one hit in 1969.

Sly and the Family Stone

Sly and the Family Stone was a popular music group in the late 1960s and early 1970s. Sly Stone (Sylvester Stewart, born 1943) started the group. The band was one of the first to be made up of men and women of both African and European Americans, which was not common at that time. Their music is a fusion of soul, rock, rhythm and blues, and funk. In 1993, Stone was inducted into the Rock and Roll Hall of Fame.

A Song of Hope

People who are free choose the way they live, work, and play. When people experience discrimination, they lose some of their freedom.

African American spirituals often provided hope when freedom seemed only a dream. "Come and Go with Me to That Land" is a song of hope for freedom and the promise of a new land. **Listen** to the recording and **identify** the rhythm patterns in the color boxes each time they occur.

Sing this spiritual and respond to its energy by clapping and swaying to the music.

▲ Dr. Martin Luther King Jr. leading a civil rights march on Washington, D.C., 1963

CD 18–5
MIDI 24

Come and Go with Me to That Land

African American Spiritual

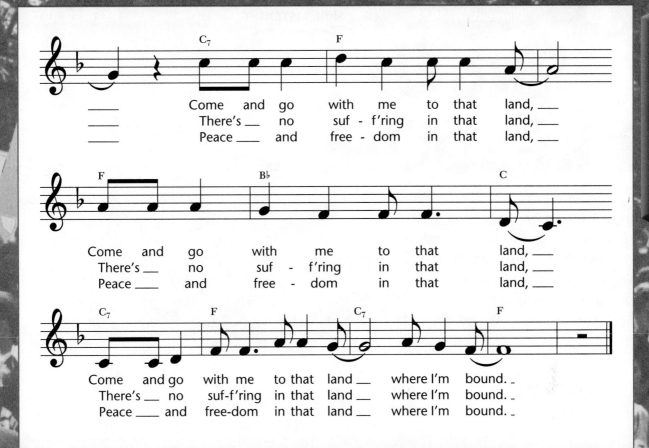

Come and go with me to that land, ___
There's ___ no suf - f'ring in that land, ___
Peace ___ and free - dom in that land, ___

Come and go with me to that land, ___
There's ___ no suf - f'ring in that land, ___
Peace ___ and free - dom in that land, ___

Come and go with me to that land ___ where I'm bound. _
There's ___ no suf-f'ring in that land ___ where I'm bound. _
Peace ___ and free-dom in that land ___ where I'm bound. _

Recorder Countermelody

Play this recorder part to accompany
"Come and Go with Me to That Land."

SING OF FREEDOM

African Americans who were freed from enslavement frequently used spirituals to express the importance of freedom. As you **sing** "Oh, Freedom," notice the timbre of the singers who perform the vocal accompaniment.

CD 18–7

OH, FREEDOM

African American Spiritual

1., 4.   Oh, _____ free - dom!   Oh, _____ free - dom!
2.   No   more   cry - in',   No   more   cry - in',
3.   There'll   be   sing - in',   There'll   be   sing - in',

Oh, _____ free - dom   o - ver   me. _____
No   more   cry - in'   o - ver   me! _____
There'll   be   sing - in'   o - ver   me! _____

And   be - fore   I'd   be   a   slave,   I'll   be   bur - ied   in   my   grave,

And   go   home   to   my   Lord   and   be   free. _____

Keyboards Add Timbre

Add a new timbre by playing these three chords to accompany
"Oh, Freedom."

Sing for Freedom

Performers and composers often combine several songs to create a longer work.

Listen to how Odetta combines *Oh, Freedom* and *Come and Go with Me (to That Land)* into one performance.

CD 18–9

Oh, Freedom and Come and Go with Me

African American Spirituals as performed by Odetta

This example of Odetta's singing showcases the low alto range of her voice.

MUSIC MAKERS

Odetta

Odetta Holmes Felious Gordon (born 1930, in Birmingham, Alabama) is a much-loved singer of African American folk music. She is known by the single name, Odetta. Her parents recognized her musical talent and encouraged her to sing. As a child, she took singing lessons and taught herself to play the guitar. She became famous in the early 1950s as an exciting interpreter of African American folk music. She has made many recordings that show off her unusual vocal range, which runs from coloratura to low alto. In 1999, President Bill Clinton presented Odetta with the National Endowment for the Arts' Medal of Arts.

Make Your Own Arrangement

Create your own choral arrangement. Use two songs that share a similar topic, and combine them into one larger work. Connect the two songs with an instrumental interlude.

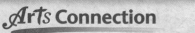

Arts Connection

Appliquéd cotton coverlet from the mid-eighteenth century ▲

A Song Of Nature

Taking care of the earth is an important part of life. Native American art and music often reflect respect for the earth, animals, and people. As you **sing** "Zuni Sunrise Call," picture the earth at daybreak.

CD 18–10

Zuni Sunrise Call

Zuni Native American Song

Noh ay loh ah noh ay loh ah

Wah ah day oh nah wee yahn nah lay

Ah _____ day oh nah wee yahn nah lay

Nah yah nah ah wee oh _____ mee tehn lah lay

Nah yah nah ah wee oh _____ mee tehn lah lay _____

◀ The American Indian Dance Theater is a large troupe of musicians and dancers that tours throughout the United States. Members perform dances that encourage a deeper understanding of Native American heritage.

Pictured are examples of Zuni traditional carvings from natural materials. The carvings of animals and people are very small. ▶

Utah

Colorado

New Mexico

Zuni Reservation

Arizona

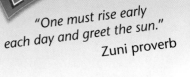

"One must rise early each day and greet the sun."
Zuni proverb

Celebrate Sunrise

Native Americans have a deep appreciation for nature. This composition for Native American flute also celebrates sunrise.
Listen to *Daybreak Vision* as you follow the melodic contour on the listening map.

CD 18–11
Daybreak Vision

written and performed by R. Carlos Nakai
Nakai blends traditional and contemporary elements in his compositions for Native American flute.

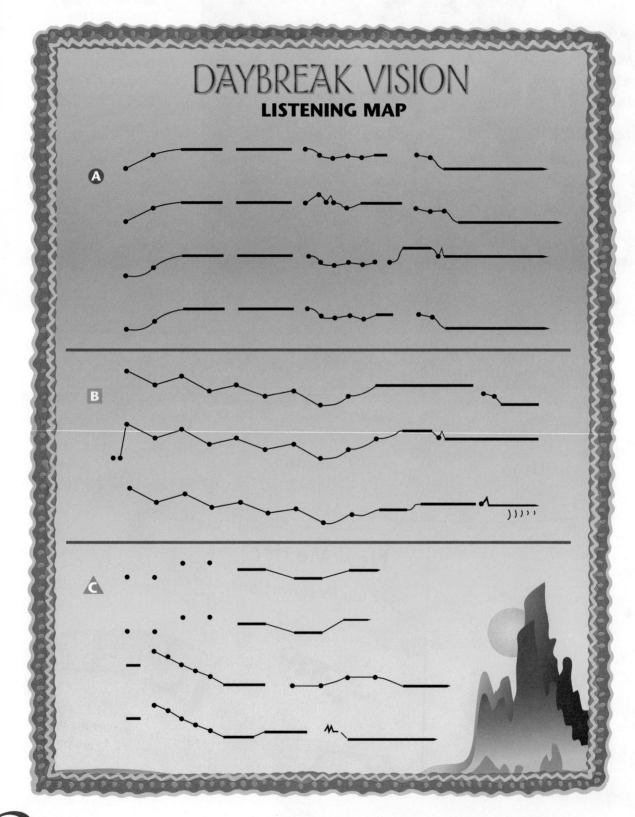

DAYBREAK VISION
LISTENING MAP

A

B

C

Protecting the Earth

People who live in different countries share concern for the earth. **Listen** to *Garden of the Earth*, a song reflecting that sentiment.

Garden of the Earth

Traditional Folk Song from Russia as performed by the Dimitri Pokrovsky Singers with the Paul Winter Consort

Paul Winter traveled to Russia fifteen times to learn about the country's musical heritage before creating this arrangement of *Garden of the Earth.*

Garden of the Earth

by Paul Winter and Paul Halley

There's a garden 'round the Earth,
There's a home beneath the sun,
In the beauty of this garden,
We will hear a thousand songs.
Many voices, many tongues,
From the mountains to the sea,
Sing of beauty all around us
In this ancient harmony.
For the glory of the Earth,
For the glory of the sun,
We will sing of life together
And forever live as one.

MUSIC MAKERS
Paul Winter

Paul Winter (born 1931) is known for his fusion of world music from various cultures with jazz. He founded the Paul Winter Consort in 1967 and explored non-Western music through this group. Winter became interested in and involved with environmental issues and has worked to join music and nature together. He even attempted to communicate with whales and used those sounds in several of his works.

Common Ground

What is a community? It's a group of people who share something in common. The people in these photographs work together in an Israeli *kibbutz*.

Learn to **sing** "*Zum gali gali.*" Then sing the refrain and verse together to create a partner song. The repeated refrain creates a common ground that unites the song.

MIDI Use the MIDI song file of *"Zum gali gali"* to experiment with texture. You can duplicate tracks to add more layers or substitute instruments for other timbres.

One If By Land, Two If By Sea

The earth's people travel in many ways. One popular form of travel is by ship on the ocean. Until the twentieth century, worldwide travel and commerce were possible only by ship. What impact did later forms of transportation have on the world's environment?

Sing "The Ship that Never Returned," a popular hit from the late nineteenth century. **Identify** the form of the song.

CD 18–17
MIDI 26

The Ship that Never Returned

Words and Music by Henry C. Work

VERSE

1. On a sum - mer's day when the waves were
2. There were sad fare - wells, There were friends for -
3. "We will live in peace and ___ joy to -

rip - pling with a gen - tle and a peace - ful breeze.
sak - en and her fate ___ is ___ still un - learned.
geth - er and en - joy ___ all ___ I have earned."

A ___ ship set sail with a car - go
But a last poor man set ___ sail, Com -
So, they sent him forth with a smile and

lad - en for a port a - cross the sea.
man - der on a ship that nev - er re - turned.
bless - ing on a ship that nev - er re - turned.

REFRAIN

B♭

Did she ev - er re - turn? No, she

E♭   B♭

nev - er re - turned, and her fate is still un -

F♭₇   B♭   E♭

learned. And ___ one last man set sail, Com -

B♭   F₇   B♭

man - der, on a ship that nev - er re - turned.

A Variation in Words

Another way people travel is by railway, including subways and cross-country trains. **Listen** to this variation of "The Ship that Never Returned." This humorous version of the song tells of the effect of a subway fare increase on one unfortunate rider.

CD 18–19
M.T.A

by Jacqueline Steiner and Bess Lomax Hawes as performed by the Kingston Trio

This song is also known as "Charlie on the M.T.A."

◀ The Kingston Trio

MIDI Use the song file for "The Ship that Never Returned" to experiment with arranging the song in different styles.

Sing Together in Harmony

Welcome to another year of choral music. This year, you will take a journey on a musical landscape composed of rhythm, melody, harmony, and form. With each new song, your awareness of how these musical elements relate to each other will help you understand the composer's technique for creating a song. At the end of this journey, you will no longer be just a visitor to the musical score. It will be a place where you will feel right at home.

Come, let's **sing** "Sail Away" and begin our musical tour.

CD 18–20
MIDI 27

Sail Away

Words and Music by Malcolm Dalglish (adapted)

Dark   clouds __ hide   the   sun, _____

Rain comes down _ and the riv-ers _   run. _   Riv-ers run _ down to the sea, _

_____   and   when you've got _ your lib - er - ty, _____

__   *Don't you want to   sail   a - way? _____

* "Don't you" is pronounced "donchiew"

UNIT 11

We Sing!

Choral singing brings people together in harmony. Groups of people all over the world sing songs together. There are choral songs about every subject imaginable. As long as people keep singing, the tradition of choral music continues!

Back to tempo, lively

Don't you want to sail a-way, don't you want to sail a-way? Don't you want to sail a-way, don't you want to sail a-way? Don't you want to sail a-way, don't you want to sail a-way? Don't you want to sail a-way, don't you want to sail a-way? Sail

A GREETING SONG

Nearly all cultures have songs to say hello and goodbye. "*O, Desayo*" is an Angolan "hello" song. In Angola, in southwestern Africa, Portuguese is the official language, but most Angolans speak Bantu. The word *menina* indicates "smallness" and in this song means "little girl."

Singing Tips

Look at the three syncopated rhythm patterns in the color boxes. Practice speaking each pattern before singing it. When you sing "*O, Desayo*," separate *O* from *Desayo* with a tiny space of silence, and then accent the consonant *D*, of *Desayo*, to enhance the vocal expression of the syncopated rhythm.

Reading Music Tips

Before singing the song, practice the pitch patterns in measures 10–11. Practice speaking the rhythm patterns in the color boxes on a neutral syllable and then with the words of the song.

Knowing the Score

Music symbols and terms give you directions about how to sing the song. Find and discuss these symbols and terms: refrain, coda, and repeat signs. If you were drawing a map of how this song is to be performed, how would it look?

Sing a Greeting

Sing "*O, Desayo,*" focusing on pitch and good breathing skills. Imagine that the pitch is an archery target and you are singing to the center of the bull's eye.

CD 18–22
MIDI 28

O, DESAYO

Folk Song from Angola
Arranged by Elliot A. Levine, Edited by Henry Leck

REFRAIN

O, Des - ay - o! _____ O, Des - ay - o!

Each time to next verse
Last time to Coda

O, Des - ay - o! Me - ni - na, O, Des - ay - o!

VERSE

1. Rains are o - ver, it's fine and shin - y wea-ther, O, Des - ay - o!

to Refrain

Fine and shin - y day for a get - to - ge - ther, O, Des - ay - o!

We Sing!

Ninga drummers from Burundi,
West Africa, in traditional dress ▶

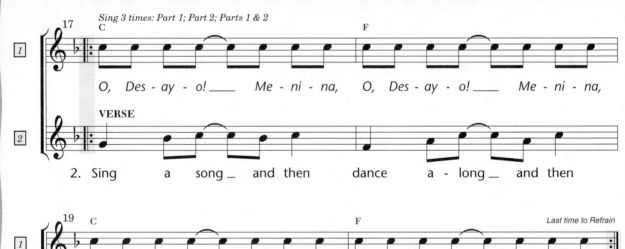

Sing 3 times: Part 1; Part 2; Parts 1 & 2

1

O, Des - ay - o! ___ Me - ni - na, O, Des - ay - o! ___ Me - ni - na,

VERSE

2

2. Sing a song _ and then dance a - long _ and then

1

Last time to Refrain

O, Des - ay - o! ___ Me - ni - na, O, Des - ay - o! ___ Me - ni - na.

2

drink a cup _ and then stay for sup - per then.

A Song of FREEDOM

Whenever groups of people have their liberties limited, they have developed songs that speak of their longing for freedom. "Freedom Is Coming" grew out of people's frustration with *apartheid*, a national policy of racial segregation once associated with South Africa.

Singing Tips

"Freedom Is Coming" can be sung while walking. Use good breathing skills and vowel shapes to help you sing with good intonation. When singing the word *freedom*, accent the first syllable.

Listen carefully to your fellow singers to maintain good blend within parts and good balance between voice parts.

Reading Music Tips

Read the shaded rhythm patterns in part 1 by clapping and speaking. Then sing them with words. **Read** and practice the shaded rhythm pattern in part 2.

Knowing the Score

Identify and discuss the purpose of repeat signs and the markings for ending 1 and ending 2. How many times is each section sung? Describe how the closing bar (or end bar) looks. How is it different from a repeat sign?

▲ *Peaceful Protest* by John Roome

Freedom Is Coming

Collected by Anders Nyberg

Freedom Song from South Africa
Arranged by Henry Leck

do — Oh, free - dom, _ oh, free - dom, _ oh,

do — (know.) Free-dom is com-ing, free-dom is

free - dom. _____ Oh,

com - ing, free-dom is com - ing, oh yes, I

▲ Nelson Mandela

▲ *A Fair Deal,* woodcut
by Margaret Gradwell

We Sing!

Unit 11 **415**

1 yes, I __ know, __ oh yes, I __ know, __ oh

2
3 know, oh yes, I know, oh yes, I

1 yes, I _____ know. _____ Oh
My

2
3 know, oh yes, I __ know, oh yes, I

1 spir - it __ knows, __ my spir - it __ knows, __ my

2
3 know(s). My spir - it knows, my spir - it

▲ *Life* by William Zulu

▲ *Freedom of religion, belief and opinion* by Dina Cormick

▲ *Freedom and Security of the Person* by James Mphahlele

A Pledge of Loyalty

This patriotic melody has become one of the most cherished in England. The lyrics speak of love for one's country. It was sung at Princess Diana's wedding and again at her funeral.

Singing Tips

Each verse of "I Vow to You, My Country" has three sections: **a** **b** **a**. Each section, in turn, is made up of two phrases. Sing the phrases *legato* on the syllable *noo* to achieve a flowing phrase line. Focus on good breathing skills to sing with accuracy and expression.

Reading Music Tips

Many measures in this song contain dotted rhythm patterns. Look in measure 7 and speak the rhythm pattern using rhythm syllables. Identify other dotted rhythms in the song.

Knowing the Score

The keyboard accompaniment for this song is included in your book. In which measures does the keyboard play alone?

CD 18–27
MIDI 30

I Vow to You, My Country

Words by Sir Cecil Spring-Rice

Melody by Gustav Holst
Arranged by R. Osborne

With emotion

Keyboard

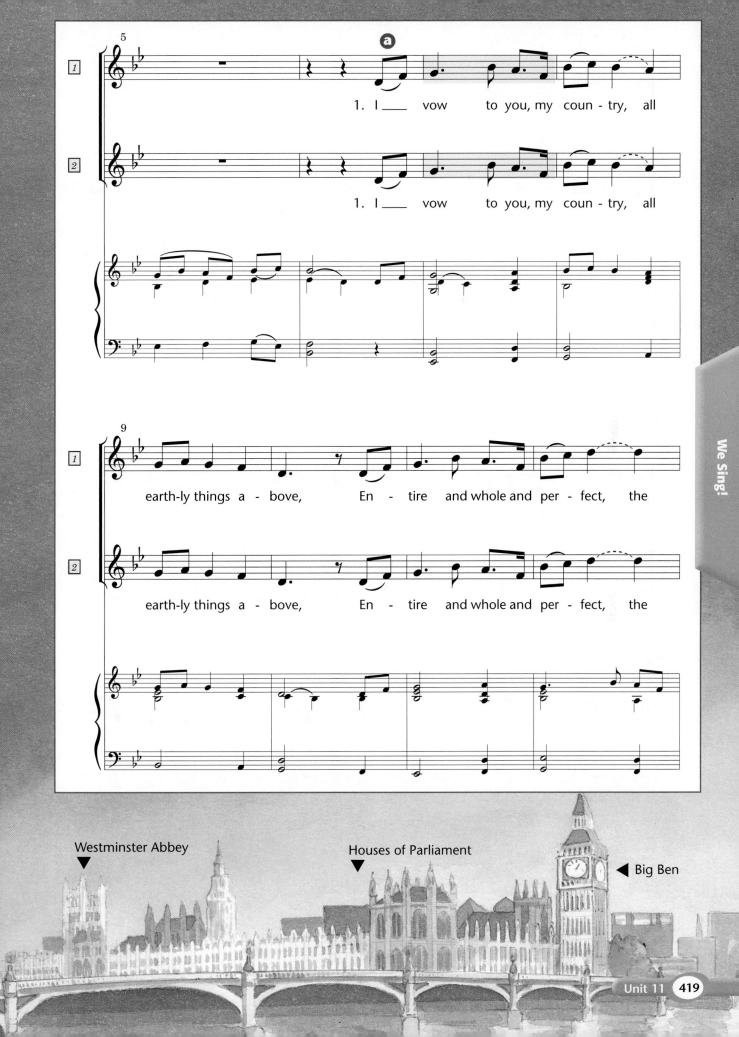

Tune In

The words of "I Vow to You, My Country" were written by Sir Cecil Spring-Rice, who was an English ambassador to the United States.

◄ White Cliffs of Dover

fi - nal sac - ri - fice.

fi - nal sac - ri - fice.

2. Home - land   the coun-try that I love, hold

2. Home - land   the coun-try that I love, hold

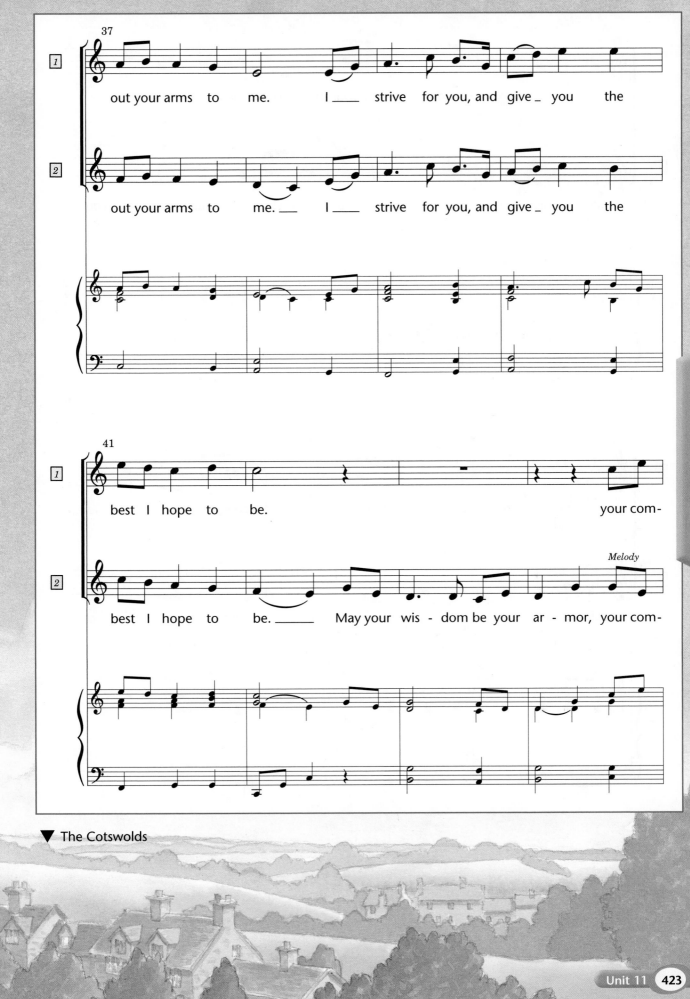

▼ The Cotswolds

A Famous Melody

Listen to *Jupiter* by Gustav Holst. **Identify** where the melody of "I Vow to You, My Country" begins.

Jupiter

from *The Planets*
by Gustav Holst

In *The Planets*, Holst composed a movement for each planet, except Earth and Pluto. (Pluto had not yet been discovered.) He composed *The Planets* between 1914 and 1916.

Stonehenge

We Sing!

A Conga from Cuba

"*Uno, dos, y tres*" is a spirited conga from the Caribbean country of Cuba. The conga is a dance originally developed by enslaved Africans living in Cuba.

Move to the rhythm of the conga as you **sing** the song.

Singing Tips

Listen to the recorded Spanish Pronunciation Practice for this song. Words beginning with a *q*, such as *quien*, are pronounced with a *k* sound, as in *kitchen*. Words beginning with a *c*, such as *con* and *Cuba*, are also pronounced with a *k* sound.

Reading Music Tips

Compare the rhythm patterns in measures 4 and 12. Are they the same, or different? Practice tapping and speaking each pattern before singing it. **Compare** the pitch patterns in measures 4 and 12. Are they the same, or different?

Read the melody using pitch syllables and hand signs.

▲ Cuban conga dancers and musicians

Knowing the Score

This song is arranged in Ⓐ Ⓑ form. In which measure does the B section begin? In which measure is *D.C. al Coda* located? What does this abbreviation mean?

Tune In

In 1938, Cuban-born musician Desi Arnaz (1917-1986) performed a series of concerts in Miami, Florida. His performances made conga dance music popular in the United States.

◀ **The Vinales Valley in western Cuba**

Uno, dos, y tres

(One, Two, and Three)

English Words by Don Kalbach

Words and Music by Rafael Ortiz
Arranged by Carlos Abril

Children playing in the
Miel River in eastern Cuba

In Search of Peace

"*Hine mah tov*" is a traditional Jewish melody. This text is commonly known as a song of peace. The translation of the Hebrew text is: "Behold, how good and pleasant it is for brethren to dwell together in peace."

Singing Tips

Hebrew is an easy language to sing. **Listen** to the recorded Pronunciation Practice for this song. The *ch* sound in Hebrew is pronounced like the *ch* sound in Bach.

Reading Music Tips

Compare the rhythm patterns in measures 5 and 13. How are they different? Practice tapping and speaking each pattern before singing it. **Compare** the pitch patterns in measures 5 and 13.

Knowing the Score

This song is arranged in Ⓐ Ⓐ Ⓑ Ⓐ form. In which measure does the Ⓐ section return? How is the Ⓐ section different the second time it appears?

Hine mah tov

Hebrew Folk Song
Arranged by Henry Leck

We Sing!

A Carol from Spain

"*Ríu ríu chíu*" is a Spanish Christmas carol from the Renaissance period, c. 1450–1600. It was sung in the courts of the nobility. It can be sung *a cappella*—without instruments—or with instruments *doubling* the parts.

Singing Tips

The tempo marking of *allegro moderato* indicates that this song should be sung moderately fast, as if you were singing it as part of a celebration. Use correct vowel shapes and good breathing skills, especially when singing the Spanish words in the refrain.

Reading Music Tips

This song has frequent meter changes that follow the rhythm of the words. The meter is felt as one, two, or three beats per measure.
Read the melody by using pitch syllables and hand signs.

Knowing the Score

At the end of the song you will see the Italian markings *D.C. al Fine*. What does that mean in English? In which measure does *Fine* appear by itself?

Ríu ríu chíu

Sixteenth Century Carol from Spain
Arranged by Henry Leck

de - ra. Dios guar-do el lo - bo de nues-

de - ra. Dios guar-do el lo - bo, el lo - bo de nues-

tra cor - de - ra. 1. Now is come the time to sing with joy and

tra cor - de - ra.

praise. Sing-ing of the birth, we've known through - out our

age. May we come to - geth - er with hope and peace and

D. C. al Fine

love.   Shar-ing with each oth - er the sym-bol of the dove.

2. As we find this season clear with warmth within us,
   Maybe we will see the meaning of forgiveness.

   See in one another growing day by day,
   Toward a closer, loving time we all would pray.   *Refrain*

3. So with treasured gifts and hope for years to come,
   May we seek the meaning of the newborn Son.

   Living life together with hope and truth and love,
   Sharing what we have through the love from up above.   *Refrain*

4. Now with celebration we gather far and near,
   Seeking new relation with those we hold most dear.

   As we come together, we hope for bright days long,
   So we join together and we sing this song.   *Refrain*

Visit **Take It to the Net** at *www.sfsuccessnet.com* to learn more about Renaissance Music.

Arts Connection

▲ *A Concert* (16th century, School of Palma Vecchio). During the Renaissance (1450–1600) there was renewed interest in art, music, and the value of humankind. More scientific exploration occurred than ever before. Artists Leonardo da Vinci and Michelangelo, writer William Shakespeare, explorer Christopher Columbus, and scientist Galileo lived during this period. Many consider the Renaissance period the "Golden Age" of the arts.

A Renaissance Christmas

Listen to another version of *"Ríu ríu chíu."*

CD 19–12
Ríu ríu chíu

**Sixteenth Century Carol from Spain
as performed by The Sixteen**

The Sixteen is one of Great Britain's finest choirs. They have toured throughout Europe, America, and Asia.

A WADING BIRD

When Europeans first traveled to Hawaii, they found a people who sang beautiful songs about their beloved land and sea.

Singing Tips

Listen to the Pronunciation Practice to learn the lyrics. Pay special attention to the sounds of the vowels. Use good breathing skills to help maintain accurate intonation for the long, sustained tones and for repeated tones. (See page 442.)

Reading Music Tips

Each phrase begins with a *do-re-mi* or *do-mi-so* pattern. **Sing** these patterns using pitch syllables and hand signs at the beginning of each phrase before singing the song.

Knowing the Score

Notice the chord symbols that are written above certain measures. They are provided so that the song can be accompanied on the *ukulele*. What is the name of the first chord to be played by the *ukulele*?

▶

The *ukulele* has been a popular instrument in Hawaii since the late nineteenth century.

'ŪLILI E

Traditional Song from Hawaii
Arranged by Wanda Gereben

1. Ho - ne a - na ko le - o e 'ū - li - li e E - ka - hi
2. Ho - ne a - na ko le - o e kō - le - a e Pe - he - a

ma - nu__ no - ho a - 'e kai Ki - a - 'i ma ka lae o__ Ke - u -
'o Ka - hi - ki? Mai - ka - 'i no. 'O - i - a 'āi - na u - lu - we - hi -

ka - ha 'O - i - a kai u - a la - na ma - li - e. 'Ū - li - li
we - hi I hu - i pū 'i - a me ke o - nao - na.

Rhythm of the Waves

"'*Ūlili E*" is a traditional Hawaiian song. You will experience the beautiful and poetic language of the native Hawaiian people when you sing this song.

Listen for the lively rhythm patterns that reflect the movements of the 'ūlili bird.

Tune In

The 'ūlili is a small bird with long legs. It runs along the beach, darting in and out as the waves come and go.

▲ Big Island, Hawaii;
view from inside a cave

'Ū-li-li ho-lo ho-lo ka-ha-kai ___ e,

'O - i - a kai u - a la - na mā -

1. li - e. 'Ū-li-li li - e. ___

2.

Last time to Coda

D. C. (Verse 2)

Coda

li - e. ___

▲ Waipio Valley, Hawaii, with waterfall

▲ Volcano steam on the Big Island

Scat Cat!

Doo-doo n' doo-bee-doo! What an unusual way for the jazz "cats" to sing. These nonsense syllables, called scat, are meant to help the singer sound like a musical instrument. One of the most famous scat singers was Louis Armstrong. His *scat* singing made him world famous. Armstrong was also known for his trumpet playing and his distinctive, husky-sounding voice.

Singing Tips

When you **sing** "Now's the Time," emphasize the accented notes.The scat syllables should be slurred together and not cleanly separated when sung.

Reading Music Tips

Compare the lowest pitches in measures 7 and 8. Are they the same or different? Focus your attention on singing each pitch accurately. Using good vocal energy, enunciate the first consonant of each nonsense syllable with vigorous energy.

Knowing the Score

The third section of this song, which begins in measure 39, is written in call-and-response style. Which voice part is given the call, and which part the response?

◄ Louis Armstrong

Sing "Now's the Time" in a *legato* style using the scat syllables.

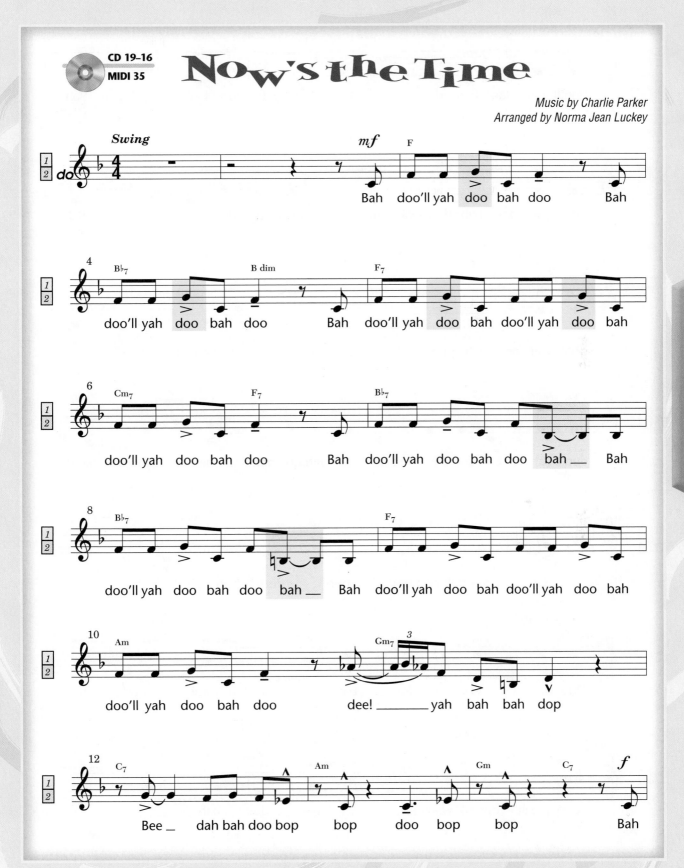

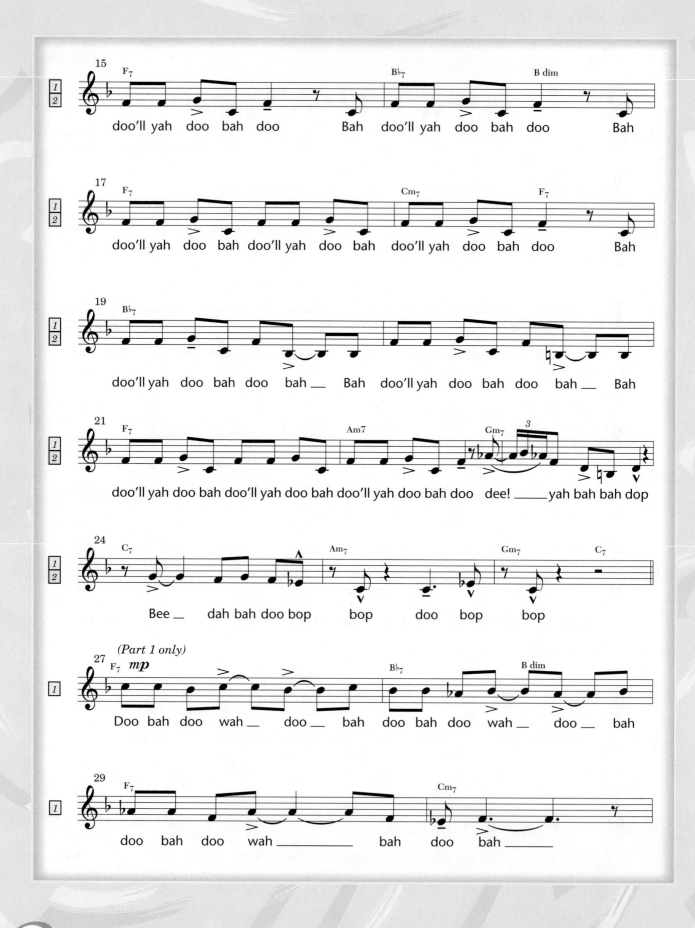

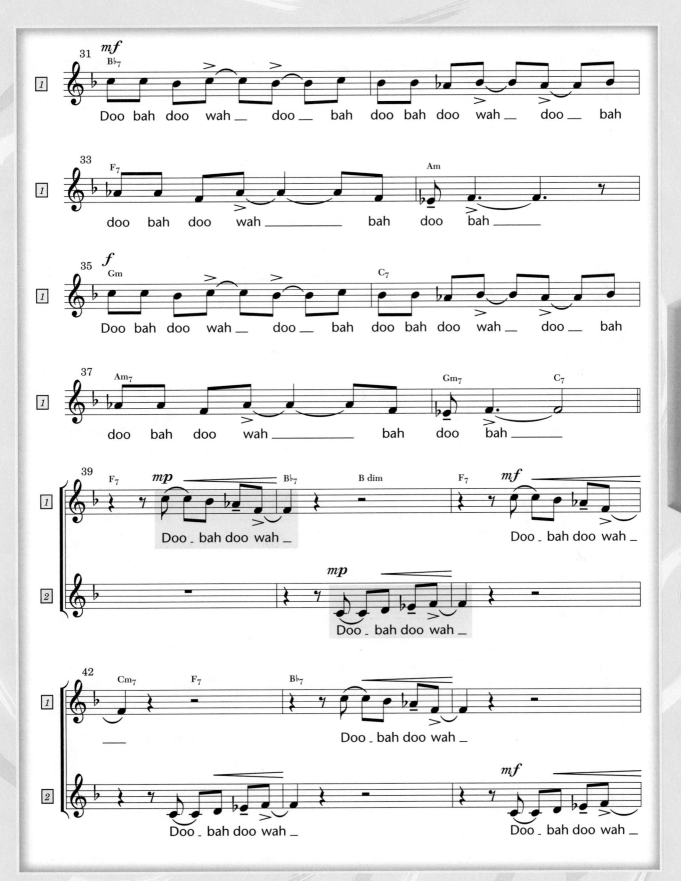

Listen to Charlie Parker's original recording of *Now's the Time.*

CD 19–18

Now's the Time

written and performed by Charlie Parker

Parker's recording of *Now's the Time* made this song famous.

MUSIC MAKERS

Charlie Parker

Charlie Parker (1920–1955) was a famous jazz performer on the alto saxophone. He and another musician, Dizzy Gillespie, contributed to the popularity of "bebop" in the 1940s and 1950s. Bebop, or "bop," was a change from the swing band sound that was popular earlier. Bop performers had more freedom in using off-beat accents (called syncopation), difficult harmonies, and solo improvisation. Bop was performed at such a fast tempo that it was almost impossible to dance to the music, so the audience had to sit and listen.

Celebrate Winter

Winter festivals are popular in areas of the world where winter means snow and freezing temperatures. This picture envisions a beautiful snowy day. Imagine a sleigh ride down a long hill.

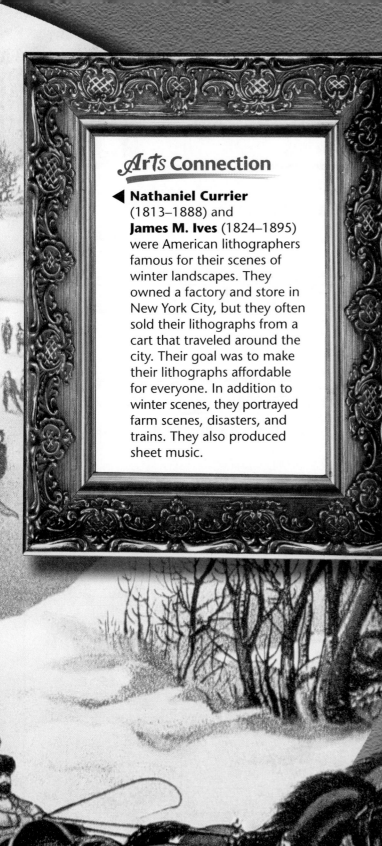

Arts Connection

◄ **Nathaniel Currier** (1813–1888) and **James M. Ives** (1824–1895) were American lithographers famous for their scenes of winter landscapes. They owned a factory and store in New York City, but they often sold their lithographs from a cart that traveled around the city. Their goal was to make their lithographs affordable for everyone. In addition to winter scenes, they portrayed farm scenes, disasters, and trains. They also produced sheet music.

Holidays in Song

All over the world, people come together for celebrations. Some celebrations recognize holidays, others observe the changing seasons, and still others honor life's milestones.

Sing of Snow

Many people celebrate the beginning of the winter season.
Sing "Winter Wonderland" and think of ways you might celebrate winter.

CD 19–19

Winter Wonderland

Words by Dick Smith

Music by Felix Bernard

Sleigh-bells ring, are you lis - t'nin'? In the lane snow is glis - t'nin', a beau-ti-ful sight, we're hap-py to - night, walk-in' in a win-ter won-der land! Gone a-way is the blue - bird; here to stay is a new bird. He sings a love song, as we go a - long, walk-in' in a win-ter won-der-land. In the mead-ow we can build a snow - man, then pre-tend that he is Par - son Brown.

He'll say, "Are you mar - ried?" We'll say, "No man, but
you can do the job when you're in town!" Lat - er on, we'll con-
spire, __ as we dream by the fire, ___ to face un - a - fraid, _ the
plans that we made, _ walk - in' in a win - ter won - der - land.

Classical Sounds of Winter

Sleigh riding was very fashionable in the late 18th century. In some European countries snow was brought in from the mountains to the city for this purpose. Leopold Mozart, Wolfgang's father, wrote *A Musical Sleigh Ride* about this pastime.

Listen to the musical sounds of winter portrayed in this selection.

CD 19–21
A Musical Sleigh Ride

by Leopold Mozart

Mozart used brass instruments and jingle bells to add a festive sound to *A Musical Sleigh Ride.*

Fall Fun

It's a late October night. Unusual sounds can be heard in the distance. You may even detect a strange rhythmic snapping sound. Could it mean a Halloween visit from a certain "creepy" family?

Before you **sing** "The Addams Family," practice snapping, on cue, along with the recording.

CD 19–22

The Addams Family

Words and Music by Vic Mizzy

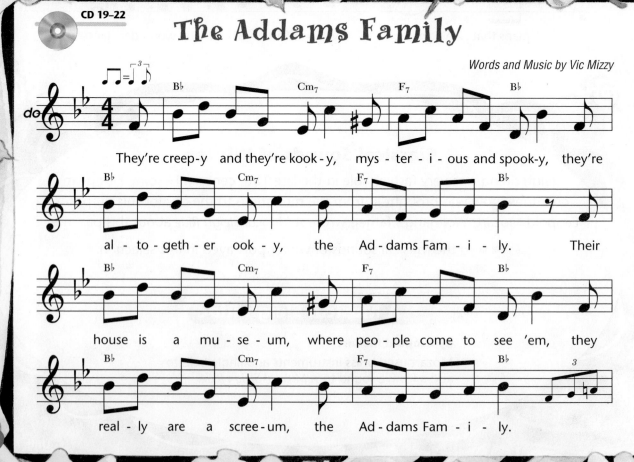

They're creep-y   and they're kook-y,   mys - ter - i - ous and spook-y,   they're

al - to - geth - er   ook - y,   the   Ad - dams Fam - i - ly.   Their

house is   a   mu - se - um,   where   peo - ple come to   see 'em,   they

real - ly   are   a   scree - um,   the   Ad - dams Fam - i - ly.

A Spooky Dance

Listen for the "skeleton dancers" in this piece for orchestra. How many melodic themes do you hear?

CD 19–24

Danse macabre

by Camille Saint-Saëns

To give this symphonic poem a special "spooky" feeling, the composer instructs the solo violinist to adjust one of the instrument's strings to be out of tune.

finger snaps
(Spoken) Neat   Sweet

Petite   So   get your cape or shawl on,   a

broom-stick you can crawl on, we're gon-na pay a call on the

Ad - dams Fam - i - ly.

Element: TEXTURE/HARMONY | **Skill: SINGING** | **Connection: SOCIAL STUDIES**

Sing a Song of Thanks

Many cultures and countries celebrate a bountiful harvest. The United States Congress declared Thanksgiving a legal holiday in 1941 and set aside the fourth Thursday in November for its celebration.

Celebrate the Harvest

Sing the festive song "Come, Ye Thankful People, Come" in two-part harmony.
Notice that part 2, the lower part, is highlighted.

CD 19–25

Come, Ye Thankful People, Come

Words by Henry Alford

Music by George J. Elvey

1. Come, ye thank - ful peo - ple, come, Raise the song of
2. All the bless - ings of the field, All the stores the

har - vest home; All is safe - ly gath - ered in Ere the win - ter
gar - dens yield; All the fruits in full sup-ply, Rip - ened 'neath the

storms be - gin; God, our Mak - er, doth pro - vide For our wants to
sum - mer sky; All that spring with boun-teous hand Scat - ters o'er the

be sup - plied; Come to God's own tem - ple, come,
smil - ing land; All that lib - 'ral au - tumn pours

Raise the song of har - vest home.
From her rich o'er - flow - ing stores.

An Autumn Song

The song "*Quả câu gió bay*" is the story of a boy who falls in love with a girl and gives her his coat, hat, and ring as tokens of his affection. When he returns home and is questioned by his parents regarding the missing articles, he tells them that the wind on the bridge took them away.

Sing this well-known song from Vietnam. It is often sung during spring and autumn harvest festivals.

CD 20–1

Quả câu gió bay
(The Wind on the Bridge)

English Words by Bryan Louiselle   *Folk Song from Vietnam*

1. Yêu   nhau   cời ___ áo   ý ___ a   cho ___ nhau.
1. My   love,   take my   coat   as   a   sign   of   my   love,

Về ___ nhà   dối ___ rằng   cha   dối ___ mẹ ___ a ___ ý ___ a.
Though, when I   go ___ home,   I   shall ___ have   to   tell ___ this ___ tale:

Rằng   a   ý ___ a ___ qua   cầu.   Rằng   a   ý ___ a ___ qua ___ cầu.
When   I   was ___ stand-ing   on the bridge,   When   I   was ___ stand-ing   on the bridge,

▲ During spring and autumn harvest festivals in Vietnam, participants dress in their finest, most traditional costumes to represent their villages.

Tình   tình   tình   gió_____   bay,   Tình   tình   tình   gió_____   bay.
A   strong wind blew the coat a - way,   A   strong wind blew the coat a - way.

2. *Yêu nhau cởi nón ý a cho nhau.*
   Về nhà dối rằng cha dối mẹ a ý a.
   Rằng a ý a qua cầu. Rằng a ý a qua cầu.
   Tình tình tình gió bay,
   Tình tình tình gió bay.

3. *Yêu nhau cởi nhẫn ý a cho nhau.*
   Về nhà dối rằng cha dối mẹ a ý a.
   Rằng a ý a qua cầu. Rằng a ý a qua cầu.
   Tình tình tình đánh roi,
   Tình tình tình đánh roi.

2. My love, take my hat as a sign of my love,
   Though, when I go home,
   I shall have to tell this tale:
   When I was standing on the bridge,
   When I was standing on the bridge,
   A strong wind blew the hat away,
   A strong wind blew the hat away.

3. My love, take this ring as a sign of my love,
   Though, when I go home,
   I shall have to tell this tale:
   When I was standing on the bridge,
   When I was standing on the bridge,
   A strong wind made me drop the ring,
   A strong wind made me drop the ring.

Holidays in Song

A HARVEST SONG

Native American people on the East coast use song and dance to celebrate planting, growing, and harvesting food. The Native American "Green Corn Song" is sung by many tribes. Traditionally, the first part is sung by an elder woman, representing the corn-chooser; then other women join in. Today, the song can be sung by a combination of men and women.

Listen to "Green Corn Song," a harvest song that has been sung for hundreds of years.

CD 20–5

GREEN CORN SONG

Part 1
Sing 4 times

Traditional Native American Song

Ya - nee - ga - wais   Ya - nee - ga - wais _____

Ya - ha - nee - ga - wais

Part 2

Ho   lah   da gay   kway   hai   hai   wan

D. S.

nay - oh   Ho   la   da gay   kway   hai   hai   wan   nay - oh

462

A Native American dancer at the Schemitzun festival. This event features Native American dancers, drummers, and entertainers from more than 500 tribal nations across North America.

A Chanukah Celebration

People of the Jewish faith celebrate Chanukah, the Festival of Lights,
for eight days usually in December. **Sing** "Oy, Hanuka" and join in the celebration.

CD 20–7

Oy, Hanuka
(O, Chanukah)

English Words by Judith Eisenstein *Yiddish Folk Song*

Oy, Ha - nu - ka, Oy, Ha - nu - ka, a yom - tov a shey - ner, A
lu - sti - ker, a frey - le - kher, ni - to nokh a - zoi - ner. __
O, Cha - nu - kah, O, Cha - nu - kah, come light the me - no - rah. __
Let's __ have a par - ty, we'll all dance the ho - rah. __

Al - le nakht in drey - dl shpi - ln __ mir,
Gath - er round the ta - ble, we'll give you a treat,

Zu - dik hey - se lat - kes, est on a shir. Gesh -
Shin - ing tops to play with and lat - kes to eat; And

vin - der, tsindt kin - der, Dee di - nin - ke likh - te - lekh ohn.
while we are play - ing, The can - dles are burn - ing __ low,

Zingt "Al Ha - ni - sim," loibt Gott far di ni - sim, Un
One for each night, they __ shed a sweet light to re -

1.
kumt gi - kher tan - tsn in kohn.
mind us of days long a - go,

2.
kumt gi - kher tan - tsn in kohn.
mind us of days long a - go.

464

Arts Connection

Lighting the Chanukah Lamp by
Dora Holzhandler, 1996 ▶

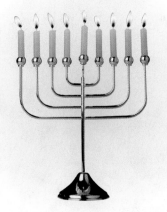

Play a Festival Song

Play these ostinatos to
accompany *"Oy, Hanuka."* The
hand drum part should be
omitted on line 4 of the song.

A Rockin' Holiday Song!

"Rockin' Around the Christmas Tree" was written in the 1950s, when rock 'n' roll was young.

Sing this upbeat song and **move** to the beat.

Create a rhythmic accompaniment that reflects the form of the song.

CD 20–11

Rockin' Around the Christmas Tree

Words and Music by Johnny Marks

A C ... G₇

Rock-in' a - round the   Christ-mas tree, _   at the Christ-mas par - ty hop. _
Rock-in' a - round the   Christ-mas tree, _   let the Christ-mas spir - it ring. _

G₇

Mis - tle - toe   hung where   you   can   see ___   ev - 'ry
La - ter we'll   have   some   pump - kin pie ___   and we'll

1. G₇   C   2. G₇   C

cou - ple   tries   to   stop.   do some car - ol - ing.

B F   Em

You will get a   sen - ti - men-tal   feel - ing when you hear ___

voic - es sing - ing, "Let's be jol - ly, Deck the halls with boughs of hol - ly."

Rock-in' a - round the Christ-mas tree, have a hap - py hol - i - day.

Last time to Coda

Ev-'ry-one danc-ing mer - ri - ly in the new old - fash-ioned way.

Coda

new old - fash - ioned way.

A Musical Lullaby

This beautiful carol, "*Still, Still, Still,*" is from Austria, a country that receives lots of snow in winter. Find Austria on a map of Europe, and then decide why Austria is a popular country for winter sports.

CD 20–14

Still, Still, Still
(Sleep, Dearest Child)

English Words by Ruth Martin (adapted)

Traditional Carol from Austria

1. Still, ___ still, ___ still, weils Kind - lein ___ schla - fen ___
2. Schlaf, ___ schlaf, ___ schlaf, mein ___ lie - bes ___ Kind - lein ___
1. Sleep, ___ sleep, ___ sleep, my ___ dear - est ___ child, now ___
2. Dream, ___ dream, ___ dream, a ___ love - ly ___ shin - ing ___

will. Ma - ri - a ___ tut es nie - der - sing - en,
schlaf. Die Eng - el ___ tun schön mu - si - zie - ren
sleep. The guard - ian ___ an - gels dear - ly ___ love you,
dream. A - cross the ___ deep blue heav - ens ___ yon - der,

sei - ne ___ gro - sse Lieb dar - bring - en.
bei dem ___ Kind - lein ju - bi - lie - ren.
Sing - ing ___ soft - ly there a - bove you.
Light - ly from star to star you'll ___ wan - der.

Still, ___ still, ___ still, weils Kind - lein schla - fen ___ will.
Schlaf, ___ schlaf, ___ schlaf, mein lie - bes ___ Kind - lein ___ schlaf.
Sleep, ___ sleep, ___ sleep, my ___ dear - est ___ child, now ___ sleep.
Dream, ___ dream, ___ dream, a ___ love - ly ___ shin - ing ___ dream.

Accompanying a Carol

When groups go caroling, they often choose a portable instrument to add harmony. To accompany "*Still, Still, Still,*" **play** these chords on the Autoharp or guitar.

A CHRISTMAS *Spiritual*

Some African American spirituals are about Christmas. This spiritual, "Rise Up, Shepherd, and Follow," is in call-and-response form.

Sing the song, taking turns as the soloist for the "call" sections.

A Spirited Spiritual

Listen to this exciting performance of *Rise Up, Shepherd, and Follow.* What voice types do you hear in the choir?

CD 20–18

Rise Up, Shepherd, and Follow

African American Spiritual

This arrangement of *Rise Up, Shepherd, and Follow* is performed by The Century Men. Buryl Red is the conductor.

Can you hear a second African American spiritual in this recording? What is it?

Rise Up, Shepherd, and Follow

African American Spiritual

VERSE

Solo   C

do

1. There's a star in the East on Christ - mas morn,
2. If you take good __ heed of the an - gel's words,

Chorus
C   B♭   G

Rise up, shep - herd, and fol - low.

Solo   C   3

It will lead to the place where the babe is born, _____
You'll for - get your __ flocks, you'll for - get your herds, _____

Chorus
D₇   G₇   C

Rise up, shep - herd, and fol - low.

REFRAIN
C   B♭

Fol - low, fol - low, Rise up, shep - herd, and

G   C   3

fol - low.   Fol - low the star of Beth - le - hem, _____

D₇   G₇   C

Rise up, shep - herd, and fol - low.

Holidays in Song

Carols for Christmas

Christmas is celebrated with Spanish-language songs in many parts of the world. *"Las Navidades"* is from Puerto Rico, an island in the Caribbean that is a commonwealth of the United States.

Sing the rhythm of *"Las Navidades"* using rhythm syllables.

CD 20–21

Las Navidades
(The Christmas Season)

English Words by Shelley Belgard

Traditional from Puerto Rico

1. Por fin lle - ga - ron   las Na - vi - da - des
2. Con tam - bo - ri - les   güi - ro y ma - ra - cas
1. The Christ-mas sea - son   is here a - gain now,
2. We play the gui - ro   and the ma - ra - cas,

las fies - tas rea - les   de nues - tro lar.
mi se - re - na - ta   a - le - gre va.
a cel - e - bra - tion   with - in our home.
while we are sing - ing   our joy - ful song.

Fies - ta de to - dos   nues - tros an - he - los,
De - se - o a to - dos   por des - pe - di - da
And we all long for   this hap - py sea - son,
And so we wish you   a Mer - ry Christ - mas,

nues - tros des - ve - los, y   nues - tro a - fán.
a - ños de vi - da y fe - li - ci - dad.
with great ex - cite - ment and joy - ful hearts.
a joy - ful New Year, and hap - pi - ness.

A Carol from Catalonia

Catalonia is a region in northeast Spain known for its beautiful beaches and mountains. People who live there speak both Spanish and Catalan.

Sing this Catalonian carol using pitch syllables.

How many examples of repetition can you **identify** in the melody?

CD 20–25

El desembre congelat
(Cold December)

English Words by Aura Kontra

Fifteenth-Century Melody from Catalonia

1. El de - sem - bre con - ge - lat, Con - fós es re - ti - ra.
2. El pri - mer Pa - re caus - á, La nit te - ne - bro - sa.
1. Cold De - cem - ber days pro - claim that the year is end - ing.
2. For this night the Child has come, peace to man - kind bring - ing.

A - bril de flors co - ro - nat, Tot el món ad - mi - ra.
Que a tot el món o - fus - cà La vis - ta pen - o - sa.
And a great re - splen-dent light toward the Earth is bend - ing.
An - gels greet Him in a throng, joy - ful prais - es sing - ing.

Quan en un jar - di d'a - mor Neix u - na di - vi - na flor. D'u - na
Mes en u - na mit - ja - nit bri - lla el sol que n'és eix - it. D'u - na
1., 2. God sent down His Son di - vine, Gave to man a gift sub - lime. And the

ro ro ro, d'u - na sa sa sa, d'u - na ro, d'u - na
bel bel bel, d'u - na la la la, d'u - na bel, d'u - na
shep - herds came in the dark of night And the kings brought their

sa, d'u - na ro - sa bel - la, Fe - cun - da i pon - cel - la.
la, d'u - na bel - la au - ro - ra que el cel en - a - mo - ra.
gifts where the Child lay sleep - ing, Sing - ing al - le - lu - ia.

Ring In the New!

"Deck the Hall" was originally a New Year's carol. Now it is frequently performed at Christmas celebrations.

Sing "Deck the Hall" in unison. Then add the countermelody.

CD 20–29
MIDI 37

Deck the Hall

Traditional Carol from Wales

1. {Deck   the   hall   with   boughs   of   hol - ly,}
   {'Tis   the   sea - son   to   be   jol - ly,}
2. {See   the   blaz - ing   Yule   be - fore   us,}
   {Strike   the   harp   and   join   the   chor - us,}

Fa   la   la   la   la   la   la   la   la.

Countermelody

Fa   la   la   la   la   la   la.

Don   we   now   our   gay   ap - par - el,
Fol - low   me   in   mer - ry   mea - sure,

1. Fa la la la la la la la la la.

2. Fa la la la la la la la la la.

1/2 Troll the an - cient Yule - tide car - ol,
While I tell of Yule - tide trea - sure,

1. Fa la la la la la la la la.

2. Fal la la la la la la la la.

3. Fast away the old year passes,   Sing we joyous all together,
   Fa la la . . .   Fa la la . . .
   Hail the new, ye lads and lasses, Heedless of the wind and weather,
   Fa la la . . .   Fa la la . . .

Fa La La!

"Deck the Hall" uses an old Welsh melody called "*Nos galan.*"

Listen to this modern version of *Deck the Hall.*

CD 20–31
Deck the Hall

Traditional Carol from Wales as performed by Mannheim Steamroller

The driving beat in this "electric" performance gives energy to the repeating melody.

MIDI Use the song file for "Deck the Hall" to practice the harmony part at a slower tempo.

A JOYFUL SOUND

Kwanzaa, or "first fruits of the harvest," is an African American holiday inspired by African harvest traditions. The occasion honors family, culture, and community. The celebration lasts for seven days, from December 26 through January 1.

Sing "*Heri za Kwanzaa*," a song that describes the joyous feelings of the celebration and the seven principles of the holiday.

CD 20–32

HERI ZA KWANZAA
(Happy Kwanzaa)

Words and Music by Victor Cook

(Harmony optional)

do

"Her - i za Kwan - zaa, Her - i za Kwan -

- zaa," Hap - py, hap - py Kwan - zaa,

This, we cel - e - brate. _____ _____ U -

mo - ja is u - ni - ty, Ku - ji - cha - gu - li - a, self-

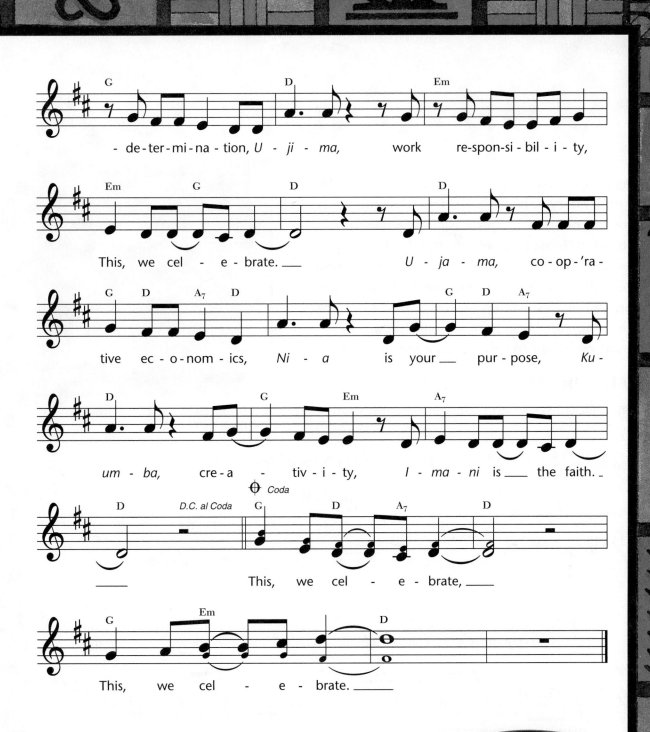

Colors of *Kwanzaa*

The colors of *Kwanzaa* are black, red, and green. Black represents black people and their African heritage. Red represents their long struggle for freedom and equality. Green represents the hills of Africa and also the future.

Happy New Year!

Many people around the world celebrate New Year's Day on January 1. New Year is Japan's most important holiday. *Shogatsu* is a three-day celebration. Most Japanese do not work during *O-Shogatsu*. House cleaning and food preparation are done earlier. Food is stored in special boxes. Many Japanese families wait up on New Year's Eve to hear the *Joya-no-Kan,* large temple bells that are rung 108 times at midnight to drive away evil thoughts.

Say It, Sing It

Sing "*Hitotsu toya,*" an *O-Shogatsu* celebration song.

▲ Temple bell at the Chion-in Temple, Japan

CD 21–1
MIDI 38

Hitotsu toya
(Temple Bells)

English Words Anonymous   *Folk Song from Japan*

1. ひ - と - つ - と - や _____ ひ - と - よ あ - く - れ - ば
1. Hi - to - tsu to - ya, _____ Hi - to - yo a - ku - re - ba
1. Tem - ple bells will chime, oh, ___ chime for the bright new year that

に - ぎ - や - か で、 に - ぎ - や - か で、
Ni - gi - ya - ka de, Ni - gi - ya - ka de,
comes to us to - night, Comes to us to - night.

お - か - ざ - り た - て - た - る ま - つ - か - ざ -
O - ka - za - ri ta - te ta - ru Ma - tsu - ka - za -
Now on ev - 'ry door there hangs a spray of love - ly

478

			Ma	tsu	ka	za	ri.
ri,							
pine,	a		spray	of	love	ly	pine.

2. ふたつとや
   ふたばのまつは
   いろよていろよて
   さんがいまつは
   かすがやまかすがやま

2. Futatsu toya,
   Futaba no matsu wa
   Iro yo te, Iro yo te.
   Sangai-matsu wa
   Kasuga-yama, Kasuga-yama.

2. Temple bells will chime, oh,
   chime for the fragrance and the
   green throughout the year.
   (2 times)
   Of the fine and healthy pine on
   Kasuga Yama, on Kasuga Yama.

3. みっつとや
   みなさんこのひは
   らくあそびらくあそび
   ふるさきこまどで
   はねをつくはねをつく

3. Mittsu toya,
   Minasan kono hi wa
   Raku-asobi, Raku-asobi,
   Furusaki komado de
   Hane o tsuku, Hane o tsuku.

3. Temple bells will chime, oh,
   chime in the merriment, the
   music, games, and dance.
   (2 times)
   People swing the battledore.
   This is the time to play.
   This is the day to play.

Add an Accompaniment!

Play this melody on mallet instruments to accompany *"Hitotsu toya."*

Play 3 times

Get in Motion!

Move to show the ringing of the temple bells as you **sing** *"Hitotsu toya."*

Classical dance at the *O-Shogatsu* festival ▶

Three Kings Day

Spanish-speaking children throughout the world celebrate *Día de los Reyes* (Three Kings Day). In Puerto Rico, Christmas celebrating begins on Christmas Eve and lasts until January 6. Children wake up on Three Kings Day to find toys and gifts. In some regions children leave empty shoes out so that visiting Wise Men can leave food or gifts.

Sing "*Los reyes de Oriente.*" Is the song based on a major or a minor scale? Next, **sing** the harmony part. How does this part relate to the melody?

CD 21–5
MIDI 39

Los reyes de Oriente
(The Kings from the East)

English Words by Aura Kontra   *Aguinaldo from Puerto Rico*

De tie-rra le-ja-na ve-ni-mos a ver-te,
From a dis-tant land, we come in ad-o-ra-tion,

Nos sir-ve de guí-a la es-tre-lla de O-rien-te.
Fol-low-ing a star, a star of fas-ci-na-tion,

¡Oh, bri-llan-te es-tre-lla que a-nun-cias la au-ro-ra,
Shin-ing star so bright, till dawn you rule the night, ___

No me fal-te nun-ca tu luz bien-he-cho-ra!
Nev-er cease to guide us with your kind-ly light. _____

Christmas Harmony

The *aguinaldo* [ah-ghee-NAHL-doh] is a folk song with lyrics that describe Christmas themes. Instruments such as the guitar, *cuatro*, *tiple*, *tres*, and *guiro* are used as an accompaniment that adds to the musical flavor of the culture.

▲ *Cuatro*

◀ *Guiro*

Participants in a Three Kings Day celebration, Puerto Rico ▼

A Song For Freedom

The words to "Lift Ev'ry Voice and Sing" were written in 1900 by James Weldon Johnson to commemorate the birthday of Abraham Lincoln. The poet's brother, J. Rosamond Johnson, set the words to music. "Lift Ev'ry Voice and Sing" is regarded as the African American national anthem.

In what ways were Martin Luther King Jr. and Abraham Lincoln alike?

Sing "Lift Ev'ry Voice and Sing" in a slow, even tempo. How would you **describe** the appropriate expression?

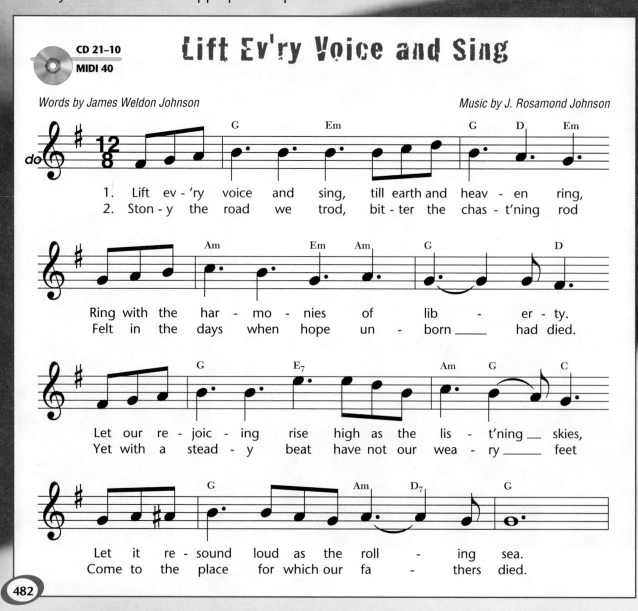

CD 21–10
MIDI 40

Lift Ev'ry Voice and Sing

Words by James Weldon Johnson   *Music by J. Rosamond Johnson*

1. Lift ev - 'ry voice and sing, till earth and heav - en ring,
2. Ston - y the road we trod, bit - ter the chas - t'ning rod

Ring with the har - mo - nies of lib - er - ty.
Felt in the days when hope un - born ____ had died.

Let our re - joic - ing rise high as the lis - t'ning __ skies,
Yet with a stead - y beat have not our wea - ry ____ feet

Let it re - sound loud as the roll - ing sea.
Come to the place for which our fa - thers died.

Sing a song full of the faith that the dark past has taught us;
We have come o - ver a way that with tears has been wa - tered;

Sing a song full of the hope that the pres-ent has brought us; _____
We have come tread-ing our path through the blood of the slaugh - tered; ___

Fac - ing the ris - ing sun of our new day be - gun,
Out from the gloom - y past, till now we stand at _____ last

Let us march on till vic - to - ry _____ is won.
Where the white gleam of our bright star _____ is cast.

MIDI Use the song file for "Lift Ev'ry Voice and Sing" to experiment with different tempos. As the tempo gets faster, how does the mood change?

Create a movement to accompany one of the eight different phrases of the song. Think about the meaning of the lyrics for your phrase.

Perform your movement while singing "Lift Ev'ry Voice and Sing." Stand motionless when you are not moving to your phrase.

Martin Luther King Jr. leading the March on Washington, D.C., March 25, 1965 ▶

Holidays in Song

Let Freedom Ring!

The Civil Rights movement did not stop with the death of Dr. Martin Luther King. This song celebrates our freedom and reminds us that securing individual freedom and civil rights for all people is a continuous struggle.

For Children Safe and Strong

Words and Music by James A. Forbes, Jr.
Arranged by Joseph Joubert

VERSE

1. We shall o-ver-come has got to be more than a free-dom song. _
2. We shall o-ver-come has got to be more than a mem-o-ry. ____
3. We shall o-ver-come has got to be more than a pro-test song. _

It's join-ing hands _ a-cross the land _ for chil-dren safe __ and strong. ..
It's a new re-solve _ to get in-volved _ in build-ing com-mu-ni-ty. ___
It's a lov-ing vow _ to learn some-how _ we all can get __ a-long. _

We shall o-ver-come has got to be more than a fer-vent prayer. _
We shall o-ver-come has got to be more than a dis-tant dream. _
We shall o-ver-come has got to be more than a res-cue plan. _

It's sac-ri-fice _ at an-y price ___ to show them that __ we care. _
It's hous-ing, health, _ and jobs right now, _ and a place on the free-dom team. _
It's a wake-up call _ to one and all. ____ It's time to hope _ a-gain. ..

REFRAIN

Oh, ____ there's a place for ev-'ry-one, _ let us face the ris-ing sun. _

____ Then we shall o-ver- come. ____

484

A Hymn for Civil Rights

"We Shall Overcome" became the anthem of the American Civil Rights movement during the early 1960s. It was also an anthem for workers in the 1940s and Chinese students in 1989.

CD 21–14
We Shall Overcome

**African American Spiritual
as performed by Louis Armstrong**

The words of *We Shall Overcome* have changed through the years but the spirit of the song remains the same.

Nobel Peace Prize Winners ▼

Rigoberta Menchú Tum

Mother Teresa

Yitzhak Rabin

Jane Addams

The Dalai Lama

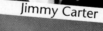

Jimmy Carter

Holidays in Song

America sings

Tune In

The melody for "America" is the melody of "God Save the Queen," the national anthem of Great Britain.

"America" was written by Samuel F. Smith to celebrate Washington's birthday. It was performed for the first time on July 4, 1831, by a group of Boston children.

Play the part below on hand bells, chimes, or resonator bells to accompany verses one and two of "America."

CD 21–15

America

Words by Samuel Francis Smith

Traditional Melody

1. My coun - try! 'tis of thee, Sweet land of
2. My na - tive coun - try, thee, Land of the
3. Let mu - sic swell the breeze, And ring from
4. Our fa - thers' God, to Thee, Au - thor of

lib - er - ty, Of thee I sing; Land where my
no - ble free, Thy name I love; I love thy
all the trees Sweet Free - dom's song; Let mor - tal
lib - er - ty, To Thee we sing; Long may our

Samuel Francis Smith, seated at the desk of Edgar Silver, founder of Silver Burdett ▶

fa	-	thers	died,	Land	of	the	Pil - grims' pride,
rocks	and	rills,	Thy	woods	and	tem - pled hills,
tongues	a -	wake,	Let	all	that	breathe par - take,
land	be	bright	With	Free - dom's	ho - ly light;

From ev - 'ry ___ moun - tain - side, Let ___ free - dom ring!
My heart ___ with ___ rap - ture thrills Like ___ that a - bove.
Let rocks ___ their ___ si - lence break, The ___ sound pro - long.
Pro - tect ___ us ___ by Thy might, Great ___ God, our King!

Our National Anthem

During the War of 1812, Francis Scott Key wrote the words to "The Star-Spangled Banner." In 1931 an act of Congress established "The Star-Spangled Banner" as the national anthem of the United States.

Practice both the melody and harmony parts for "The Star-Spangled Banner." Then **sing** in two-part harmony.

CD 21–17

The Star-Spangled Banner

Words by Francis Scott Key

Music by John Stafford Smith

1. Oh, __ say! can you see, by the dawn's ear - ly light,
2. On the shore, dim - ly seen through the mists of the deep,
3. Oh, __ thus be it ever when __ free men shall stand

What so proud - ly we hailed at the twi - light's last gleam-ing,
Where the foe's haugh-ty host in dread si - lence re - pos - es,
Be - tween their loved homes and the war's des - o - la - tion!

Whose broad stripes and bright stars, through the per - il - ous fight,
What is that which the breeze, o'er the tow - er - ing steep,
Blest with vict - 'ry and peace, may the heav'n-res - cued land

O'er the ram - parts we watched were so gal - lant - ly stream-ing?
As it fit - ful - ly blows, half con - ceals, half dis - clos - es?
Praise the Pow'r that hath made and pre - served us a na - tion!

Let's Celebrate

Music is often an important part of celebrations.

Listen to *The Fourth of July.* The music paints a lively picture of the holiday.

CD 21–19

The Fourth of July

by Morton Gould
performed by Morton Gould and his Symphonic Band

Gould's "Yankee Doodle" celebration includes fireworks and a parade.

And the rock - ets' red glare, the bombs burst - ing in air,
Now it catch - es the gleam of the morn - ing's first beam,
Then __ con - quer we must, for our cause it is just,

Gave proof through the night that our flag was still there.
In full glo - ry re - flected now __ shines on the stream.
And this be our motto: "In ____ God is our trust!"

Oh, say, does that __ Star - Span - gled Ban - ner __ yet __ wave __
'Tis the Star - Span - gled __ Ban - ner, oh, long may __ it ____ wave __
And the Star - Span - gled __ Ban - ner in tri - umph __ shall __ wave __

O'er the land ____ of the free and the home of the brave?
O'er the land ____ of the free and the home of the brave!
O'er the land ____ of the free and the home of the brave!

Holidays in Song

Music Reading Practice

Reading Sequence 1, page 10

CD 1–14
MIDI 42

Rhythm: Reading Meter in 4

Use rhythm syllables to **read** and **perform** this counter-rhythm for "Laredo."

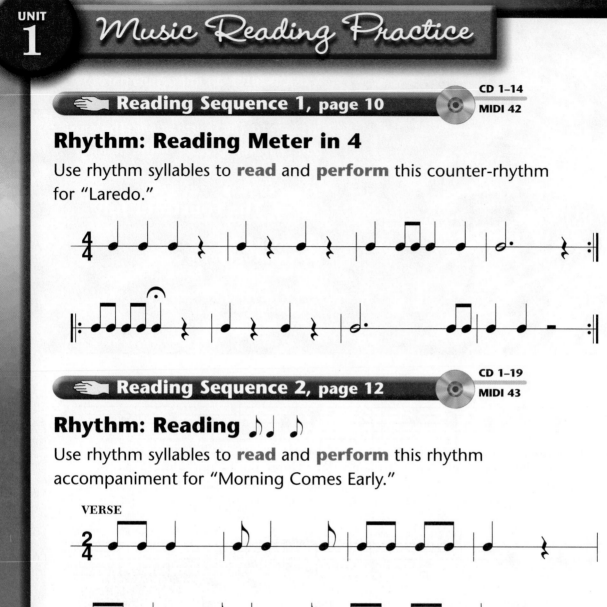

Reading Sequence 2, page 12

CD 1–19
MIDI 43

Rhythm: Reading

Use rhythm syllables to **read** and **perform** this rhythm accompaniment for "Morning Comes Early."

VERSE

REFRAIN

CD 2–3
MIDI 44

Melody: Reading Note Names (C-D-E-G-A)

Read and **sing** this countermelody for "Bound for South Australia." Use pitch syllables and hand signs.

CD 2–12
MIDI 45

Melody: Reading Pentatonic Patterns

For inner hearing practice, use pitch syllables and hand signs to **read** and **sing** this countermelody for "This Train."

Music Reading Practice

Reading Sequence 5, page 52

CD 3–11
MIDI 46

Rhythm: Reading ♩ ♫ ♩ and ♫♩

Use rhythm syllables to **read** and **perform** this two-part rhythm accompaniment for "California."

Reading Sequence 6, page 54

CD 3–18
MIDI 47

Rhythm: Reading ♩ ♫♩, ♫♩♩, and ♬♩

Use rhythm syllables to **read** and **perform** this counter-rhythm for "Drill, Ye Tarriers."

Melody: Reading *fa*

Read and **sing** this two-part countermelody for *"A la puerta del cielo."* Use pitch syllables and hand signs.

Melody: Reading *do, re, mi, fa, so,* and *la*

Read and **sing** this countermelody for *"Da pacem, Domine."* Use pitch syllables and hand signs.

CD 5–15
MIDI 50

Reading Sequence 9, page 94

Rhythm: Reading 𝅘𝅥𝅮. and 𝅘𝅥𝅮

Use rhythm syllables to **read** and **perform** this counter-rhythm for *"Himmel und Erde."*

CD 5–21
MIDI 51

Reading Sequence 10, page 96

Rhythm: Reading Dotted-Rhythm Patterns

Use rhythm syllables to **read** and **perform** this counter-rhythm for "Don't You Hear the Lambs?"

Melody: Reading *low ti*

Read and **sing** this two-part countermelody for "All Through the Night." Use pitch syllables and hand signs.

Melody: Reading *low ti*

Read and **sing** this two-part countermelody for *"Dundai."* Use pitch syllables and hand signs.

Music Reading Practice

Reading Sequence 13, page 136

CD 7–3
MIDI 54

Rhythm: Reading

Use rhythm syllables to **read** and **perform** this counter-rhythm for "Wabash Cannon Ball."

Reading Sequence 14, page 138

CD 7–8
MIDI 55

Rhythm: Reading Dotted-Rhythm Patterns

Use rhythm syllables to **read** and **perform** this counter-rhythm for "Scotland the Brave."

Melody: Reading a Diatonic Major Scale

Read and **sing** this countermelody for *"Las velitas."* Use pitch syllables and hand signs.

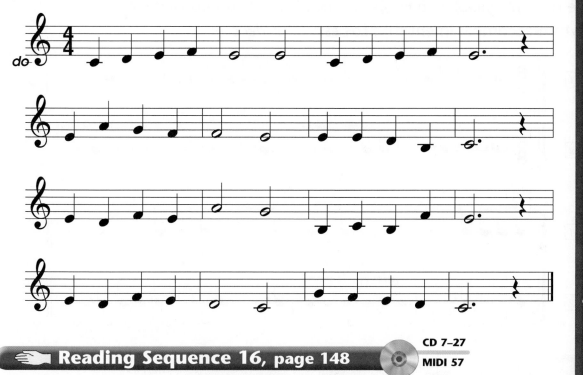

Melody: Reading a Melodic Sequence

Read and **sing** this countermelody for "Autumn Canon." Use pitch syllables and hand signs.

Reading Sequence 17, page 174

CD 8–33
MIDI 58

Rhythm: Reading in Compound Meter

Use rhythm syllables to **read** and **perform** this two-part rhythm accompaniment for "*Las estrellitas del cielo.*"

Reading Sequence 18, page 178

CD 9–10
MIDI 59

Rhythm: Reading in ⁶⁄₈ Meter

Use rhythm syllables to **read** and **perform** this rhythm accompaniment for "Blow the Wind Southerly."

Reading Sequence 19, page 188

Melody: Reading the Natural Minor Scale

Read and **sing** this countermelody for "Johnny Has Gone for a Soldier." Use pitch syllables and hand signs.

Reading Sequence 20, page 190

Melody: Reading the Harmonic Minor Scale

Read and **sing** this two-part countermelody for "Go Down, Moses." Use pitch syllables and hand signs.

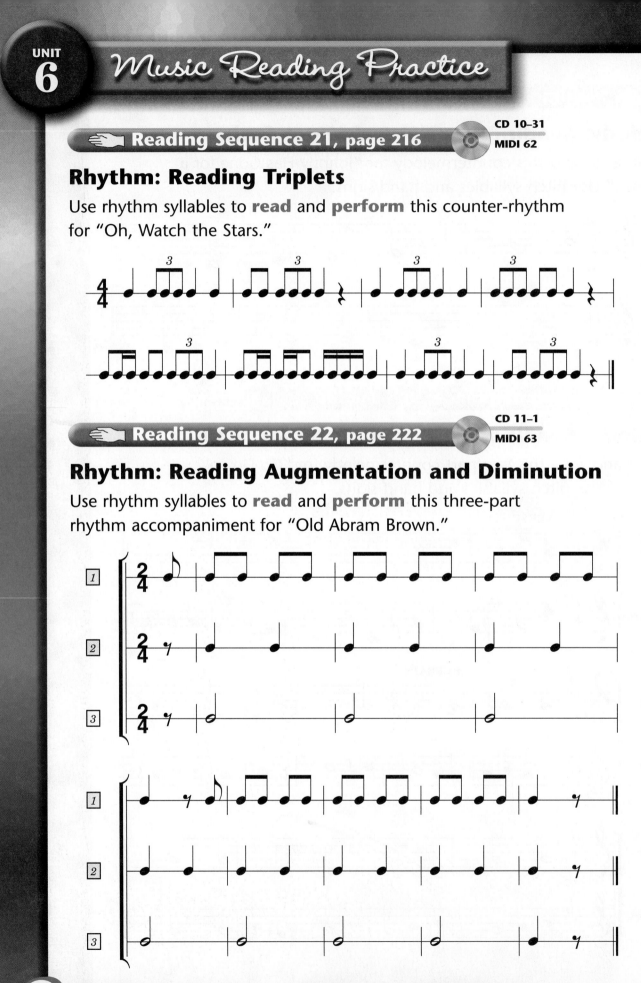

Reading Sequence 21, page 216

CD 10–31
MIDI 62

Rhythm: Reading Triplets

Use rhythm syllables to **read** and **perform** this counter-rhythm for "Oh, Watch the Stars."

Reading Sequence 22, page 222

CD 11–1
MIDI 63

Rhythm: Reading Augmentation and Diminution

Use rhythm syllables to **read** and **perform** this three-part rhythm accompaniment for "Old Abram Brown."

CD 11–18
MIDI 64

Melody: Reading in Mixolydian Mode

Read and **sing** this countermelody for "The Greenland Whale Fishery." Use pitch syllables and hand signs.

CD 11–23
MIDI 65

Melody: Reading in Dorian Mode

Read and **sing** this countermelody for "Connemara Lullaby." Use pitch syllables and hand signs.

This section of your book will help you develop your skill at playing the soprano recorder.

Getting Ready

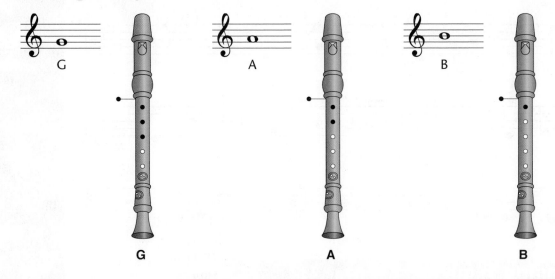

G   A   B

G   A   B

Look at the diagram for the note G. Using your left hand, cover the holes that are darkened. Press hard enough so that the holes make a light mark on each finger and thumb. Cover the tip of the mouthpiece with your lips. Blow gently as you whisper *daah*. **Play** a steady beat on the note G. After you can play G, try practicing A and B. The diagrams will help with finger placement.

Soprano, alto, tenor, and bass recorders are played together to form a consort. Sometimes the higher sound of the sopranino recorder is added.

◀ Alto

Soprano ▶

Tenor ▶

Beginning with a "B-A-G" Song

Now that you can play B, A, and G, **play** a countermelody to accompany the song "Wabash Cannon Ball," page 136. It can be played during the verse or the refrain. Choose which section you want to **sing** and which section you want to **play**.

Building Right Hand Strength

Here are two new notes. Cover the holes securely with your fingers flat, not arched, and whisper *daah*. When playing notes in the low register of the recorder, remember to use very little air.

Below is a recorder countermelody that you can **play** during the verses of "California," page 52. Find a way to tap the beat as you **sing** the refrain. Does the recorder countermelody use mostly steps, leaps, or repeats?

Adding High C and High D

Practice playing high C and high D. (Remember to move your thumb slightly away from the hole when playing D.) When you can **play** these notes, accompany the refrain of the song "Drill, Ye Tarriers," page 54, on your recorder. How is the recorder part different from the main melody? How is it the same?

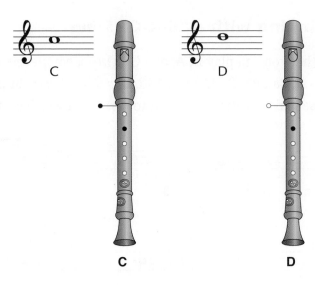

C   D

C   D

Listen to this Renaissance piece played by a recorder consort.

CD 21–20

The Honiesuckle

by Anthony Holborne
as performed by the Flanders Recorder Quartet

The English composer Anthony Holborne lived during the sixteenth century and was described as having been a "Gentleman usher" to Queen Elizabeth I.

◄ A child in sixteenth century costume playing a Renaissance descant recorder

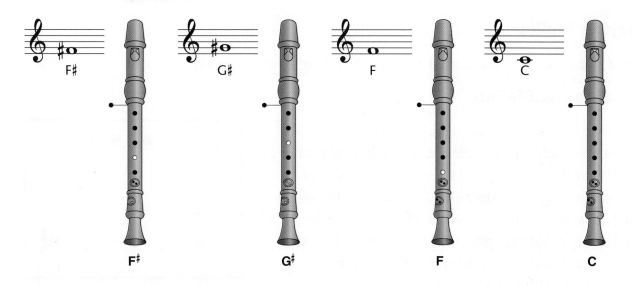

Learning Notes in Pairs

Try learning these new notes paired with notes you already know: F♯ with G; G♯ with A; F and C. This half-step rule will help you remember how to finger F♯ and G♯.

1. Think of the fingering for the note that is a half step higher than the note with the sharp.

2. Skip a hole on your recorder and then cover the next two holes.

New Recorder Challenges

When you can play F♯ and G♯, play this countermelody with "Laredo," page 10.

Use the diagrams above to learn to play F and low C. **Play** this countermelody during the refrain of *"A la puerta del cielo,"* page 60.

Practice each countermelody slowly as you become familiar with these new notes.

Mallet Instruments

Playing Mallets

When using mallets to play barred instruments, follow these simple suggestions.

Holding the Mallets

Fold your fingers and thumbs around the mallet handle—the thumb should lie alongside the handle, but the pointer finger should not sit on top of the mallet. The backs of your hands should face the ceiling. Grip the handles on the hand grips, but not at the very end. (Smaller hands may need to grip further up toward the mallet head.) Elbows should hang easily at your sides. Avoid elbows that stick out to the side or hug the body.

Striking the Bars

Strike each bar at its center, not at either end. Let your mallet strike quickly and then bounce away. If you let the mallet stay on the bar, the sound is stopped.

Matching Mallets to Instruments

It is important to choose the appropriate mallet for each instrument to make the best sound.

For special effects, use hard wood mallets or mallet handles. Avoid anything that would damage the surface of the bars.

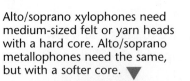

Bass instruments need large felt or yarn heads. Choose softer mallets for metallophones, and harder mallets for xylophones.

Alto/soprano xylophones need medium-sized felt or yarn heads with a hard core. Alto/soprano metallophones need the same, but with a softer core. ▼

Glockenspiels need small wood, hard rubber, or composition heads. ▼

Position

You may sit or stand while playing mallet instruments. This depends on the distance of the top of the instrument from the floor. Your body should stay straight with your arms placed easily in front of you to strike the bars.

Sit on the floor. ▶

◀ Sit in a chair to play bass instruments.

Stand ▶

◀ Sit in a chair.

Playing the Guitar

Why Play the Guitar?

The guitar is perhaps the most loved instrument in the United States, especially among young people. Most popular and folk music includes the guitar. You can very quickly learn how to begin making music with the guitar by following the suggestions included in these pages.

Types of Guitars

There are three types of guitars—nylon-string classical, steel-string acoustic, and electric. Look at these photographs and learn the names of their parts.

tuners

nut

fret

neck and fingerboard

soundhole

pick-ups

tremelo arm

tone and volume controls

toggle switch

▲ Nylon-String Classical Guitar

▲ Steel-String Acoustic Guitar

▲ Electric Guitar

Tuning the Guitar

- Guitar strings are numbered 1, 2, 3, 4, 5, 6, with the sixth string being the lowest in pitch. (It is also the thickest string.)

- You can tune the guitar using the keys of the piano. The illustration to the right shows what keys to use for tuning each guitar string.

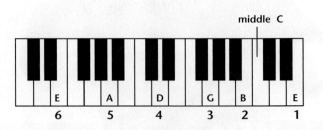

middle C

E   A   D   G   B   E

6   5   4   3   2   1

- You can also tune your guitar by using an electronic tuner, which allows you to "see" when each string is in tune.

- You can also tune the guitar by using a method called "relative tuning." Follow these steps:

1. Tune the sixth, or lowest-pitched, string to E on the piano or pitch pipe.

2. Press the sixth string on fret 5 and pluck it with your right thumb, producing the note A, which you use to tune the next, or fifth, string.

3. Reach your right hand over to the tuners, and turn the fifth-string tuner until the two sounds match. Now the fifth string is in tune.

4. Press the fifth string on fret 5, and use the pitch to tune the fourth string, repeating the tuning process as before.

5. Press the fourth string on fret 5, and use the pitch to tune the third string.

6. Press the third string on fret 4, and use the pitch to tune the second string.

7. Press the second string on fret 5, and use the pitch to tune the first string. Now you are in tune!

The Best Playing Positions

There are three ways to hold your guitar comfortably and correctly. Notice the different ways that are pictured here:

- Always raise the guitar neck slightly, because this allows the left hand to play chords without extra tension and effort.

- Always keep the front of the guitar completely vertical, because this also helps the left hand to play chords easily.

- Place the thumb of your left hand behind the neck. Keep your fingers arched as you reach around the neck to press the strings. Press the strings down onto the fingerboard by trying to pinch your thumb and fingers together. Keep your palm away from the neck.

Playing Basics

Here is some basic information on how to **play** the guitar:

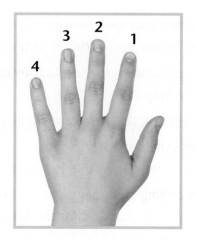

- The left-hand fingers press the strings on the frets to produce chords, which are used to accompany songs.
- The right-hand thumb brushes the strings to make the sounds.
- Notice how the left-hand fingers are numbered; you will use these numbers when you begin reading the guitar chords.

Playing Guitar Chords

- All chords have note names—these are indicated in many song scores in this book, as shown on the right. The position of the chord names tells you what chords you will use, and when you will be changing chords in the song.

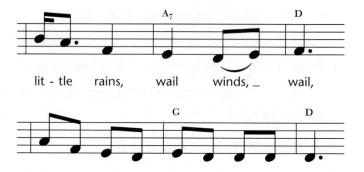

Guitar Chords Used in This Book

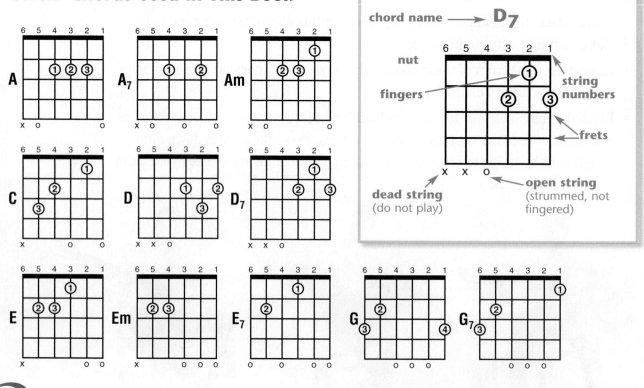

Some Hints on Practicing

- Practice right and left hand separately if it helps you, but always try to "put everything together" (both hands playing while singing the song) each time you practice. This will help you develop the "feeling" of playing, which you will never forget!

- If possible, watch yourself play in the mirror, so that you can "see" that you are actually playing and doing a great job!

- It is better to play songs slowly at an even pace and gradually build up the tempo, than to play quickly through the easy parts and slow down at the difficult parts. Playing evenly helps your mind and hands stay together!

How You Can Tell You're Improving

You are improving if you answer "yes" to more and more of these questions:

- Can you make chord changes without looking?

- Can you play at an even tempo?

- Can you sing along while you play?

- Do your fingertips hurt less when you play?

- Can you play for longer periods of time?

- Can you play some songs from memory?

Guitar

Sitting Position

For maximum support from your arms, shoulders and back, sit slightly forward on the bench with your feet resting on the floor at all times. Your knees should be just under the front edge of the keyboard. Sitting too close will push the elbows back which in turn will cause the shoulders to go up and tension to develop. You should feel a center of gravity, which will allow you to lean from side to side if necessary.

Hand Position

The most supportive hand position is the shape of your hand as it hangs naturally at your side. When you bring your hand up to the keyboard, the fingers should be slightly curved at the middle joint and the wrist should be parallel to the keyboard. You should feel a certain amount of "flexibility" in your elbows as they hang near your side. Don't be a hugger – one who keeps the elbows too close to the sides at all times. The elbow should follow through with the natural movement of your wrist.

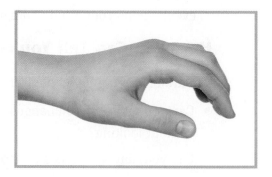

Finger Numbers

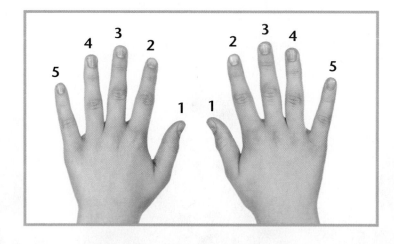

Fingering for Steps and Skips

How a melody moves determines the fingering on the keyboard. Look at the diagrams at the top of page 513. By translating the keyboard examples to one- and two-line staves, it is easy to see how right/left movement on the keyboard relates to up/down movement on the staff.

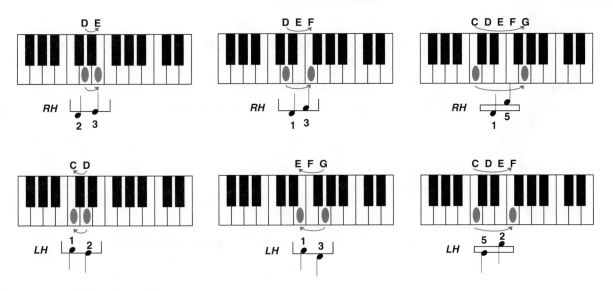

Three-Line Reading

Play the following examples. Determine a logical fingering before you begin each one.

RH   Begin on D:

LH   Begin on D:

Playing from Treble and Bass Clefs

When singing music, you have learned to follow the upward/downward direction of a melody and to determine if it moves by step, by leap, or if it stays on a repeated tone. When playing music, you must read music in the same way as well as determine where to play the notes on the keyboard. Each note in printed music indicates one place, and only one place, where it can be played.

Sound Bank

◄ *Arpa* [AHR-pah] A folk harp that has 34–36 nylon strings and spans almost five octaves. It is a diatonic instrument and must be retuned to play in a different key. The arpa is used especially for the *jarocho* music of Veracruz, Mexico. CD 21–21

◄ *Axatse* [ahks-AHT-see] An African rattle made from a gourd that is cut, emptied of its seeds, dried in the sun, and covered with loose-fitting net. Small beads or shells woven into the net create loud sounds as they hit the hollow gourd. CD 21–22

◄ *Bodhran* [boh-RAHN] A drum from Ireland made of animal skin nailed to a single-headed frame; hand-held, using a criss-cross system of cord, wire, or sticks over the open end. CD 21–23

◄ **Bongo Drums** A pair of small Afro-Cuban single-headed drums made from hollowed tree trunks that are joined together horizontally. The larger drum is placed to the player's right. The drums are played with bare hands. CD 21–24

◄ **Clarinet** A cylinder-shaped wind instrument, usually made of wood. There are holes and metal keys on the side of the clarinet and a reed in the mouthpiece. Low notes on the clarinet are soft and mellow. The middle notes are open and bright, and the highest notes are thin and resonant. CD 21–25

◄ **Conga Drum** An Afro-Cuban elongated drum. The muleskin head is struck with the hands. Pressing the head with the hand, elbow, or wrist raises the pitch. CD 21–26

◀ **Doumbek** [DOHM-bek] Arab and Turkish music feature the doumbek. It is a goblet shaped drum with a combination of a deep bass tone ("doum") and fiery, crisp treble tone ("bek"). Formally, the doumbek has a goatskin or fishskin head stretched and glued to the top. Now they are being made of cast aluminum with a synthetic head. The focus is on both high and low tones. CD 21–27

◀ **Dulcimer: Plucked** A soundbox with strings across it. The strings are usually plucked with a quill. The sound of a dulcimer is quiet and sweet. CD 21–28

◀ **Dundun** [DOON-doon] West African double-headed drums some having an hourglass shape. The ends are covered with goatskin drumheads that are fastened together with leather cords stretched down the length of the drum. These drums are known as talking or singing drums because they can match the pitch and rhythm of spoken language. CD 21–29

◀ **Erhu** [EHR-hoo] A Chinese string instrument with a long, round, hardwood neck that has two tuning pegs at the upper end. The lower end is inserted into a resonator. The instrument has two steel strings and is played with a horsehair bow that is supported by a bamboo neck. CD 21–30

◀ **Flute** A small metal instrument shaped like a pipe, with holes and keys in its side. The player holds the flute sideways and blows across the open mouthpiece. The sound of the flute is pure and sweet. Its low notes are the same ones that fifth graders sing, but it can also go much higher. CD 21–31

◀ **Guitar: Acoustic** A wooden string instrument with six strings. The player strums or plucks the strings with a pick or the fingers to play a melody or chords. When played softly, the guitar is gentle and sweet. It sounds lush and powerful when it is played louder. CD 21–32

Guitarrón [gee-tahr-ROHN] A large, round-backed, non-fretted bass guitar of Chile and Mexico. It is strung with six harp strings, and was invented around the beginning of the twentieth century. The guitarrón is either strummed or plucked, and has a rich, deep sound. CD 21–33

Hand Bells Each bell has a handle to hold for ringing. It is swung to produce a sound and has a clapper inside. They are used in sets for pitch, rhythm and tone-color. These sets can range from six to sixty that cover a range of a short melodic scale to five chromatic octaves. The music is performed by a team of four to 15 ringers, each ringer holding one hand bell in each hand. CD 21–34

Harp The symphonic harp is a large instrument with strings stretched vertically in an open, triangular frame. The player plucks the strings and operates foot pedals to play chromatic tones. Rippling chords are characteristic sounds of the instrument. CD 21–36

Harpsichord A small keyboard instrument shaped something like a piano. Because the strings are plucked, not hammered like piano strings, the sound of the harpsichord has a light, transparent quality. CD 21–35

Jarana [hah-RAH-nah] An eight-string guitar used to strum rhythmic accompaniments in various *son* (sohn), or "folk music," ensembles in Mexico. It is used especially in the central Gulf Coast area in playing *jarocho* (pertaining to Veracruz) music. CD 21–37

Koto [koh-toh] A 13 to 17-string zither with movable frets. It is known as the national instrument of Japan. The player sits on the floor, either cross-legged or in a kneeling-sitting position. Sound is produced when the player plucks the silk strings, using the fingers and thumb of the right hand, with a bamboo, bone, or ivory pick. The sound of the koto is a little like that of a harp. CD 21–38

Instrument Key: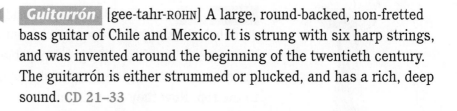

Mbira [m-BEE-rah] An African finger xylophone made of 5 to 30 or more thin metal or cane tongues attached to a sounding board. The tongues are plucked with the thumbs and forefingers. The length of each tongue determines its pitch. Each tongue of the mbira produces a soft sound. Rattles are sometimes attached to the body of the instrument. The sound may be amplified with a gourd. CD 21–39

Piano A large keyboard instrument with 88 keys and many strings on the inside. When the player presses the keys, hammers inside the piano strike the strings to make the sounds. The piano can play music in a quiet mood as well as in a loud "military style." CD 21–40

Requinto [reh-KEEN-toh] A small guitar that is used to play fast, highly improvisational melodies. The strings are plucked with a long, thin plastic pick. Like the jarana, the requinto is used in playing *jarocho* songs in the Veracruz area. CD 21–41

Saxophone A woodwind instrument invented by Adolphe Sax in the nineteenth century by placing a clarinet-type reed mouthpiece on a piece of brass tubing. The saxophone has a warm, brassy-but-mellow sound that makes it ideal in jazz ensembles. CD 21–42

Shakuhachi [shah-koo-hah-chee] A Japanese end-blown bamboo flute with a thumbhole and four finger holes. The early eighth-century instrument had five front finger holes, one thumbhole, and was made from stone, jade, or ivory. CD 21–43

◀ **Sitar** A classical Indian plucked-string instrument with seven strings over movable metal frets. Four strings are for the melody and three for the drone required of all classical Indian music. Twelve to 20 more strings below the seven, are not plucked but resonate by sympathetic vibration when the melody strings are plucked. CD 21–44

◀ **Snare Drum** A small, cylinder-shaped drum. Two heads made of calfskin or plastic are stretched over the metal shell and strings wrapped in wire (snare) are fixed to the bottom. When the player strikes the top with sticks, the snares vibrate in response. It can produce a sharp, steady, long, raspy, or rolling sound. CD 21–45

◀ **Steel Drums** Tuned percussion instruments made from oil drums. They were developed in Trinidad and are used for Caribbean-style music. Rubber-headed pan sticks are used to strike dented areas on the tops of the drums. Steel drums produce a hollow, metallic sound. CD 21–46

◀ **Synthesizer** A keyboard instrument, with keys like a piano that produces sound by means of electronics. Synthesizers come in all shapes and sizes. The synthesizer can sound like an electronic version of almost any of the standard orchestral instruments. It has a range of unusual tone qualities and sound effects. CD 21–47

◀ **Taiko** *Taiko* means "big drum," despite the fact that there are various shapes and sizes. They are used in various styles of Japanese traditional music. All *taiko* are struck with some sort of stick called *bachi*. There are *taiko* with a nailed head, and others with heads stretched over a hoop and tensioned with ropes. CD 21–48

◀ **Timpani** Large, pot-shaped drums, also called "kettledrums." The timpani can sound like a heartbeat or a roll of thunder. Unlike most drums, they can be tuned to specific pitches. CD 21–49

Instrument Key: strings   percussion   woodwind   brass   keyboard

◀ **Trombone** A large brass instrument with one of the loudest voices in the orchestra. The trombone is a long, narrow, curved tube with a bell at one end and a cup-shaped mouthpiece at the other. It has a movable metal tube, called a slide, that lengthens or shortens the tubing. The trombone can project a huge, brilliant sound, but its soft voice is mellow. CD 21–50

◀ **Trumpet** The smallest brass instrument. It has a bell at one end and a cup-shaped mouthpiece at the other. There are three valves, or buttons, on top. In its loudest voice, the trumpet has an important-sounding, brilliant tone. It can also sound soft, warm, and sweet. CD 21–51

◀ **Tuba** The largest brass instrument, with a very large bell that usually points upward. The tuba is so heavy that it may be set on a metal stand while the player sits behind it to blow into the cup-shaped mouthpiece. The tuba's low notes, the lowest of any brass instrument, are deep and dark sounding. The higher ones are hearty and warm. CD 21–52

◀ **Vihuela** [vee-WEH-lah] The vihuela is linked with the guitar and viol. The strings are plucked with six or seven pairs of unison strings. It is a large instrument with very little inward curve. Multiple roses set into the soundboard add to the unique appearance. The size suggests low pitch. It was extremely popular in Spain during the 15th and 16th centuries. CD 21–53

◀ **Violin** A small wooden string instrument that is held under the chin. The player uses a bow or plucks it with the fingers. The violin has many different voices, from a beautiful "singing" quality to a bright, playful sound. CD 21–54

◀ **Xylophone** A pitched percussion instrument that has a keyboard of wooden bars and is played with mallets. The xylophone has a bright, brittle sound that makes it effective in lively or humorous passages. CD 21–55

Glossary

Highlighted terms appear as vocabulary words on the indicated lesson pages.

AB form A musical plan that has two different parts, or sections. p. 57

ABA form A musical plan that has three sections. The first and last sections are the same. The middle section is different. p. 100

accent (>) Indicates that a note should be sung or played with more emphasis than the other notes. p. 172

accidental (♯) (♭) (♮) A sign used to show an altered pitch. The most common signs (which raise or lower a pitch by a half step) are sharps, flats, and naturals. p. 191

accompaniment Music that supports the sound of the featured performer(s). p. 418

articulation A form of musical expression using *legato, staccato,* or *marcato.* p. 87

backbeat An emphasis on the off beats: 1 **2** 3 **4**. p. 215

ballad A folk song that tells a story. p. 294

beat A repeating pulse that can be felt in most music. p. 12

blues A twentieth-century jazz style characterized by a 12-bar blues harmonic structure, flatted third and seventh notes, and slow, syncopated rhythms. p. 352

call and response A follow-the-leader process in which a melody is introduced by one voice or instrument (call) and then immediately answered by other voices or instruments (response). p. 20

calypso A style of folk music from the Caribbean that tells a story about an event or experience. p. 200

canon A musical composition in which the parts imitate each other. One part begins, or leads, and the other part follows. p. 158

changing meter A grouping of beats that changes throughout a composition; for example, the music may begin in ¾ and then change to ¼ or any other meter. p. 124

chord Three or more different tones played or sung together. p. 70

chorus A large group of singers p. 30

coda (⊕) A "tail," or short section, added at the end of a piece of music. p. 411

compound meter (⁶⁄₈) A meter in which the beat is subdivided into groups of three. p. 175

concerto A composition written for solo instrument(s) with orchestra. p. 111

contour The "shape" of a melody, determined by the way it moves upward and downward in steps and leaps, and repeated tones. p. 29

countermelody A melody that is played or sung at the same time as the main melody. p. 116

crescendo (◁══) Gradually getting louder. p. 46

decrescendo (══▷) Gradually getting softer. p. 46

descant Another melody that decorates the main tune, usually placed above the main melody. p. 114

diatonic scale An arrangement of seven different notes. It is called "major" when the *tonic*, or home note, is *do*. p. 146

duet A composition written for two performers. p. 347

duple meter The way beats in music are organized into groups of two. p. 178

dynamics The degrees of loudness and softness of sound. p. 6

ensemble A group of players or singers. p. 131

form The overall structure, or plan, of a piece of music. p. 100

forte (*f*) Loud. p. 8

fortissimo (*ff*) Very loud. p. 8

gamelan Ensembles consisting of gongs, gong-chimes, metallophones, xylophones, and drums, found in Indonesia, Malaysia, and in scattered places around the Western world. p. 319

half step The distance between one key and the next, black or white. p. 146

harmonic minor scale An arrangement of eight tones with a pattern of steps as follows: whole, half, whole, whole, half, whole + half, half. p. 192

harmony Two or more different pitches sounding at the same time. p. 34

improvise To make up the music while performing. p. 352

irregular meter A grouping of beats that moves in an irregular number of beats, such as $\frac{5}{4}$. p. 221

jazz A style that grew out of the music of African Americans, then took many different substyles, such as ragtime, blues, cool jazz, swing, bebop, and rock. It features solo improvisations over a set harmonic progression. p. 42

key The scale on which a piece of music is based, named for its tonic, or "home" tone. p. 102

key signature The musical symbol, comprising sharps or flats placed on the staff, that defines the key of a piece of music. p. 104

legato Music performed in a smooth and connected style. p. 87

major scale An arrangement of eight tones according to the following pattern of steps or intervals: whole, whole, half, whole, whole, whole, half. p. 146

marcato Music performed with stressed or accented notes. p. 87

measure ( ) A grouping of beats set off by bar lines. p. 45

melody A line of single tones that moves upward, moves downward, or repeats. p. 188

meter The way beats of music are grouped, often in sets of two or three. p. 50

mezzo forte (*mf*) Medium loud. p. 8

mezzo piano (*mp*) Medium soft. p. 8

motive A phrase that repeats in different ways. p. 59

movement Each of the smaller, self-contained sections (usually three or four) that together make up a symphony, sonata, concerto, string quartet, or suite. p. 55

natural minor scale An arrangement of eight tones with a pattern of steps as follows: whole, half, whole, whole, half, whole, whole. p. 189

ostinato A repeated rhythm or melody pattern played throughout a piece or a section of a piece. p. 32

partner songs Two or more different songs that can be sung at the same time to create harmony. p. 70

pentatonic Music based on a five-tone scale. A common pentatonic scale corresponds to tones 1, 2, 3, 5, and 6 of the major scale. p. 24

percussion Pitched or nonpitched instruments that are played by striking, scraping, or shaking. p. 64

phrase A melodic idea that is a complete musical thought, something like a sentence. p. 29

pianissimo (*pp*) Very soft. p. 8

piano (*p*) Soft. p. 8

pitch The location of a tone with respect to highness or lowness. p. 189

pizzicato On a string instrument, the plucking of the strings. p. 198

polyphonic texture Music created when two or more separate melodies are sung or played together. p. 73

quartet A composition for four voices or instruments, each having a separate part; a group of four singers or instrumentalists, each playing or singing a different part. p. 311

ragtime An early form of jazz popular from around 1890 to World War I. p. 332

refrain The part of a song that repeats, using the same melody and words. p. 56

rhythm pattern A combination of sounds and silences in the same or differing lengths. p. 53

rondo A musical form in which the first section always returns. The most common rondo form is ABACA. p. 142

round A composition in which the parts enter in succession, singing the same melody. p. 160

scale An arrangement of pitches from lower to higher according to a specific pattern of intervals or steps. p. 146

scat singing A jazz vocal style in which syllables are used instead of words. p. 84

sequence A pattern of pitches that is repeated at a higher or lower pitch level. p. 149

shanty A sailor's work song. p. 264

simple meter A meter in which the beat is subdivided into groups of two. p. 175

slur (♩‿♩) Indicates that a syllable is sung on more than one pitch. p. 170

spiritual An African American religious folk song that originated during the period of enslavement. p. 26

staccato (♩) Music performed in a separated, detached style. p. 87

style In music, style refers to the unique way in which the elements of melody, rhythm, timbre, texture, harmony, and form are handled to create a special "sound." p. 224

swing A jazz style developed in the 1930s and played by big bands. p. 82

symphony In Western art music, an ensemble consisting of multiple strings plus an assortment of woodwinds, brass, and percussion instruments. p. 55

syncopation An arrangement of rhythm in which important sounds begin on weak beats or weak parts of beats, giving a catchy, off-balance movement to the music. p. 12

tempo The speed of the beat in music. p. 98

texture The layering of sounds to create a thick or thin quality in music. p. 78

theme and variations A musical form in which each section is a modification of the initial theme. p. 184

tie (♩ ♩) A musical symbol that connects two notes of the same pitch. p. 95

timbre The special sound, or tone color, that makes one instrument or voice sound different from another. p. 66

time signature Musical symbol that indicates how many beats are in a measure (top number) and which note gets the beat (bottom number). p. 10

triple meter The way beats in music are organized into groups of three. p. 178

triplet (♩♩♩) A symbol used to show three even sounds on a beat in simple meter. p. 217

unison The simultaneous playing or singing of the same notes by two or more performers either at the same pitch or in octaves. p. 92

upbeats Beats that are sometimes called weak beats because they lead to the next note, a strong beat. p. 132

verse Refers to the section of a song that is sung before the refrain. p. 56

vocables Sung or spoken syllables that do not have a specific meaning. p. 302

whole step On a keyboard, the distance between any two keys with a single key between. p. 146

yodeling A style of singing using a rapid shift between a lower full voice and a high voice style of singing called *falsetto*. p. 347

Classified Index

Listening selections appear in *italics*.

Poems and Stories

Recorded Interviews

Credits

Design and Electronic Production: Kirchoff/Wohlberg, Inc.

Listening Maps and Music Reading Practice: MediaLynx Design Group

Photograph Credits

2 (Bkgd) Melford, Inc., Michael/Getty Images 2 (B) Gary Conner/PhotoEdit 2 (TC) ©Lester Lefkowitz/Corbis 8 Craig Lenihan/AP/Wide World 9 American Academy Inst of Arts and Letters/Getty Images 10 ©Ian Logan/Getty Images/Stone 12 © Paula Bronstein/Getty Images/Stone 16 © Stan Burnside, John Beadle, Jackson Burnside 21 Everett Collection, Inc. 24 © Bob Thomas/Getty Images/Stone 28 © Paul Harris/Getty Images/Stone 30 Indianapolis Children's Choir 31 Minnetrista Cultural Center & Oakhurst Gardens 34 Richard Nowitz/Words & Pictures/PictureQuest 36 Photofest 37 Photofest 38 ©Joan Marcus 39 Everett Collection, Inc. 46 PictureQuest 47 PictureQuest 49 Deborah Feingold/Archive Photos 51 Jose Carrillo/PhotoEdit 51 Ric Ergenbright/Corbis 52 Grabill/Getty Images 53 Corbis 54 Michael Maslan Historic Photographs/Corbis 63 National Gallery/Corbis 66 The Stock Market 67 Jack Vartoogian 68 (C) Mary Evans Picture Library 68 (B) Tim Brown/Index Stock Imagery 70 (Bkgd) ©Wes Thompson/Corbis 74 Archive Photos 74 Smithsonian Institution 76 ©Pat O'Hara/Getty Images/Stone 78 Joe Viesti/Viesti Collection, Inc. 78 Alan Kearney/Viesti Collection, Inc. 78 Jose Azel/Aurora & Quanta Productions 79 Lebrecht Collection 81 The Stock Market 82 Bettmann/Corbis 83 Getty Images 88 Bettmann/Corbis 88 Mary Kate Denny/PhotoEdit 90 © Images Coulour Library-ImageState Ltd. 91 © Images Coulour Library-ImageState Ltd. 92 (Bkgd) © Images Coulour Library-ImageState Ltd. 94 Newberry Library/SuperStock 96 David David Gallery/SuperStock 99 Mike SeegerMandi Wright/Roanoke Times 102 Smithsonian American Art Museum, Washington, DC/Art Resource, NY 104 SuperStock 109 Dan Peha/Viesti Collection, Inc. 110 Richard Cummins/Corbis 111 © John Running 111 PhotoDisc 112 Diana Ong/SuperStock 113 Getty Images 114 Tom Bean/Corbis 116 Bob Rowan/Corbis 118 Corbis 119 Steve Elmore 119 © Harald Sund/Getty Images/The Image Bank 120 Thomas A. Kelly/Corbis 121 Corbis 124 Florent Flipper/Unicorn Stock Photos 124 Steve Cole/PhotoDisc 124 CMCD/PhotoDisc 130 Ritchie Valens, portrait/Corbis 131 Federico Patellani/Corbis 134 (TR) Michael Howell/Index Stock Imagery 135 (BR) Richard Gaines 138 Robert Landau/Corbis 138 ©Richard T. Nowitz 139 Corbis 140 SuperStock 141 SuperStock 145 (BL) Musee du Louvre Paris/Dagli Orti/The Art Archive 146 © Pat O'Hara/Corbis 152 SuperStock 154 © Michael S. Yamashita/Corbis 155 Michael Ochs Archives, Venice, CA 155 Bettmann/Corbis 156 C Squared Studios/PhotoDisc 156 Jack Vartoogian 157 Ebet Roberts Photography 158 © Marko Modic/Corbis 159 American Stock/Archive Photos 160 Gianni Dagli Orti/Corbis 163 Archive Photos 164 C Squared Studios/PhotoDisc 166 Tim Thompson/Corbis 167 SuperStock 168 Brian Yarvin/Image Works 170 (Bkgd) ©Richard Hamilton/Corbis 172 (Bkgd) Harvey Lloyd/Taxi/Getty Images 174 Joan Miro, "Personages Dans la Nuit," 1950. Oil on burlap, 35 x 45 3/8 inches. The Museum of Contemporary Art, Los Angeles. The Rita and Taft Schreiber Collection. Given in loving memory of her husband, Taft Schreiber, by Rita Schreiber. Photo: Squidds & Nunos; ©2002 Successio Miro/Artists Rights Society(ARS), New York/ADAGP, Paris 176 (BL) Bart Muldes/Courtesy of Angel Romero 180 Library of Congress 180 Getty Images 182 Courtesy Central Pacific Railroad Photographic History Museum, © 2002, CPRR.org 183 Getty Images 185 Corbis 186 AP/Wide World 187 © Bettmann/Corbis 188 © MIchelle Garrett/Corbis 188 © Tria Giovan/Corbis 189 © Leonard De Selva/Corbis 190 AP/Wide World 191 Corbis 192 Corbis 193 © Bettmann/Corbis 196 © Horace Bristol/Corbis 196 © Fukuhara/Corbis 196 SuperStock 197 © Michael Boys/Corbis 197 The Granger Collection, New York 198 SuperStock 198 The Granger Collection, New York 198 PhotoDisc 199 Hulton Getty/Archive Photos 202 (Bkgd) ©Pablo Corral Vega/Corbis 204 Michael Ochs Arcives, Venice, CA 205 SuperStock 208 Corbis 208 CBS Photo Archive/Archive Photos 209 Stone 210 From the collection of Mitch McGeary, www.rarebeatles.com 211 SuperStock 212 Jon Hammer Collection/Archive Photos 218 John Higginson/Getty Images 219 Chris Hellier/Corbis 220 Culver Pictures Inc. 223 Archive Photos 225 Archive Photos 229 Corbis 230 Blank Archives/Archive Photos 231 Clifford Ashley/New Bedford Whaling Museum 232 (Bkgd) McIntyre, Will & Deni/Getty Images 234 (B) McIntyre, Will & Deni/Getty Images 235 (BR) ©Bettmann/Corbis 236 Getty Images 236 © Images Colour Library-ImageState Ltd 237 ©Andy Sacks/Getty Images/Stone 238 Cindy Loo/Corbis 238 © Images Colour Library-ImageState Ltd 239 Michael Ochs Archives, Venice, CA 240 © Ted Spiegel/Corbis 242 © Andy Sacks/Getty Images/Stone 245 Jack Vartoogian 248 The Granger Collection, New York 249 Ebet Roberts Photography 249 © Bettmann/Corbis 250 Jasper Johns, "Map", 1963, 60"x93", Encaustic and Collage on Canvas, Private Collection.© Jasper Johns/Licensed by VAGA, New York, NY. Photo by David Lees/Corbis 250 Dream Maker Software 257 Lebrecht Collection 259 Corbis 260 (Bkgd) ©David Muench/Corbis 260 (TR) ©David Muench/Corbis 261 (BL) Jill Trinka 265 SuperStock 267 Atlantic Coast Line - Seaboard Cost Line Railroads Historical Society 272 Tria Giovan/Corbis 272 M. Westlight Stock/Corbis 273 Getty Images 273 Corbis 274 Tria Giovan/Corbis 276 Robert Holmes/Corbis 277 Bettmann/Corbis 278 David Spindel/SuperStock 278 Bettmann/Corbis 278 Getty Images 281 (BL) ©TedWilliams/Corbis 282 Corbis 283 Everett Collection, Inc. 284 Popperfoto/Archive Photos 285 Bettmann/Corbis 285 Corbis 286 ©Jason Lauré 286 Wally McNamee/Corbis 286 ©Jason Lauré 288 American Stock/Archive Photos 288 © Images Colour Library-ImageState Ltd 288 Getty Images 290 H Isachar/Art Directors & TRIP Photo Library 290 Wolfgang Kaehler 290 Dan Polin/Lights, Words, and Music 290 Judy Griesedieck/Corbis 291 © Robert Frerck/Getty Images/Stone 296 Jack Vartoogian 296 Hulton-Deutsch Collection/Corbis 310 © M. Angelo/Corbis 310 Sergio Dorantes/Corbis 311 Turtle Island Records 312 Ebet Roberts Photography 315 Christie's Images/Corbis 318 Wolfgang Kaehler 319 William Waterfall/©PACIFIC STOCK 319 Wolfgang Kaehler 320 David Farrell/Lebrecht Collection 321 Corbis 322 Tim Thompson/Corbis 323 Photo courtesy of John J. van Gool from his website http://www.lutherie-van-gool.nl 324 Jan Butchofsky-Houser/Corbis 325 Robert Frerck/Odyssey Productions 326 (Border) ©Robert van der Hilst/Corbis 332 Outline Press Ltd. 334 Culver Pictures Inc. 335 Frank Driggs/Archive Photos 337 Reprinted with permission of the publisher, Children's Book Press, San Francisco, CA. Art copyright © 1998 by Michele Wood. 338 © Hulton-Deutsch Collection/Corbis 339 The Granger Collection, New York 340 The Granger Collection, New York 341 Lebrecht Collection 342 Culver Pictures Inc. 342 © Murray & Associates/Picturesque/PictureQuest 342 © Bettmann/Corbis 342 © Mosaic Images/Corbis 342 © Hulton-Deutsch Collection/Corbis 342 The Granger Collection, New York 342 Lebrecht Collection 347 Michael Okoniewski/AP/Wide World 348 Carving by Mike Kotz/Valley Road Woodcarvers; Photo by Jim Quarles 349 AP/Wide World 351 MGM Records/Archive Photos 351 Culver Pictures Inc. 351 AP/Wide World 353 Lebrecht Collection 355 ©Bob Krist/Getty Images/Stone 356 © Bettmann/Corbis 357 © Bettmann/Corbis 358 Lebrecht Collection 359 AP/Wide World 359 Photofest 360 Getty Images 362 © James L. Amos/Corbis 363 Lebrecht Collection 364 Ebet Roberts Photography 364 Getty Images 364 Neal Preston/Corbis 366 M. Schwarz/Image Works 366 Alan Oddie/PhotoEdit 366 Mary Kate Denny/PhotoEdit 366 AFP/Corbis 368 © World Perspectives/Getty Images/Stone 370 (Bkgd) ©Pablo Corral Vega/Corbis 378 © Digital Vision/PictureQuest 380 Neal Preston/Corbis 381 © Digital Vision/PictureQuest 382 Private Collection/SuperStock 384 Bettmann/Corbis 385 Getty Images 386 (TR) Elena Rooraid/PhotoEdit 386 (BL) Peter Chadwick/©Dorling Kindersley 387 (BR) Peter Chadwick/©Dorling Kindersley 388 (CL) Stephen McBrady/PhotoEdit 388 (BC) David Young-Wolff/PhotoEdit 388 (TR) ©Dorling Kindersley 390 Getty Images 390 Getty Images 394 Getty Images 395 Christe's Images/SuperStock 396 © Bob Krist/Corbis 397 SuperStock 397 Theo Westenberger 399 Ebet Roberts Photography 400 Ted Spiegel/Corbis 400 © David Rubinger/Corbis 403 (BL) Michael Ochs Archives 412 © Bruno De Hogues/Getty Images/Stone 416 Dina Cormick 416 William Zulu 417 James Mphahlele 426 (CR) ©Wolfgang Kaehler/Corbis 426 (Bkgd) adalberto Rios/Getty Images 428 (Bkgd) ©Andrea Pistolesi/Getty Images 439 Lebrecht Collection 440 © David Olsen/Getty Images/Stone 441 A. Daniel Lease 442 Ebet Roberts Photography 442 Douglas Peebles/Corbis 442 Philip Rosenberg Photography 443 © Roger Ressmeyer/Corbis 443 G. Brad Lewis 444 © William P. Gottlieb from the Library of Congress Collection 451 Bob Parent/Archive Photos 452 The Granger Collection, New York 456 Orion/Paramount/Kobal Collection 461 Dr. Barbara Cohen 462 Toni Parker Johnson/Mashantucket Pequot Tribal Nation 463 Mashantucket Pequot Tribal Nation 464 CMCD/PhotoDisc 465 (TR) Bridgeman Art Library International Ltd. 465 (TL) CMCD/PhotoDisc 468 © Paul Almasy/Corbis 470 © Frere Marc, Taize/Gene Plaisted, OSC/The Crosiers 471 © Frere Marc, Taize/Gene Plaisted, OSC/The Crosiers 476 Lawrence Migdale/Stone 478 Kenneth Hamm/Photo Japan 478 © Images Colour Library-ImageState Ltd 479 Michael S. Yamashita/Corbis 481 AP/Wide World 482 Corbis 482 PhotoDisc 483 Bettmann/Corbis 484 © Jim Zuckerman/Corbis 485 Fernando Morales/© AFP 485 Bettman/Corbis 485 Hulton - Duetsch Collection/Corbis 485 Reuters/Ian Waldie/Archive Photos 485 Ron Sachs/CNP/Archive Photos 485 © Bill Wittman 486 Jeff Greenberg/PhotoEdit

Design and Electronic Production: Kirchoff/Wohlberg, Inc. Listening Maps and Music Reading Practice: Medialynx.

Illustration Credits

6 Tony Caldwell 6 Steve Barbaria 8 Steve Barbaria 14 Patrick O'Brien 17 Patrick O'Brien 18 Elizabeth Rosen 20 Elizabeth Rosen 22 Arvis Stewart 26 Vilma Ortiz-Dillon 26 Nancy Freeman 28 Vilma Ortiz-Dillon 32 Donna Perrone 32 Beatrice Lebreton 35 Michael Di Giorgio 42 Michael Dinges 44 Michael Dinges 50 Fabricio Vanden Broeck 56 Marni Backer 58 Fabricio Vanden Broeck 60 Gail Piazza 65 Tony Nuccio 68 Tom Leonard 86 David Galchutt 88 David Galchutt 98 Bob Karalus 100 Enrique O. Sanchez 103 Enrique O. Sanchez 103 Vilma Ortiz-Dillon 107 Neecy Twinem 108 Todd Leonardo 123 Vilma Ortiz-Dillon 134 Donna Perrone 136 Don Madden 178 Arvis Stewart 184 Tom Leonard 194 Oki Han 200 Jennifer Bolten 202 Michael Di Giorgio 207 Jennifer Bolten 213 Tuko Fujisaki 216 Eileen Hine 222 Tuko Fujisaki 226 Michael Di Giorgio 228 Michael Di Giorgio 230 Craig Spearing 233 Michael Di Giorgio 248 Annette Cable 248 Antonio Cangemi 249 Debbie Maze 266 Chris Duke 267 Chris Duke 268 Tony Nuccio 268 Bob Berry 269 Chris Duke 270 Joe Boddy 290 Sarah Larson 294 Antonio Cangemi 296 Antonio Cangemi 298 Bradley Clark 300 Bradley Clark 302 Gerardo Suzan 304 Michael Di Giorgio 304 Gerardo Suzan 306 Michael Di Giorgio 306 Gerardo Suzan 314 Jean & Mou-Sien Tseng 328 Roger Leyonmark 344 Craig Spearing 346 Craig Spearing 354 Steve Barbaria 359 Dan Brawner 370 Michael Di Giorgio 372 Pat Paris 374 Pat Paris 376 Pat Paris 392 Linda Wingerter 396 Jennifer Bolten 397 Michael Di Giorgio 399 Jennifer Bolten 400 Antonio Cangemi 402 Andrew Wheatcroft 406 Jennifer Hewitson 408 Jennifer Hewitson 418 Bob Karalus 420 Bob Karalus 422 Bob Karalus 424 Bob Karalus 430 Ron Himler 431 Ron Himler 432 Ron Himler 434 Debbie Maze 436 Debbie Maze 456 David Galchutt 458 Arvis Stewart 460 Chi Chung 466 Claude Martinot 472 Marni Backer 474 Esther Baran 476 Beatrice Lebreton 480 Vilma Ortiz-Dillon 481 Vilma Ortiz-Dillon

Acknowledgments

Credits and appreciation are due publishers and copyright owners for use of the following:

4: "God Bless America," Words and Music by Irving Berlin. Copyright 1938, 1939 by Irving Berlin. Copyright © 1965, 1966 (Renewed) by Irving Berlin. Copyright Assigned to the Trustees of the God Bless America Fund. This arrangement Copyright © 2003 by the Trustees of the God Bless America Fund. International Copyright Secured. All Rights Reserved. Used by Permission. 6: "Get on Your Feet" Words and music by John DeFaria, Clay Ostwald and Jorge Casas. Copyright © 1988 Foreign Imported Productions & Publishing, Inc. (BMI) International Rights Secured. All Rights Reserved. Reprinted by permission. 10: "Laredo" English words © 1988 Silver Burdett Ginn. 14: "Éliza Kongo" from *Brown Girl in the Ring* by Alan Lomax. Copyright © 1997 by Alan Lomax. Reprinted by permission of Pantheon Books, a division of Random House, Inc. 18: "Day-O," from *Folk Songs of Jamaica*. Complied by Tom Murray. © 1951 Oxford University Press. Used by Permission. All Rights Reserved. 25: "Arirang" English words © 1995 Silver Burdett Ginn. 28: "Morning Has Broken." Reprinted by permission of Harold Ober Associates Incorporated. Copyright © 1957 by Eleanor Farjeon. 32: "Funwa alafia" (Welcome, My Friends) English words © 2002 Pearson Education, Inc. 36: "Oklahoma" from *Oklahoma!* Music by Richard Rodgers, words by Oscar Hammerstein II. Copyright 1943 by Williamson Music. Copyright Renewed. This arrangement Copyright © 2001 by Williamson Music. International Copyright Secured. All Rights Reserved. Used by Permission. 42: "Be Bop" by Toyomi Igus from I SEE RHYTHM p. 19. Text copyright © 1988 by Toyomi Igus. Reprinted with permission of the publisher, Children's Book Press, San Francisco, CA. 44: "Choo Choo Ch'Boogie," Words and music by Vaughn Horton, Denver Darling and Milton Gabler. Copyright 1945 (Renewed) RYTVOC, Inc. This arrangement © 2001 RYTVOC, INC. All Rights Reserved. Reprinted by permission of Hal Leonard Corporation. 46: "Stand By Me" featured in the Motion Picture *Stand By Me*. Words and music by Ben. E. King, Jerry Leiber and Mike Stoller. © 1961 (Renewed) Jerry Leiber Music, Mike Stoller Music and Mike & Jerry Music LLC. This arrangement © 2001 Jerry Leiber Music, Mike Stoller Music and Mike & Jerry Music LLC. All Rights Reserved. Used by permission. 50: "Adelita" English words © 1991 Silver Burdett Ginn. 57: "Away to America" Words and Music by Linda Williams. Copyright © 1983 by Hal Leonard Corporation. This arrangement copyright © 2001 by Hal Leonard Corporation. International Copyright Secured. All Rights Reserved. Used by Permission. 58: "La Ciudad de Juaja" (The City Of Juaja), English words by Ruth De Cesare, John Donald Robb Archives of Southwestern Music, College of Fine Arts, University of New Mexico. Used by permission of John Donald Robb Trust. 60: "A la puerta del cielo" (At the Gate of Heaven) English words © 2002 Pearson Education, Inc. 67: "Ye jaliya da" a folk song from West Africa. Used by permission, DWADD. 71: "Live in the City" Music by Buryl Red, words by Bryan Louiselle. © 2000 Generic Music and Frog Prince Music. Used by permission. 72: "Play a Simple Melody" from the Stage Production "Watch Your Step." Words and music by Irving Berlin. Copyright © 1914 by Irving Berlin. Copyright Renewed. This arrangement © 2001 by the Estate of Irving Berlin. International Copyright Secured. All Rights Reserved. Used by Permission. 77: "Let Freedom Ring" Words and music by Buryl Red. © 2000 Generic Music. Used by permission. 84: "Teach Me To Swing" Words and music by Kirby Shaw. Copyright © 1997 Kirby Shaw Music. International Copyright Secured. Reprinted by permission. 86: "The Voices of Pride" Words and music by Ned Ginsburg. © 1991 by Ned Ginsburg. Reprinted by permission. 90: "De colores" English words © 1988 Silver Burdett Ginn. 92: "Chiapanecas" English words © 2005 Pearson Education, Inc. 97: "Don't You Hear the Lambs?" from *Folk Songs North America Sings* by Richard Johnston. 1984 by Caveat Music Publishing Ltd., copyright assigned 1988 to G Ricordi & Co. (Canada) Ltd. Used with permission. 106: "Dundai" English words © 2002 Pearson Education, Inc. 108: "Jo'ashila" (Walking Together) Traditional Navajo song from Roots and Branches. Courtesy World Music Press. 114: "The Ash Grove" Arrangement © 2002 Pearson Education, Inc. 116: "Roll On, Columbia" Words by Woody Guthrie.

Index of Songs